3D PRINTING & LASER CUTTING

A Railway Modelling Companion

Jeff Geary & Dave Renshaw

Ian Allan
PUBLISHING

First published 2016

ISBN 978 07110 3841 7

Published by Ian Allan Publishing Ltd, Addlestone,
Surrey, KT15 2SF

Printed in Bulgaria

Visit the Ian Allan Publishing website at
www.ianallanpublishing.com

Contents

Introduction

First, a confession. When Kevin Robertson of Ian Allan Publishing approached us in March 2015 with the suggestion that we write a book on 3D printing, our first reaction was, 'But we've never done any 3D printing!' However, Kevin persuaded us that as railway modellers with the best part of a century's computer programming experience between us, this shouldn't be much of a problem. So we agreed to give it a go. This book is therefore the story of a journey of discovery. Like any beginners, we made plenty of mistakes, but in some ways this is a benefit. We have documented our failures as well as our relative successes, and it is often the case that more can be learned from failure than from success. Hopefully, the reader will learn from our early mistakes, and not repeat too many of them!

Second, an explanation. Notwithstanding what has just been said, the reader may be perplexed that mistakes made and lessons learned in one chapter seem, in some cases, to be repeated again later! This is because the projects were done by two of us, and not necessarily in the same order as they appear in the book. Some parts of Chapter 5, for example, were completed before Chapter 4 was even started.

The book is structured in four parts. The first part, comprising Chapters 1 and 2, describes the technicalities. Chapter 1 explains some of the theory behind computer-aided design (CAD). Chapter 2 reviews a selection of the many CAD programs available. We took a decision early on to restrict ourselves to software that is free of charge. In part, this was because we did not feel qualified to recommend one program rather than another, having (at the outset at least) only limited experience. The other reason was that with free software you can pick and mix. Some packages are better suited than others for certain tasks, and the reader will see that we have used a variety of different programs in the creation of our models. Had we spent several hundred pounds on a commercial package, we would probably have felt obliged to use it for everything, just to get our money's worth!

The second part of the book, Chapters 3, 4 and 5, is about the process of building 3D models, from lineside structures to rolling stock and locomotives. The reader is encouraged to follow these to get a feel for the different approaches taken by different programs. You might not want any cable ducting on your layout, but the exercise of building some on your computer will be instructive.

The third part of the book is about the process of 3D printing itself. Chapter 6 reviews the different technologies and their strengths and weaknesses. It also describes the 3D printer we used to build the examples in this book. This was purchased as a kit of parts to keep down the cost. The price was not dissimilar to that of a decent locomotive kit, and it took a lot less time to build! In Chapter 7 we present some practical advice, most of it learned the hard way by making mistakes, working out where we went wrong then figuring out a better way.

The final part of the book, Chapter 8, is about laser cutting and etching. We look at the equipment available and a range of example projects.

What are our conclusions? First of all, it has to be stressed that it is early days for 3D printer technology. No doubt before very long the kind of printer we used will be extremely old hat. Certainly this technology will not allow you to print a locomotive that would rival one of Mr Beeson's masterpieces. High-quality printing is possible but comes with a serious price tag, whether you are looking to purchase the machinery or buy time via a bureau.

However, there are good reasons why you might want to look into 3D printing. Firstly, there are projects, such as buildings, lineside structures and fairly simple items of rolling stock, where the quality of print obtainable from a low-cost machine today is perfectly adequate. Secondly, the skills you develop in using 3D software will still be applicable to building much higher-quality models on the printers of the future.

When it comes to laser cutting and etching, the technology is 'good to go' and is a hugely powerful tool for precisely cutting and etching parts for all manner of structures. The drawback is price; this may well be too high for most modellers, but there are companies offering cutting services and it is quite conceivable that a club might make the investment. Over time, prices may well come down to a point where they are more generally affordable. An encouraging development is that some of our larger libraries are starting to set up 'makerspace' areas to offer 3D printing and laser cutting facilities to the public.

We can foresee a time when 2D and 3D software skills will be just as much a part of our hobby as the ability to use a soldering iron or wield a paintbrush. So why not have a go? Download some free software and, in the words of one of the 3D websites we review in Chapter 2, 'Start tinkering now'!

Acknowledgements

We would like to thank Kevin Robertson, Nick Grant, Alistair Plumb and Sue Frost of Ian Allan Publishing both for the initial idea and for their assistance in the book's production. Thanks are also due to Jane Kennedy of Oakwood Press, and Greg Martin, who runs the RailAlbum website, for their permission to use some of their material in illustrations, which are credited accordingly. Finally, thanks to Iain Henderson and Roger Stonham, two friends who have given us some sound initial advice and, in the case of Roger, generous amounts of time on his laser cutting machine.

1

Basic concepts

In this chapter we introduce the concept of a three-dimensional drawing. It is by means of such a drawing that the 3D printer is instructed what to print. We shall explain some of the technical jargon that inevitably crops up whenever computers are involved.

What is CAD?

CAD is an acronym for Computer Aided Design. In essence it is an application program that runs on a computer enabling the user to make an accurate engineering drawing. In the era before CAD, a draughtsman would work at a drawing table, such as that depicted in Figure 1-1 and, by means of squares, compasses, rulers and protractors, would produce the drawings from which parts could be made and assembled into a locomotive, ship, bridge or tunnel. Each such project might involve dozens or even hundreds of drawings, so a manufacturing business of any size would employ a great many draughtsmen in a large drawing office such as the rather splendid example depicted in Figure 1-2.

Many copies of these drawings would be required in the workshops. The process used for copying the drawings employed a blue pigment, and the copies were thus known as blueprints. Unfortunately, the blue pigment faded over time and the copies had only a limited life. Also, the chemical reaction used in the copying involved the production of large amounts of highly pungent ammonia. The process was thus labour-intensive, and therefore costly, impermanent, and very smelly. Few tears were shed when it was rendered obsolete by CAD. (As an aside, one of the authors got his first programming job in the 1960s, before CAD existed. A friend, who had just started in a drawing office, remarked 'Computer programming is a dead end, because in a few years computers will program themselves, but there'll always be a need for draughtsmen'. Sadly, the author has lost touch with the maker of this spectacularly wrong prediction!)

Drawings and images

We must first distinguish what we mean by a CAD drawing as distinct from the more general idea of an image. CAD does not work with images – it can only work with drawing files.

An image might be a photograph taken with a digital camera, or it might be a picture you have scanned, or downloaded from the internet. A typical file type is '.bmp' (for bitmap). Bitmap images are made up of tiny little squares called pixels (an abbreviation for 'picture elements'), each pixel having attributes describing its colour and brightness. A photograph taken by a digital camera,

ABOVE Figure 1-1 Advert for a draughtsman's table, 1863. *Public domain image (https://commons.wikimedia.org)*

LEFT Figure 1-2 Harland & Wolff's drawing office, 1912. *Painting by Karl Beutel from Wikimedia Commons under Creative Commons licence*

for example, might contain 2,000 rows each of 3,000 pixels. When such an image is stored on a computer's disc the resulting file is a representation of the colour and brightness of each of these pixels. When the image is displayed on the computer screen, which might only be 1,000 by 1,500 pixels, it must be squeezed by making each 'screen' pixel an average of the colour and brightness of four (2 x 2) adjacent pixels of the original image. If we wish to zoom in on the image, for example to blow up an area covering just 200 by 300 pixels of the original image so that it fills the whole screen, the computer will simply repeat each pixel 5 x 5, i.e. 25 times. The resulting loss of quality is amply demonstrated in Figure 1-3, in which the inset picture shows the effect of zooming in on the locomotive's shed plate.

Consider now Figure 1-4, which is a CAD drawing file. The file type ('por') is a rather old one, hardly used nowadays. However, it is chosen here because it is stored in plain text format and is both clear and concise (the same CAD drawing saved in the more usual 'dxf' file format would occupy more than 2,000 lines of text!). This demonstrates the essential difference between a drawing file and an image. Figure 1-4 doesn't look much like a drawing, and indeed it isn't one. Rather, it is a series of *instructions* for making a drawing. The file describes eight entities: six lines, an arc and a polygon. Each entity comprises a line of text describing what it is (line, arc, etc.) followed by one or more lines of numerical data specifying where and how it is to be drawn. Take, for example, the first entity. This is a line specified by the numbers 0, 0, 0, 3.4, 3.4, 3.4, 1.8. The first few numbers (which all happen to be zeroes in this example) indicate the way in which the entity is to be drawn, i.e. as a continuous, dotted or dashed line, the colour to be used, etc. Following this comes the positional data, which defines the start and end points of the line. The points are specified by their horizontal and vertical distances from the origin of an xy grid. Referring to Figure 1-5, the horizontal measurement is called the x coordinate of the point, and the vertical measurement is the y coordinate. For example, point P is at x = 3.4 and y = 3.4. Point Q is at x = 3.4 and y = 1.8. These happen to be the start and end points of the first line described in the drawing file of Figure 1-4. The drawing file thus instructs the computer to draw a line from point P to point Q.

The file *describes* a drawing rather than simply storing an image of it. The beauty of this arrangement is that the lines are mathematically perfect. That is, they are infinitesimally thin and perfectly straight. Their start and end points are at exact locations, not 'the nearest pixel to…'. They

```
header
C:\dwgs\nut.por
Save As...
Autodesk, Inc.
Drafix CAD for Windows

line
0 0 0 3.4 3.4 3.4 1.8
line
0 0 0 3.4 1.8 3.9 1.8
line
0 0 0 3.9 1.8 3.9 3.4
line
0 0 0 3.9 3.4 3.4 3.4
line
0 0 0 3.4 3 3.9 3
line
0 0 0 3.4 2.2 3.9 2.2
arc
0 0 0 1.7 2.6 0.4 0 6.2831853071796
poly
0 0 0 0 1 0 0 0 6
2.4 3
1.7 3.4
1 3
1 2.2
1.7 1.8
2.4 2.2
eof
```

ABOVE *Figure 1-3*
Illustrating the effect of zooming in on a bitmap image.

LEFT *Figure 1-4*
An example of a CAD drawing file.

suffer from none of the blurring evident in Figure 1-3, however much they are magnified. Of course, when such a line is actually rendered in pixels on a computer screen or printer it will lose its perfection. However, the quality of the line will be the same whether it is rendered at a scale of 1:1 or 1,000:1. In case you're wondering what the drawing described in Figure 1-4 is, it is in fact a plan and elevation of a hexagonal nut, as illustrated in Figure 1-6.

In Figure 1-7 a CAD drawing of the locomotive pictured in Figure 1-3 is shown, together with a 'zoomed-in' view of the engine shed plate. This has been scaled up by 2,000% from the original plate on the front of the smokebox; however, there is no loss of precision as in Figure 1-3. If we scale up a section of the Cartazzi axlebox on the trailing wheels by a similar factor, you can see several examples of hexagonal bolt, again with no loss of precision. The difference between Figures 1-7 and 1-3 is not just aesthetic. For reasons we shall see later, the shed plate in Figure 1-7 is potentially 3D-printable, while that in Figure 1-3 is not.

1

[Figure 1-5: xy grid with axes y = 0 through y = 5 and x = 0 through x = 5, showing point P near (3.5, 3.5) and point Q near (3.5, 1.8)]

ABOVE *Figure 1-5* Representing two points on an xy grid.

BELOW *Figure 1-6* The drawing described by Figure 4.

BOTTOM *Figure 1-7* The effect of zooming in on a CAD drawing.

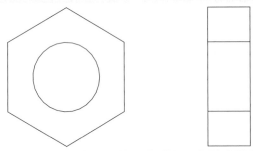

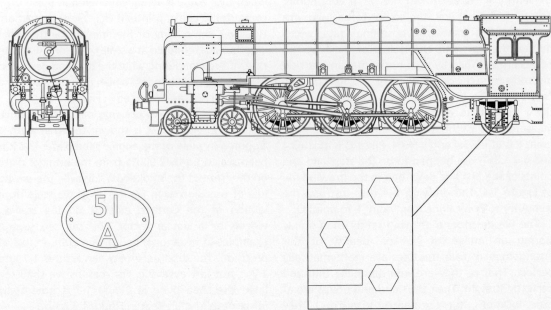

3D drawings

What has been described so far is a two-dimensional drawing file, but to make a solid object we need to describe it in three dimensions. This is not at all as easy as might be thought, unless the object happens to be a regular geometrical shape, such as a cube or sphere. Remember that our CAD file, from which the object will be created, does not contain images. It contains only numerical data from which to construct an image to display on a screen or to be printed. Lines, arcs, circles, etc, are easily described by their start, end or centre points, but how does one go about describing a three-dimensional object in such a manner?

The answer is to use an xyz grid, as illustrated in Figure 1-8. Imagine that the sheet of paper holding the xy grid of Figure 1-5 has been laid flat on a desk, and a third dimension, z, has been added, with z representing the height of a given point above the surface of the desk. For example, point A is directly above the point x = 1, y = 3 and is at a height of z = 2. You can imagine it as being perched on the top of a stick (shown in blue) whose length is 2 and whose base is at x = 1, y = 3. Point B is above the point x = 3, y = 2 at a height of z = 2.7. We say that point A's coordinates are (1,3,2) and those of point B are (3,2,2.7). We could specify a line AB by giving the coordinates of its start and end points in three-dimensional space, as against the two-dimensional line that would be specified by points P and Q of Figure 1-5.

We come now to the most crucial step of all. If we add a third point, C, to Figure 1-8 we can define two more lines, namely from B to C and from C to A, and having three lines enables us to specify a

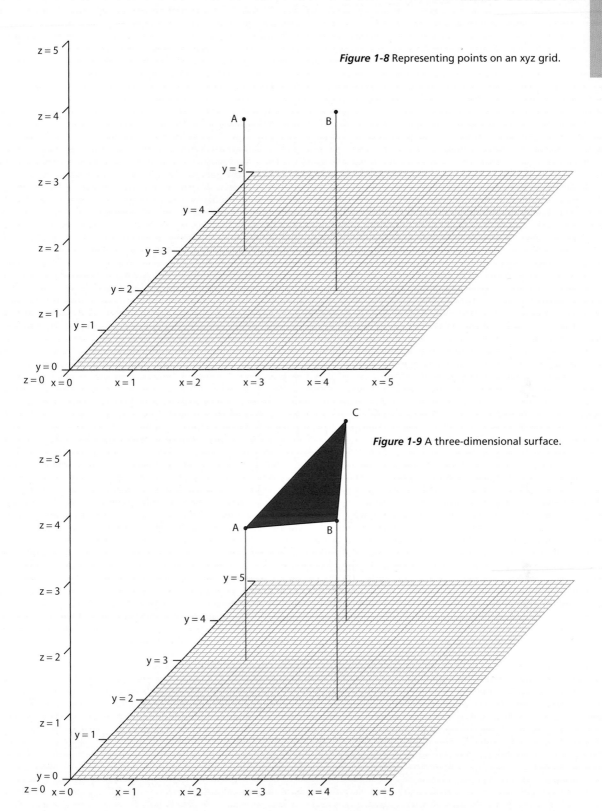

Figure 1-8 Representing points on an xyz grid.

Figure 1-9 A three-dimensional surface.

triangular *surface*, ABC, the edges of which correspond to the three lines. Such a surface is the fundamental building block of a 3D drawing, and is shown in yellow in Figure 1-9. Objects in a 3D drawing are built up from a large number of such triangular surfaces, known as *facets*. Each of the points A, B and C is a *vertex* (plural *vertices*), and the three lines AB, BC and CA are known as its *edges*. By putting together a number of such facets, we can represent three-dimensional objects, and the three-dimensional object thus formed is known as a *mesh*.

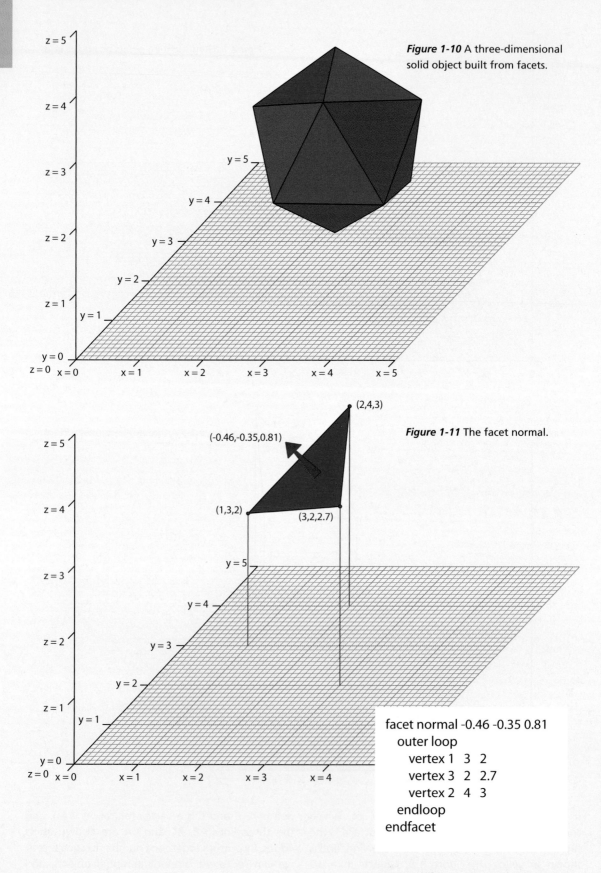

Figure 1-10 A three-dimensional solid object built from facets.

Figure 1-11 The facet normal.

```
facet normal -0.46 -0.35 0.81
  outer loop
    vertex 1  3  2
    vertex 3  2  2.7
    vertex 2  4  3
  endloop
endfacet
```

ABOVE *Figure 1-12* A snippet of stl file describing the facet in Figure 1-11.

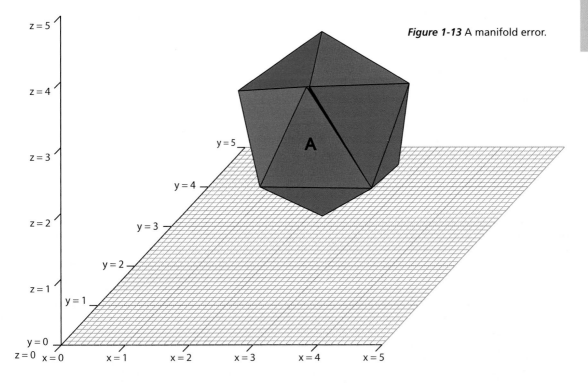

Figure 1-13 A manifold error.

For example, in Figure 1-10 we have built up a mesh from 20 such facets, and it is approximately spherical. If we used a great many more than 20 facets, the mesh would look much more like a perfect sphere.

To represent such an object in a 3D drawing file, we need to specify the x, y and z coordinates of the vertices of each of its facets. There is one further requirement, which is not quite so obvious. The way the object in Figure 1-10 is drawn, it looks like an approximately round solid body. However, exactly the same set of vertices could equally well represent a void, or bubble, inside a larger solid. Consider, for example, the inside surface of a hollow sphere such as a football. To determine which way the surfaces face we need one further piece of information. This is the *facet normal*. Here, the word 'normal' is used in its geometrical sense of being at right angles to a given surface. The facet normal always points *outwards* from the surface of which the facet is a part. For example, in the case of a hollow sphere the facet normals on the outer surface will point away from the centre of the sphere, while those on the inside will point towards the centre of the sphere. In Figure 1-11 we show the normal to the facet illustrated in Figure 1.9 as an outwards-pointing arrow. Its direction is represented as -0.46 units in the x direction, -0.35 units in the y direction and +0.81 units in the z direction from the centre of the facet. Notice also that each of the vertices is labelled with its x, y and z coordinate rather than the letters A, B and C.

A common file format to represent 3D objects is the 'stl' file type (for STereoLithography). The facet shown in Figure 1-11 would be represented by the snippet of code shown in Figure 1-12. Like the drawing file shown in Figure 1-4, this file is not an image of the facet, but a description of how to draw the facet. The stl file for a real-life 3D object would contain many hundreds or thousands of such instructions. The purpose of a 3D CAD program is to take in our description of a solid object and convert it into facets, calculating the x, y and z coordinates of the vertices that comprise the mesh representing the object.

Criteria for 3D printability

Essentially, when we print an object such as the approximate sphere depicted in Figure 1-10, we ask the 3D printer to fill the whole space *inside* the object with plastic, or whatever material we are printing with. The 'inside' of the object is defined by the direction of the facet normal arrows, all of which point outwards. If we had defined a second smaller sphere inside the larger one, but with its facet normal arrows pointing inwards, we would fill the space *inside* the outer sphere but *outside* the inner one, thus creating a hollow spherical object rather than a solid one.

There are some essential criteria that a mesh must satisfy before it can be 3D printed. The most important is that its surface or surfaces must be continuous. In technical jargon, all surfaces must be what are known mathematically as 2-manifolds.

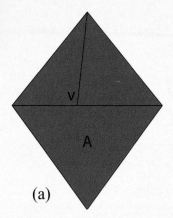

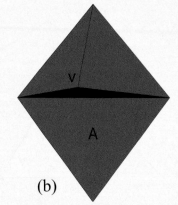

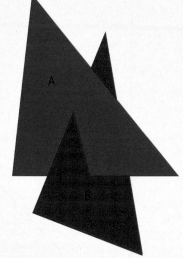

(a)

(b)

ABOVE *Figure 1-14* The vertex-to-vertex rule.

RIGHT *Figure 1-15* Intersecting facets.

For example, in Figure 1-13 the topmost vertex of the triangular facet labelled A does not quite coincide with the vertices of its neighbours. This causes a gap, shown in black, in the surface, which makes it non-continuous. Therefore it does not enclose a finite volume and cannot be 3D-printed. This is an example of a *manifold error*.

We now see why the high precision of a CAD drawing is a necessary requirement, and why the low quality of an image won't do. The vertices shared by adjacent faces must have *exactly* the same coordinates. The displacement illustrated in Figure 1-13 might only be tiny, but it would still render the object unprintable.

Another requirement that must be satisfied is the vertex-to-vertex rule, namely that each triangle must share exactly two vertices with each of its adjacent triangles. Figure 1-14 illustrates a configuration that contravenes this rule. At (a) we see that facet A has three vertices on its upper edge. This is illegal because, as far as the software is concerned, the edges are not properly connected. At (b) we see why. By moving vertex V very slightly we see that there is in fact a degenerate facet between facet A and the other two. Although this facet has zero area, since its three vertices are in line at (a), it still prevents proper connection between A and the other two facets, and therefore constitutes a leak.

Another problem that can arise is that of intersecting facets. This situation is illustrated in Figure 1-15, where triangles A and B intersect one another. This can cause problems for the 3D printer because a triangle might lie partly inside and partly outside the mesh. 3D printers do not like internal edges and faces.

Some 3D CAD programs not only create triangles but also faces formed from polygons – particularly four-sided ones known as quads. These can suffer from a defect that is never encountered with triangular facets, namely non-flat faces. With three vertices it is always possible to find a plane that includes all three. However, if we introduce a fourth vertex, this could lie outside the plane of the other three. This gives rise to a non-flat face, which our slicing program might not like.

Mesh processing and slicing

To ensure that none of the above errors creep into our 3D drawing, we can employ a mesh processing program. Sometimes mesh checking and fixing is built into our 3D CAD program, while sometimes it is an add-on that we have to install. Other 3D CAD programs do not have any mesh processing capability, so we have to install a separate program to do this for us.

Typical things we ask our mesh processing program to do are to get rid of duplicate vertices – i.e. where two vertices lie very close together, merge them into one, which gets rid of problems like that in Figure 1-13. We can also ask it to remove non-manifold edges, which fixes problems such as that in Figure 1-14 and, to some extent, Figure 1-15. However, you might find that in doing so it removes large chunks of your model, so it is a good idea to check for manifold errors as you go along rather than at the end, to help identify the source of any problems. Figure 1-16 illustrates a buffer beam, made up of 680 triangular facets, in a mesh processing program called Meshlab, of which more later. Building this buffer beam will be one of our examples later in the book.

The output from such a program goes into a *slicing* program, which, as its name implies, takes horizontal slices across the mesh and describes

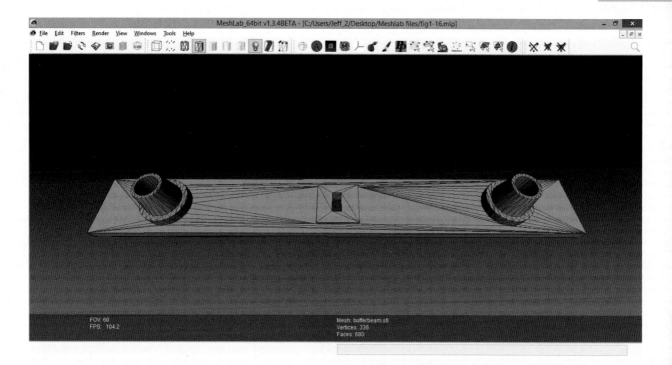

ABOVE *Figure 1-16* A 3D mesh.

RIGHT *Figure 1-17* Printing in slices.

these slices in a language called G-code. The G-code instructions tell our printer where to move to in the xy plane, when to start and when to stop printing, where to move to next, and so on. Once our first slice is printed, either the print head moves up (in the z direction) or the print bed moves down, and the next slice is printed on top of the first.

'Printing' in this context can mean one of several things. On cheaper 3D printers it generally means extruding molten plastic, usually PLA (PolyLactic Acid), through a nozzle in a process called 'Fused Filament Fabrication' (FFF). On more expensive machines, a laser beam can be used to sinter (cause to coalesce by heat and compression) metallic dust in a process called Selective Laser Sintering (SLS). We shall discuss these and other technologies in detail later in the book.

Figure 1-17 illustrates how our buffer beam would be printed, with, of course, greatly exaggerated thickness of slices. At the top of the diagram the individual slices are shown separately. At the bottom, they are shown as they would be printed, one on top of the other.

In the remaining chapters of the book, we shall review some of the software available for 2D and

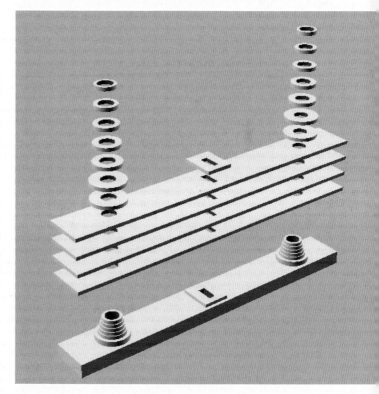

3D CAD and mesh processing/slicing. Then we shall describe some examples using a selection of this software to build lineside structures, rolling stock and locomotives.

2

CAD Software

In this chapter we will review some of the software available for making CAD drawings. We have taken a decision that all the software we use in this book, and therefore everything reviewed here, should be free of charge. It is possible to spend many thousands of pounds on a CAD package, but the likelihood of this being worthwhile to the average railway modeller is remote. There are packages available that will meet most, if not all, of a modeller's needs at no cost. Most can be downloaded from the internet and installed on your computer in a matter of minutes. It should be stressed that the inclusion of a package in this chapter does not constitute a recommendation, nor does the exclusion of a particular package necessarily mean anything other than that the authors have no direct experience of it. Indeed, there may well be some excellent packages out there that the authors have never heard of. A search for 'CAD software' from www.downloads. com yields (at the time of writing) more than 750 suggestions. We have not tried them all!

Blender

Blender is a bit like Marmite – try it, and you will either love it or hate it. There are people who have tried to get to grips with *Blender* and have given up in despair, advising anyone who'll listen that Blender is a serious threat to your sanity. At the other extreme, a contributor to one of the many Blender forums says 'I love *Blender* so much that I'm thinking of getting a tattoo'! How can a software package inspire such extremes of reaction?

The main reason that some people find *Blender* exasperating is its user interface, which is unconventional to say the least. For example, with almost every program you've ever used things are selected by clicking on them with the left mouse button (LMB). Not so with *Blender*. Clicking the LMB sets the position of the 3D cursor, which is the location at which new objects will be added. To select an object, *Blender* uses the right mouse button (RMB), and this can take some getting used to. The way the mouse works in *Blender* can be disconcerting. In most applications, clicking on something then moving the mouse will 'drag' that something around the screen. Letting go of the mouse button will 'drop' the something in that location. Not so with *Blender*. Click with the RMB and drag the object a little way, then release the RMB. The object will continue to move around with the mouse, even with no button pressed! To 'drop' the selected object, you need to click the LMB. Incidentally, a three-button mouse, or a two-button mouse with a wheel that can be used as a third button, is virtually essential.

To users whose experience is mainly with 'point and click'-type user interfaces, *Blender* can seem overwhelmed by keyboard shortcuts. Most applications recognise a few standard ones like **Ctrl-O** to open a file, **Ctrl-S** to save, **Ctrl-P** to print, and so on. However, *Blender* takes the keyboard shortcut to new levels. There are 60 alphabetic, numeric, punctuation and function keys on a standard keyboard, and this means that there are a total of 480 possible combinations of these keys with **Shift**, **Alt** and **Ctrl**. Sometimes it can seem as if Blender uses every single one of them! For example, in **Edit** mode you can press **Shift-Alt-Ctrl-M** to highlight non-manifold edges and vertices! All of the keyboard shortcut functions can also be accessed via menus and various editor windows, but the route to them can be cryptic!

However, if you can persevere with *Blender* and master its somewhat quirky user interface, you will find that it has some real positives. Firstly, it is truly free, open source software. Unlike many other so-called 'free' packages, Blender is not a cut-down version of a commercial package that is offered free of charge in the hope that you will buy an upgrade. Nor does it demand your e-mail address and bombard you with advertising. The Blender Foundation is a Dutch public benefit corporation set up by the original author of *Blender*, Ton Roosendaal. Its software is distributed free of charge to give the world-wide internet community access to 3D technology.

A second point in favour of *Blender* is the range of features and facilities it offers. It contains a lot more than just 3D CAD capabilities – far more, in fact, than the average railway modeller will need to do 3D printing. It has facilities for creating surface textures, colours, light and shade. It can do shadows and reflections. It has extensive facilities for animation, so you can make movies with *Blender*. To some extent this explains why its user interface is of necessity a lot more complicated than the 'point and click' style.

Thirdly, *Blender* has a thriving user community, not least in the model railway world. Forums, tutorials, on-line manuals and a wealth of practical advice are available online. A selection of these

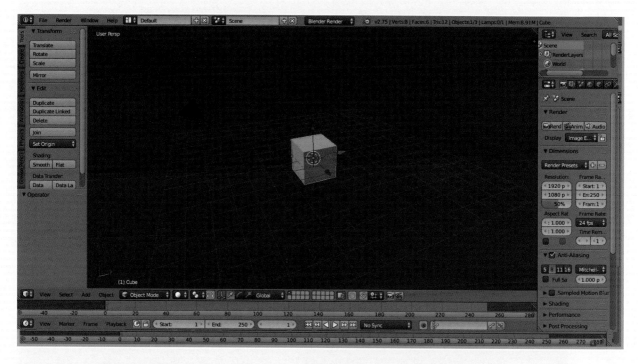

ABOVE *Figure 2-1 Blender* default startup screen.

resources is listed in Appendix 1. One of particular interest is the RMWeb Laser Cutting, 3D Printing and CAD special interest group.

So, if you decide to give *Blender* a try, here's how to go about it. Go to the website http://www. blender.org/download, select the operating system appropriate for your computer (Windows, Mac, Linux) and click 'download'. The download takes only a few moments, and the installer works like a dream, with no nonsense about having to register as a user or restart your computer. On starting *Blender* you will be presented with the screen shown in Figure 2-1.

This default startup screen contains five windows, each of which can display whatever you select by clicking the small icon at the extreme top left or bottom left of the window. For example, the window running across the top of the screen is displaying an 'i' icon – it is an information window. At the left side, not quite at the bottom of the screen, there is an icon with a cube. This relates to the main window, which is a 3D view of the startup object: a cube, illuminated by a lamp and viewed by a camera. We shall not have much use for the latter, so select them (RMB) and press the **Del** key. In the extreme bottom left is another window icon with a clock; this is a timeline window, used for

doing animation. Again, we shall not need this for 3D printing, so we can get rid of it. To do this, move the mouse pointer to the hatched area just left of the 3D view window icon. The mouse cursor will then change to a cross: left click and drag this down over the hatched area in the timeline window, and the latter will disappear together with its window. To the right are two further windows: an outliner, which displays a hierarchical list of the objects in the 3D view, and a properties editor, which can be used to display and edit properties of the currently active entity. This is an important tool. The icons to the right of it offer choices of the entity whose properties you can edit. Click on the little cube icon ('object') and you will see the current location, size and rotation of the currently selected object. Try typing new numerical values for these and observe the effect on the cube.

On the left side of the 3D window is the tool shelf. The visibility of this can be toggled by the **T** key. Click on the **Tools** tab, then on **Translate**, **Rotate** and **Scale** in turn and move the mouse around in the 3D window. This gives you an alternative way to change things around. Left click when you want the translating, rotating or scaling to stop. Now click the **Create** tab and try adding some more cubes, spheres, cones, etc, to the scene (see Figure 2-2). Remember to left click to set the 3D cursor to the point where you want the new object to be

added. Get a feel for using the mouse by right clicking and dragging objects around, and left clicking where you want to park them. Try zooming in and out with the mouse wheel, and spinning the whole scene by moving the mouse with the centre button, or wheel, pressed down. You can make yourself seasick if you do this for too long!

One important thing we will need is the 3D Printing add-on to *Blender*. To activate this, go to the File menu on the top (info) window and click **User Preferences**. Select the **Add-ons** tab and under **Categories** click **Mesh**. From the list of Mesh add-ons check the one called '**Mesh : 3D Print Toolbox**'. The 3D Print tools enable us to check for things like manifold errors as described in the previous chapter.

TOP *Figure 2-2* Various 3D objects.

ABOVE *Figure 2-3* Customised *Blender* startup screen.

We now want to save a customised startup screen, so select all the objects in the 3D view (the 'A' key is useful here, to **Select/Deselect All**) and delete them. By the way, do not worry that the **3D Print Toolbox** has disappeared from the toolshelf – it is only there when there is at least one object in view. On the menu at the bottom of the screen click **View > Left** and click the **Ortho/Perspective** toggle as necessary to get an orthographic view. This will give us a standard side elevation view, which is generally the best starting point for a 3D

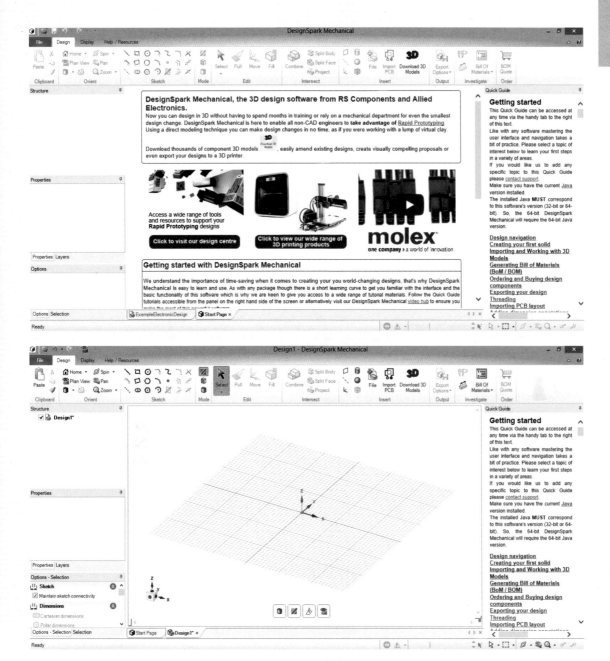

TOP *Figure 2-4 DesignSpark Mechanical* startup screen.

ABOVE *Figure 2-5 DesignSpark Mechanical* New Project screen.

drawing. Finally, on the **File** menu click **Save Startup File**. Our new customised startup screen is as shown in Figure 2-3. This will be the starting point for all Blender-based examples later in the book.

DesignSpark Mechanical

For those who prefer a more conventional user interface, *DesignSpark Mechanical* might be worth a look. It is one member of a suite of tools being made available for free by RS Components (http://

www.designspark.com). *DesignSpark Mechanical* provides a good range of 3D CAD capabilities but maintains a reasonably simple and uncluttered user interface. It doesn't have the rendering and movie-making features of more complex programs like Blender as it focuses clearly on mechanical design, which helps significantly with the lightweight feel.

There is more than enough capability for the majority of model railway 3D printing projects and you can export your models in stl file format. Installation is simple, though currently the only supported platform is Windows (32 or 64bit).

Figure 2-4 shows the main screen as it appears when you start the program. The program assumes you will be connected to the internet and will need to be at least every 30 days so that it can check your licence. Don't panic – it can be used happily offline, although you will lose some of the quite slick help functions. The central section of the screen is taken up with a 'start' page advertising interesting stuff from the distributor (hey, it's free software – you gotta let them try to sell you something!). You can happily close this screen using the 'X' on the tab at the bottom of the panel.

If we go ahead and close this panel and any example panels the program decides to show us, we end up with a blank area in the centre of the screen. If we now create a new design project by clicking **File > New Design** we get the screen shown in Figure 2-5.

If you are online you will get quick guide information in the pane on the right – in this case it is about getting started. The help is pretty good in this program. If you hover the mouse pointer over any of the icons and options in the various toolbars you get a snippet of help that is often enough for you to figure out whether you are looking in the right place.

Along the top of the screen are several groups of icons that are the tools you will need to make your 3D drawing (Figure 2-6). The **Orient** options, which can be found towards the left end of the toolbar, allow you to change the view, spin, pan and zoom in or out. Next come a group of icons

called **Sketch**; these provide tools to draw lines, rectangles, circles, arcs, etc, on a two-dimensional grid. These can then be turned into three-dimensional objects using the **Pull** tool in the **Edit** group. To the right of this are an important group of tools that allow you to combine three-dimensional objects, either by merging them together, or using one object to intersect with another. The Insert group allows you to add ready-made 3D objects to your drawing, either standard shapes like cubes and cylinders, or complete models either from stl files or downloaded from the web. The **Output** options include the all-important facility to export your model in stl format ready for 3D printing.

Figure 2-7 shows a Pennsylvania Railroad concrete track bumper made with *DesignSpark*.

The main body of the bumper was created as a rectangle in plan view, then 'pulled' upwards to make it into a solid body. The top rear edge was then selected and the **Chamfer** tool used to apply the rear sloping angle. In the side view a curved line was drawn matching the radius on the top of the bumper; this was then pulled into a curved plane

BELOW TOP *Figure 2-6* DesignSpark Mechanical toolbar.

BELOW BOTTOM *Figure 2-7* DesignSpark Mechanical track bumper model.

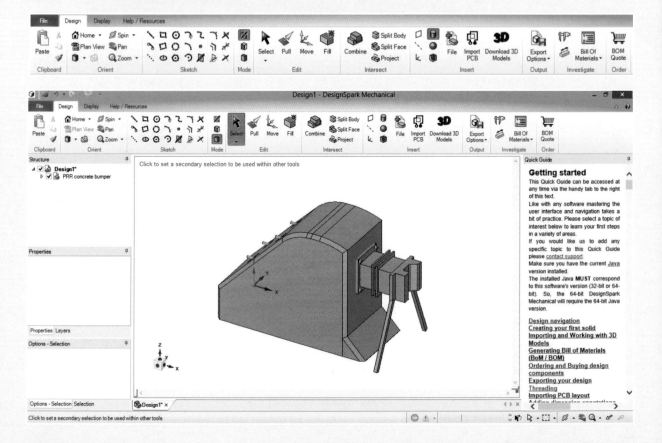

that was used with the **Combine** tool to cut away the top. Another rectangular box was drawn and merged with the front of the block. This was again chamfered to give the angled face at the bottom front of the object. This gave the basic concrete block that, as you can see, has a small chamfer on all its edges. To do this all the edges were selected by holding the **Ctrl** key and clicking each edge, then all were chamfered using the **Pull** tool in one go.

In a similar way you can round off edges, create fillets in corners or extrude faces. All in all this is a very powerful program that avoids being too daunting by presenting thousands of options all at once. There is a fair amount of help information available from the distributor, creators and user community.

Autodesk Fusion 360

Fusion 360 is a full-blown commercial CAD product with a large range of capabilities. Luckily, at the time of writing a free licence is available to educators, hobbyists or small start-up businesses. As with most of the other programs reviewed here there is more than enough functionality for the average model railway 3D printing project.

The user interface of *Fusion 360* is clean and uncluttered, even though it has a large range of capabilities including rendering and animation. These capabilities are nicely stowed away out of sight unless you are using them, so for those of us who just want to model objects they don't get in

BELOW *Figure 2-8 Autodesk Fusion* 360 start screen.

the way. The start screen for *Fusion 360* is shown in Figure 2-8.

The screen shows the toolbar and screen set up while in **Model** mode, which is where we need to be. Each of the items on the toolbar has a dropdown list containing many functions, and opening the **Create** list will show a range of primitive objects, including complex things like spirals and threads, that can be built by specifying a few parameters. You can also create arbitrary shapes and 'sculpt' them by moving around faces and vertices.

In the top right-hand corner of the main screen area you can see a cube, which is the way you control the current viewing angle. The initial is the 'home' view, but if you click on a face of the cube you can see the front, back, left and right. You can also click on an edge of the cube to look at the model from that angle or return to the 'home' view by clicking on the small house-shaped button that appears to the top left of the view control if you mouse over it. You can also pan and rotate the view using the buttons on the toolbar at the bottom centre of the work area.

Figure 2-9 shows a model – an LNER lineside ballast bin – opened in *Fusion 360* and drawn to the correct size for a 4mm/1ft scale model. The **Chamfer** modifier has been selected and you can see a panel on the right-hand side of the screen where parameters can be entered and hints are given as to what to do next. Along the bottom of the screen is a long line of icons that is a 'breadcrumb trail' documenting all the operations

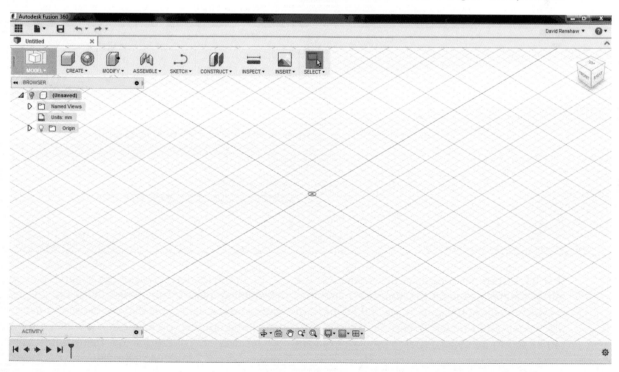

BELOW *Figure 2-9* Using the chamfer modifier in *Fusion 360*.

BOTTOM *Figure 2-10* *OpenSCAD* startup screen.

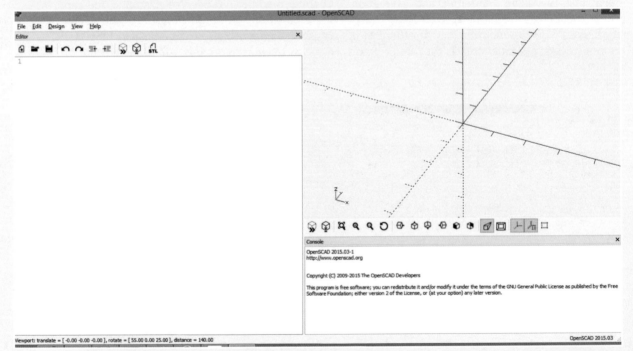

that have been performed on this model. On the left of the main screen is the **'Browser'** panel that provides details of the units in use and the parts of the model, listed under **'Bodies'**. Individual parts can be selected as well as being shown or hidden using these entries.

Up in the top left corner of the screen is an icon resembling nine small squares. Clicking on this opens up the data panel that contains information on all the projects you have been working on and allows you to collaborate on them with other people – not something you find in every CAD program! From this panel you can bring in models in many different formats by uploading them to your project, where they are converted into Fusion 360 format in the cloud rather than doing all the conversion on your machine. This capability requires you to set up an Autodesk account, which also opens up a number of other facilities

Fusion 360 has functions that can help specifically with 3D printing. You can use the '3D print' item on the **File** menu or right click on one or more of the body entries in the browser and use the '**Save as STL**' option. From here you can either simply save in stl format or send the model to another of Autodesk's tools, **Meshmixer** or **Print Studio**.

As you would expect from a sophisticated program of this type, there is plenty of help with context help panels popping up when you hover the mouse over icons and menu items. There is a lot in here, but it's fairly accessible.

OpenSCAD

While *DesignSpark* and *Fusion 360* employ fairly conventional 3D CAD user interfaces, this program is, in its way, even more unconventional than Blender. *OpenSCAD* (pronounced 'Open-Ess-CAD') is a free CAD tool available on multiple platforms under the GNU Public Licence. It's essentially a very simple tool and differs from most other CAD programs in that it is not built around the idea of dragging and dropping objects using the mouse. Instead the model is described by specifying it in a text format. The very simple start screen is shown in Figure 2.10.

To the left is a text editor window into which you can type object definitions, to the right is a panel in which the model is rendered, and below this is a pane showing status information.

So if there are no icons, buttons and drag-and-drop, how the heck do you define a model? It's actually quite simple, especially if you have ever done any sort of computer programming. There is a small range of native objects you can create directly. For instance, to create a cube with 10mm sides at the origin we type the single line shown in Figure 2-11.

It looks very much like a bit of computer code, even ending with a semicolon. If we want to move it to somewhere other than the origin we can use a 'translate' function, and to rotate it we use the 'rotate' function. Interestingly, we put the translate and rotate definitions in front of the definition of the cube. It's a bit like using reverse polish notation on a desktop calculator in the '70s! The line of code shown in the inset to Figure 2-12 gives us the result shown.

To get complex shapes there are solid geometry Boolean functions that allow basic shapes to be merged together or cut one from another. It all works surprisingly well, and of course if you need to change the size of something you can go into the script and change a few values, and the model updates. The scripts can get quite large, but there are options for including components into other components so you can subdivide things. Figure 2-13 shows the LNER ballast bin modelled in *OpenSCAD*.

BELOW *Figure 2-11* A simple cube in *OpenSCAD*.

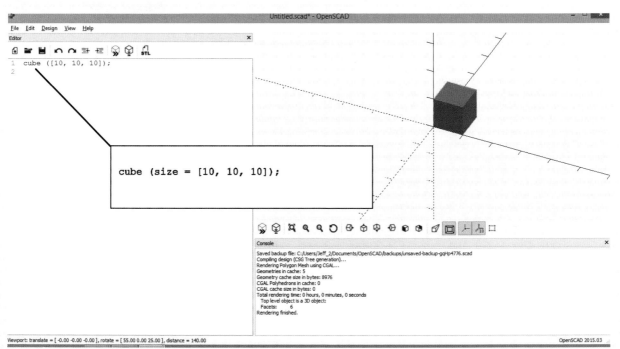

BELOW *Figure 2-12* Moving and rotating in *OpenSCAD*.   **BOTTOM** *Figure 2-13* The LNER ballast bin in *OpenSCAD*.

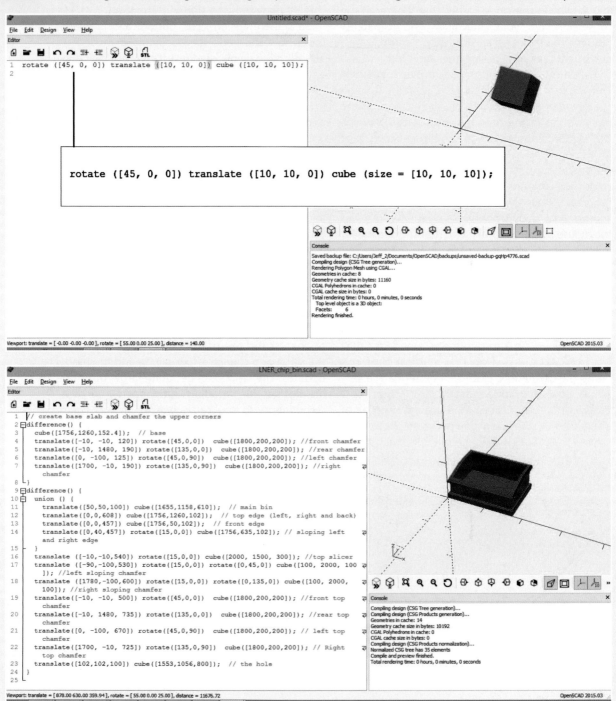

If you have never done any programming, *OpenSCAD* may not be for you. However, it can provide a very succinct way of describing some quite complex models in certain circumstances, as we shall see later in the book.

Sketchup Make

Unlike the 3D CAD tools reviewed so far, the user interface of which can be somewhat daunting, *Sketchup Make* is a doddle to use. However, its simplicity arises in part from its limited range of capabilities. Sketchup was originally a Google product, but is now marketed by Trimble and comes

BELOW *Figure 2-14* *Sketchup Make* default startup screen.   **BOTTOM** *Figure 2-15* Making a solid object.

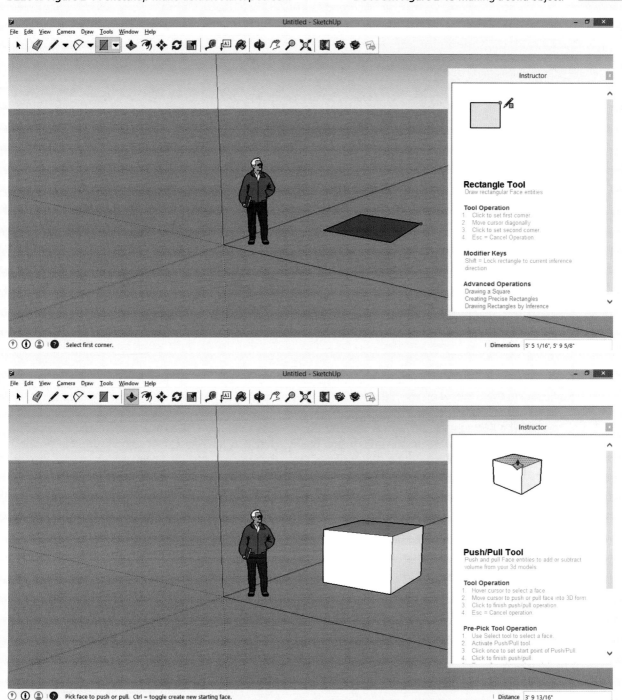

in two forms. *Sketchup Make* is free of charge, but limited in capabilities. *Sketchup Pro* is, at the time of writing, £331 for a single user licence, but a lot more capable. You can download a trial copy of *Sketchup Pro* free of charge for 30 days. However, we are in this chapter focussing on free software, so we shall concentrate on *Sketchup Make*.

The software can be downloaded from http://www.Sketchup.com, where you can also view some very helpful video tutorials about getting started with the program. On loading Sketchup, you will be presented with the screen shown in Figure 2-14.

The screen couldn't be simpler. Along the top are a series of basic drawing and editing tools.

BELOW *Figure 2-16 Sketchup* customised startup screen.

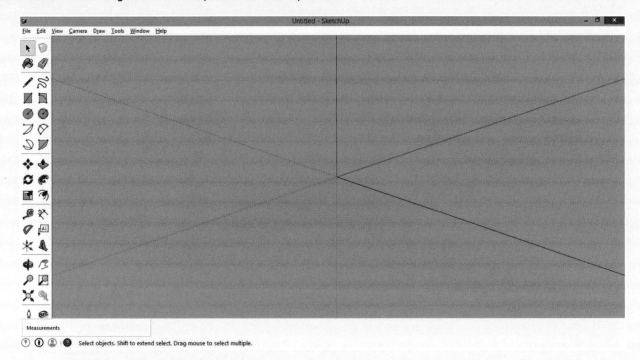

Close to the origin is a very helpful fellow who will tell you, in the window on the right, what the tool you've just selected is for, and how to use it. As you can see, the **Rectangle** tool has been selected, and the very straightforward instructions have been followed to draw a rectangle on the xy plane. On the toolbar, to the right of the **Rectangle** tool, is the **Push/Pull** tool; if we select this we can turn our rectangle into a solid object simply by pulling it upwards (Figure 2-15). This is how Sketchup works. There are no solid objects that you can select directly – everything is made by drawing in two dimensions then using the **Push/Pull** tool to create a solid. It is all extremely simple and straightforward.

After a very short time you may find that you don't need the helpful fellow and his instructions, so click on the man, delete him and close the instructions window. To get the full range of tools, go to the **View** menu, select **Toolbars**, uncheck the **Getting Started Tool Set** and click **Large Tool Set**. Click also on **Measurements** – this will give you a useful display of the measurements of what you're drawing. Unlike *Blender*, Sketchup works in real units of measurement, which makes things a lot easier. You can click **Window > Preferences > Template** and, instead of **Simple Template**, click on the **Construction Documentation Template**. You can choose to work in feet and inches or in millimetres. Finally, click **File > Save As Template**,

and this will then become your default startup screen (Figure 2-16).

So, if *Sketchup Make* is free and so easy to use, why would we want anything else? The answer is that it is limited in its facilities. Trimble's hope is that using *Sketchup Make* will whet your appetite so that you go ahead and purchase *Sketchup Pro*. There are several things that you simply can't do in *Sketchup Make*. One of them, and particularly important from a 3D printing point of view, is that you can't export stl files directly. Since virtually all 3D printing requires data in stl format, this is a problem. Fortunately, it can be overcome. There are a number of free software packages that will convert a file format that *Sketchup Make* can output into stl format. One such is *Meshlab*, which will be reviewed later. There are numerous other limitations to *Sketchup Make*. However, if you only want to create simple lineside structures and the like, *Sketchup Make* may be the CAD tool for you.

Autodesk Tinkercad

This is one of the simplest 3D modelling programs you could wish for. You don't even need to download any software: *Tinkercad* runs in your web browser. Simply go to http://www.tinkercad.com (Figure 2-17) and accept the invitation to start tinkering!

You will need to register online as a *Tinkercad* user. There is a basic tutorial video, which teaches

BELOW *Figure 2-17* Tinkercad startup screen.   BOTTOM *Figure 2-19* A kitchen table.

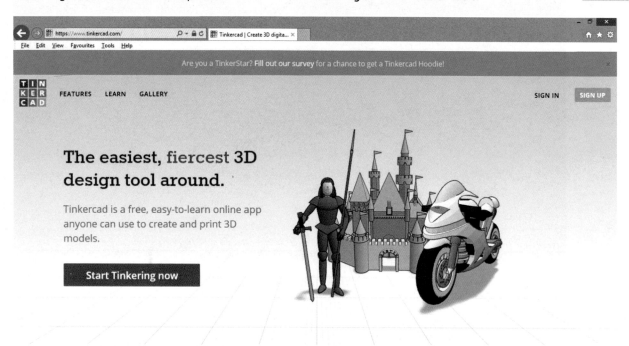

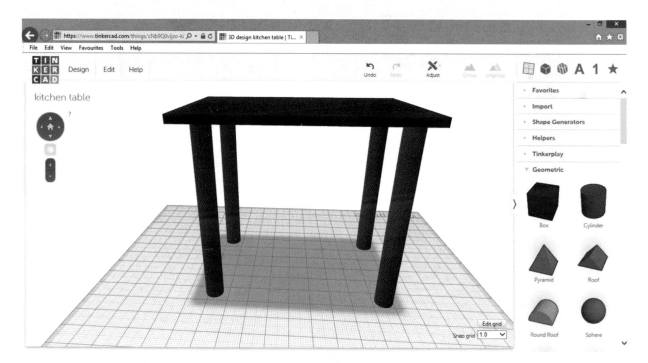

you the rudiments, and a series of lessons. It is all very easy and a lot of fun!

Basically, the idea is to build things by dragging and dropping basic geometric and custom shapes, then modifying them and combining them in various ways to build real objects. It is as easy as playing with a set of child's building bricks. For example, the kitchen table in Figure 2-19 was built from a cube and four cylinders in less than a minute, after watching the tutorial video for the first time! Having built your table, which is saved for you to the cloud, you can then download it to your computer as an stl file for 3D printing.

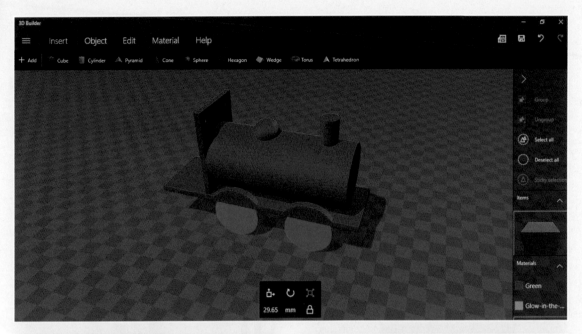

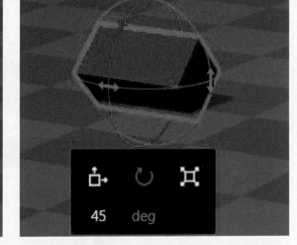

Microsoft® 3D Builder

This, like TinkerCAD, is a very simple tool for creating basic models. It came to the authors' attention when we upgraded one of our computers to Windows 10. 3D Builder is pre-packaged with Windows 10 so if you upgrade (or buy a new computer) you will find it in your 'Apps' list. Along the top of the screen (figure 2-19) you will see the 'Insert' menu item, which lets you add basic 3D shapes to your model (cubes, cylinders etc.). To the right of this, the 'Object' menu gives you options to manipulate complete objects, e.g. to make duplicates or mirror images. Next, the Edit menu contains, amongst other things, options to merge, intersect or subtract objects from one another. To the right of the screen are options to group multiple objects into a single object and various

TOP *Figure 2-19* Microsoft *3D Builder*.

ABOVE LEFT *Figure 2-20* Scale tool.

ABOVE RIGHT *Figure 2-21* Rotate tool.

selection options. The tools you will probably use most are those within the little rectangle at the centre bottom of the screen. On the left is the 'Move' tool - use this to move the selected object around in 3 dimensions. On the right is the 'Scale' tool which allows you to expand or contract an object. The little padlock toggles you between locked and unlocked aspect ratio - i.e. scaling in all three dimensions, or just one dimension (figure 2-20). In the centre is the 'Rotate' tool (figure 2-21). Use this to rotate the object around a selected axis.

The remarkable ease of use of both 3D Builder and TinkerCAD comes at a price, however. A lot of the complexity in other 3D CAD programs arises from the wide range of capabilities and options available. Clearly, for these programs to be quite so easy to use means that their facilities are limited. However, if you just want to print something simple and don't want to spend a lot of time and effort, 3D Builder or TinkerCAD may be for you.

DraftSight

DraftSight is a 2D CAD program, free for individual use, from Dassault Systems. Because it is restricted to two dimensions, it is not suitable for creating 3D meshes. However, we mention it here for two reasons. First, it is often useful to have a couple of 2D drawings of an object you wish to print in 3D – for example, a plan and an elevation, to use as background images on your 3D modelling screen. Second, if you want to do some laser cutting, a 2D drawing file is what you require. There are numerous other free 2D programs available, too many to review them all, but we use *DraftSight* to build one of our examples later in the book, so we mention it here.

Figure 2-22 shows the *DraftSight* startup screen. Many people don't like a black background, but fortunately *DraftSight* lets you change a great many things about the user interface. To get a more conventional white background, click **Tools > Options > System Options** and under **Display** select **Element Colours** and change the **Model Background** to white. There are plenty of other things you can customise in the **Options** window, such as where your files are to

be saved to or opened from, what file types to use as default, drawing units, and so on (Figure 2-23).

In use, *DraftSight* is fairly straightforward, although the mouse sometimes doesn't quite do what you might think it should. Down at the bottom of the screen is the **Command** window. Most drawing is done using the mouse, but certain actions require text input. A useful feature of this window is that it provides an audit trail of everything you've done so far. You can make this window bigger or smaller by dragging its top edge. On the left side of the screen is the **Palette** area. By default, this displays the **Home palette** when *DraftSight* starts up, and this exhorts you to purchase *DraftSight Professional* or to look at the learning tools on the web; you can close this to get more drawing space. Another palette that fits into the same area is the **Properties** palette, which is useful for editing the numerical properties of drawing entities. Access this via **Tools > Properties**.

DraftSight is able to write files in a range of dxf and dwg formats, so is suitable for creating files for laser cutting.

LibreCAD

Another free 2D package that is well worth a look is *LibreCAD*. Unlike DraftSight, which requires you to give an e-mail address to which it will send you periodic promotional and advertising material, *LibreCAD* is truly free, open-source software. You are politely invited to consider making a donation to

BELOW *Figure 2-22 DraftSight* startup screen.

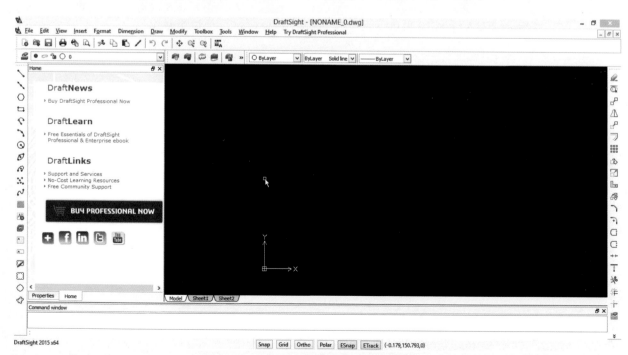

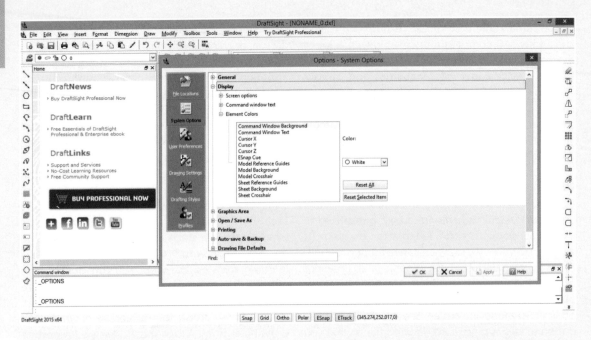

the *LibreCAD* community, and if you make extensive use of it you should consider this.

the *LibreCAD* community, and if you make extensive use of it you should consider this.

LibreCAD grew out of an earlier 2D CAD package called *QCAD*, which had a very similar user interface to that of *AutoCAD*, one of the leading commercial packages (and very expensive!). *LibreCAD* thus has a similar look and feel to *AutoCAD* and has an extensive range of options.

However, it is a work in progress and this can be frustrating. For example, although the **Edit** menu contains **Copy** and **Paste** as options, they do not seem to work. So, you decide to look in the manual to see what you're doing wrong. Click **Help > Manual** and at

ABOVE *Figure 2-23* *DraftSight* Options window.

the time of writing you get a message saying 'OOPS NO MANUAL!' and explaining that a new manual is being written. You are directed to a work in progress document and various wikis and forums. Here you will find that **Copy** and **Paste** are being developed, but meanwhile you are offered a workaround: to copy something from one drawing file into another, use **File > Import Block** to import the whole drawing, then delete the bits you don't want!

Nevertheless, *LibreCAD* can produce some nice 2D drawings and scores well on the ease-of-use scale. We shall use *LibreCAD* to create some fancy brickwork later in the book.

BELOW *Figure 2-24* A *LibreCAD* 2D drawing.

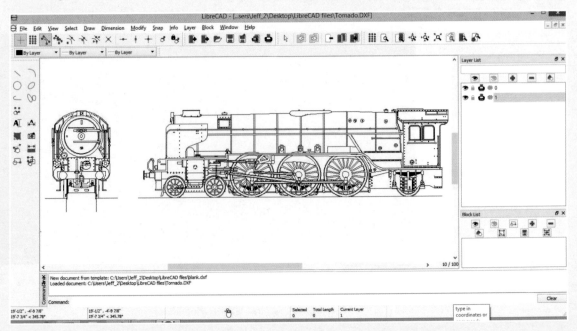

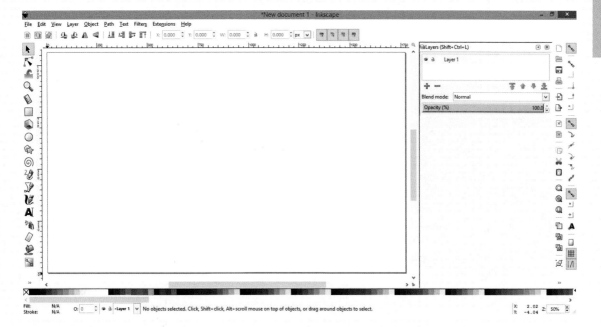

Inkscape

Inkscape is a free vector graphics drawing program. It is not intended to be CAD software, but is a versatile tool for graphic designers, illustrators and the like. However, it has a wide range of drawing capabilities and has become popular for the creation of etching and cutting files. We will use *Inkscape* to draw one of our laser cutting examples later in the book.

Figure 2-25 shows the *Inkscape* main screen set up and ready to go, in this case with an A4 page in landscape mode. The size of the page you are working on can be adjusted in the document properties option, selecting from a range of presets or specifying a custom size – very useful when working with odd-sized sheets of material.

The user interface of *Inkscape* is fairly conventional, although there are a huge range of tools and options and consequently by default there are toolbars with icons on all four sides of the screen. The main tool menu is on the left of the screen, and selecting a tool from here causes the top toolbar to change with appropriate options. The panel on the right displays different settings dialogs based on which of the buttons in the lower area of the pane is clicked. This is where you adjust things like line colours, fill patterns and layers.

Inkscape is able to read and write a wide range of file formats, including dxf, which is useful for creating files for laser cutting.

Meshlab

Meshlab is a mesh processing program, developed by the Information Science & Technology Institute (ISTI) in Pisa, Italy. It is designed to check, repair, edit and render large 3D meshes, such as those that arise from 3D scanning. As such, most of its capabilities are beyond what we require to print railway models. However, it may be a useful tool to have in your 3D workshop for a couple of reasons. First, it can be used to check meshes for manifold errors of the type described in Chapter 1, and to repair any such errors it may find. Second, and possibly more importantly, it can import and export a wide range of file types. This means that programs that are not able to write stl files, such as *Sketchup Make*, can write in one of the 20-odd formats that *Meshlab* understands. *Meshlab* can then export the mesh in stl format suitable for 3D printing.

Meshlab is free of charge, open-source software made available by ISTI under the terms of the GNU Public Licence. You can download it from http://www.sourceforge.net, and you can watch some splendid tutorials featuring Mr P on Youtube. Just look for MrPMeshLabTutorials.

Figure 2-26 shows a mesh imported into *Meshlab* and checked for manifold errors. This mesh is in fact a Stanier chimney, the construction of which will be described later in the book. As you can see, it is free from any such errors. If it was not, *Meshlab* could probably fix them. Our principal use for *Meshlab* will be to convert meshes from one format to another, as will be described later. Another free mesh processing program that you might like to try is *netfabb Basic*. This, like *Sketchup Make*, is a 'free' version of a program you have to pay for – *netfabb Professional* – so be prepared for exhortations to upgrade!

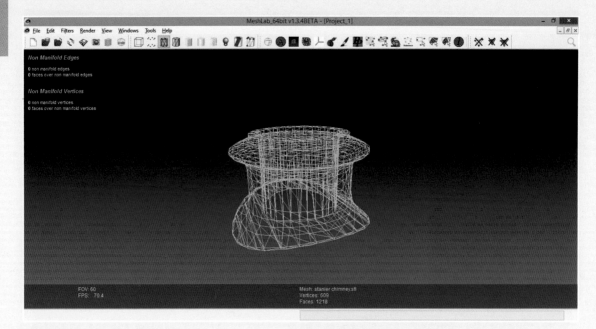

ABOVE *Figure 2-26* *Meshlab* screen   BELOW *Figure 2-27* A buffer beam in *Slic3r*

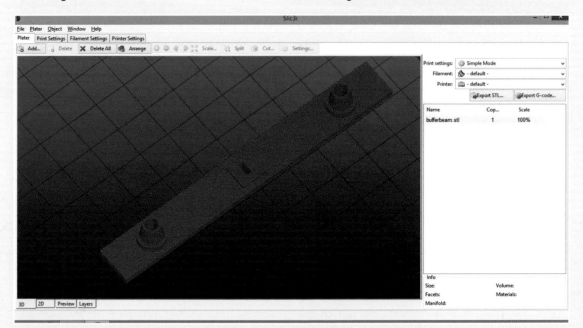

Slic3r

Slic3r (pronounced 'slicer') is a slicing program, as explained in Chapter 1. It takes a file in stl format and converts it into a series of instructions to a 3D printer. These instructions are in a language called G-code, which was originally developed for numerically controlled machine tools such as lathes, millers, grinders, etc. Figure 2-27 shows a buffer beam loaded into *Slic3r*.

On the right of the screen you will see an option to export this as G-code. The result (or, rather, a small snippet of the resulting file) is illustrated in Figure 2-28. Text to the right of a semi-colon is

comment – it is ignored by the 3D printer and is there purely to help human readers! The first few instructions lift the nozzle from the printer bed, wait for the nozzle temperature to reach 200°C, then lower the nozzle to print the first slice. There follow a large number of G1 codes, which are linear moves to the specified x and y coordinates, extruding the indicated amount of plastic material. These print our first slice. The nozzle will then be moved up (in the z direction) to print the next slice, and so on.

Slic3r has a lot more capability than this, however. It can create support structures, for example. If we want to print a horizontal surface some distance

```
bufferbeam.gcode - Notepad
File  Edit  Format  View  Help
M107
M104 S200 ; set temperature
G28 ; home all axes
G1 Z5 F5000 ; lift nozzle

M109 S200 ; wait for temperature to be reached
G21 ; set units to millimeters
G90 ; use absolute coordinates
M82 ; use absolute distances for extrusion
G92 E0
G1 Z0.350 F7800.000
G1 E-2.00000 F2400.00000
G92 E0
G1 X48.668 Y88.274 F7800.000
G1 E2.00000 F2400.00000
G1 X50.820 Y87.481 E2.07096 F1800.000
G1 X52.000 Y87.375 E2.10761
G1 X148.000 Y87.375 E5.07798
G1 X150.259 Y87.772 E5.14894
G1 X152.247 Y88.915 E5.21990 F1800.000
G1 X153.726 Y90.668 E5.29087
G1 X154.519 Y92.820 E5.36183
G1 X154.625 Y94.000 E5.39848
G1 X154.625 Y106.000 E5.76978
G1 X154.228 Y108.259 E5.84074
G1 X153.085 Y110.247 E5.91170
G1 X151.332 Y111.726 E5.98266
G1 X149.180 Y112.519 E6.05363
G1 X148.000 Y112.625 E6.09028
G1 X52.000 Y112.625 E9.06064
```

Slic3r
File Plater Object Window Help
Plater Print Settings Filament Settings Printer Settings

General

Layer height: 0.2 mm
Perimeters: 3 (minimum)
Solid layers: Top: 3 Bottom: 3

Infill

Fill density: 20 %
Fill pattern: Honeycomb
Top/bottom fill pattern: Rectilinear

Support material

Generate support material: ☑
Pattern spacing: 2.5 mm
Contact Z distance: 0.2 (detachable) mm
Don't support bridges: ☑
Raft layers: 0 layers

Speed

Perimeters: 60 mm/s
Infill: 80 mm/s
Travel: 130 mm/s

ABOVE LEFT *Figure 2-28* The buffer beam as G-code

ABOVE RIGHT *Figure 2-29 Slic3r* Print Settings tab

above the printer bed, *Slic3r* will generate a series of supports that prevent the surface from sagging while it cools; once the model is complete, these can be snapped off. It can create a raft – a solid bed upon which our model can be printed – often useful for structures that do not have a solid base themselves. It can save material by filling the interior of objects using a lower density than the exterior surfaces. All of these options and more are set up using the **Print Settings** tab (Figure 2-29).

Slic3r is free of charge, open-source software and can be downloaded from http://www.slic3r.org/download.

Operating systems

In the accompanying table we indicate what platforms can be used to run the various programs reviewed in this chapter (as of 2016). Note that *Tinkercad* runs in your web browser, so the operating system is irrelevant.

Hands on

In the next three chapters we shall use a selection of the software reviewed above to draw some lineside structures, rolling stock and locomotive components. The reader is encouraged not just to read these chapters, but also to download the relevant software from the World Wide Web and to follow the examples. You may not actually need any cable ducting or fireless locomotives on your layout, but these are not included because of what

OPERATING SYSTEMS			
Program	**Windows**	**Mac**	**Linux**
Blender	✓	✓	✓
DesignSpark Mechanical	✓	✗	✗
Fusion 360	✓	✓	✗
OpenSCAD	✓	✓	✓
Sketchup Make	✓	✓	✗
3D Builder	✓	✗	✗
DraftSight	✓	✓	✓
LibreCAD	✓	✓	✓
Inkscape	✓	✓	✓
Meshlab	✓	✓	✓
Netfabb Basic	✓	✓	✓
Slic3r	✓	✓	✓

they are. Rather, they are included to demonstrate particular 3D drawing techniques and to give you a feel for how to use them. You need not print them – if you don't need them on your layout this would be a waste of material. However, by treating them as a series of exercises, you will develop a feel for how to use the software to build whatever you want.

Where we use a program for the first time, we have endeavoured to provide detailed mouse-click by mouse-click instructions. However, when a program has been used before, we assume the reader has already become familiar with the program basics, so we give more general guidance.

Lineside structures

In this chapter we demonstrate the basic steps of making a 3D drawing, and for this we will build some simple lineside structures. Among the techniques we will demonstrate are: 'extruding' a 2D shape to form a 3D object, combining objects by adding or subtracting one object to or from another, and forming an array of objects in three-dimensional space. We shall also include an example where the parametric interface of *OpenSCAD* allows us to build in just a few dozen lines of code a structure that would be extremely tedious to build in any other way.

Concrete cable trunking

For our first example, we will produce some simple concrete cable trunking, a feature seen alongside the tracks on most railways these days. We shall use *DesignSpark Mechanical*.

The cable ducts usually come as two parts, a 'U' section concrete trough and a lid. The duct we wish to model is delivered in 1 metre lengths and is 220 millimetres wide and 170 millimetres deep. We will work in real world units and scale later, so to start with we create a rectangle 1,000mm by 220mm.

In *DesignSpark*, click **File > New Design**, and switch to **Plan View**. Select the **Rectangle** drawing tool from the toolbar and click and drag out a rectangle on the drawing surface. We can either drag out to exactly the size we want or overtype the dimensions shown and press **Enter**. We should end up with something like this.

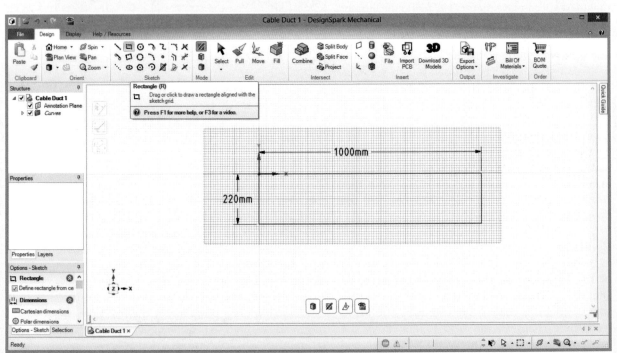

Figure 3-1 The initial rectangle

This is a 2D object, but what we want is a 3D rectangular box. To do this we 'pull' or 'extrude' the top face of the rectangle upwards by 170mm. Switch back into the 'home' view, then select the **Pull** tool from the toolbar and click on the face of the rectangle. Again we can drag it to the exact dimension we require or type in the size and press **Enter**. We end up with our first solid object.

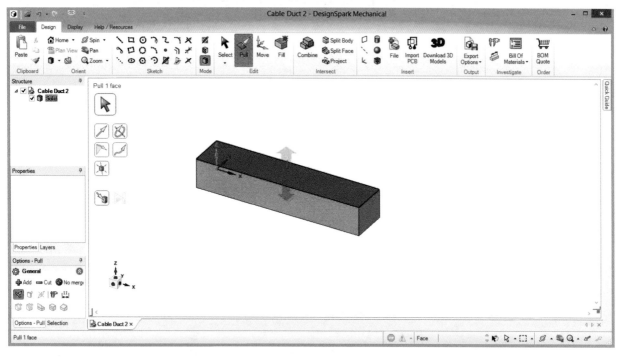

Figure 3-2 A 3D box

We now create another rectangular box 150mm wide, which is the width of the open section of the ducting, and a little longer than the first, say 1,200mm. Switch to plan view (if it's greyed out, click the top surface of the first box). Draw the rectangle, then switch back to 'home' view and pull it to be about 180mm deep. This gives us something like this.

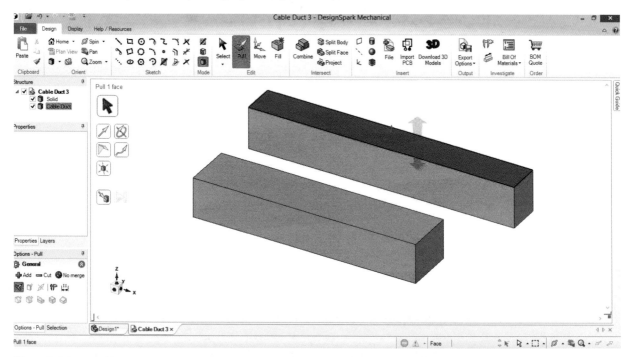

Figure 3-3 A second box

Now we cut out the 'U' section from the cable duct. We do this using the second solid object we have created. Switch to top view, select the second solid by triple-clicking it and, using the **Move** tool, move it over the first using the arrow-heads, so it is centralised on it.

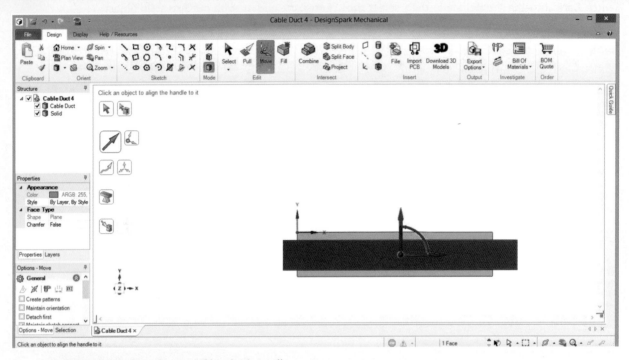

Figure 3-4 Position the second box horizontally

Switch to one of the end views ('left' or 'right') using the little blue cube icon, then position the second box vertically so that we can see the 'U' shape we are after (note that we have renamed our first solid 'Cable Duct' in the structure pane on the left).

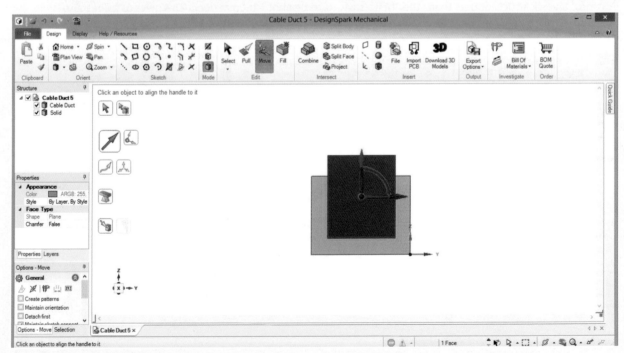

Figure 3-5 Position vertically

Next we use the **Combine** tool to subtract the second box from the first to give us our cable duct shape. Click anywhere to deselect the second box, then select **Combine** from the toolbar and uncheck the 'Keep Cutter' box in the options pane. Select the Cable Duct as the target object, then the second solid as the cutter (Figure 3-6). Delete the 'intersection' object by clicking it and – hey presto! We have our cable duct (Figure 3-7).

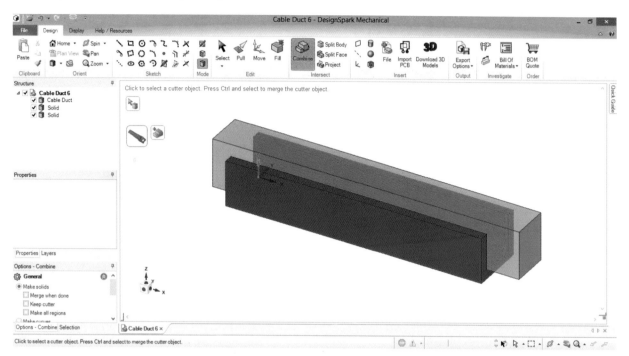

Figure 3-6 Subtract the boxes

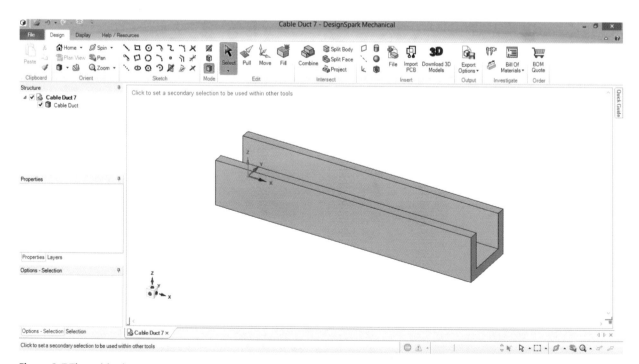

Figure 3-7 The cable duct

We can create a lid for the duct in a very similar manner. Create two rectangular boxes both 1 metre long, one 220mm wide and 40mm thick, the other 145mm wide and 50mm thick (Figure 3-8).

Position these two boxes one on top of the other so that we have a lid with a stepped section that would fit into the 'U' section of the cable duct as in figure 3-9.

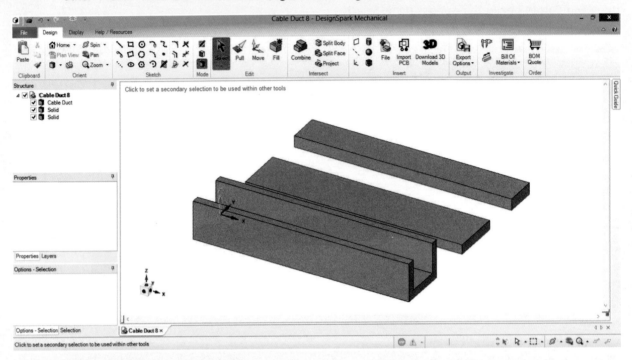

Figure 3-8 The lid components added

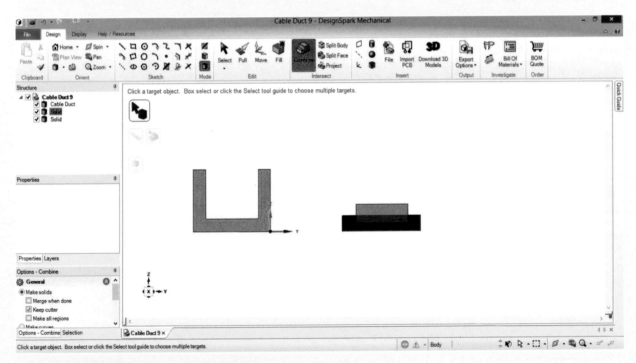

Figure 3-9 The lid components in position

This time we use the **Combine** tool to merge the two solids together rather than cut one out of the other. To do this, we hold down the **Ctrl** key while selecting them, and end up with both our component shapes on the workbench.

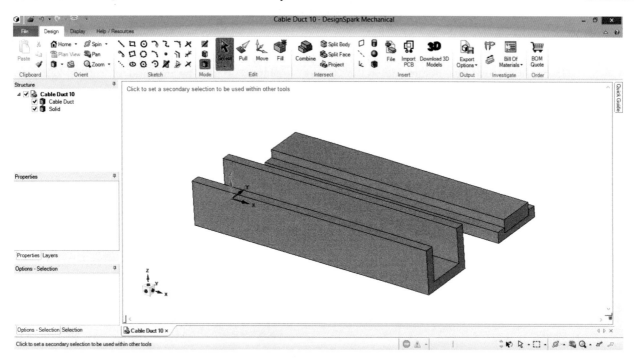

Figure 3-10 The lid components united

We could at this stage decide to print the objects as they are, but as they are going to be pretty tiny in most scales it seems hardly worth firing up the printer for just one pair. We will therefore create a sprue of parts. Using more rectangular box shapes drawn in exactly the same manner, we create a sprue round the pair of components, as shown.

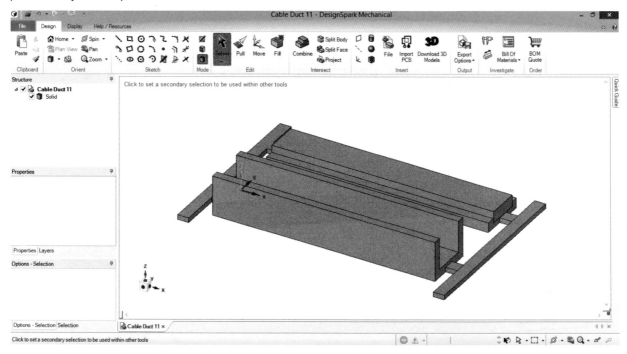

Figure 3-11 The duct parts fitted to sprues

We can now make multiple copies of the pair and merge all the pairs into a longer sprue. First, we rotate the parts by 90 degrees so that our longer sprue runs across the printer workspace. To do this, use the **Move** tool again, but this time instead of dragging in the direction of the 'axis' arrows, drag it around the blue 'rotate' arc – see Figure 3-12. Now use the **Move** tool, holding down the **Ctrl** key, to make multiple copies of our sprue, and the **Combine** tool to combine them into a single long sprue containing eight duct sections and eight lids, as in Figure 3-13.

Our final task is to export this sprue in **stl** file format. To do this we use the **Export Options** tool towards the right-hand end of the toolbar. We now have a completed stl file describing all the intricacies of our model. OK, so there isn't much intricacy in this particular item, but hopefully you are getting the idea of how we can build up complex shapes by merging or cutting out very basic shapes. Look around the railway and see how many things are basically combinations of rectangular boxes.

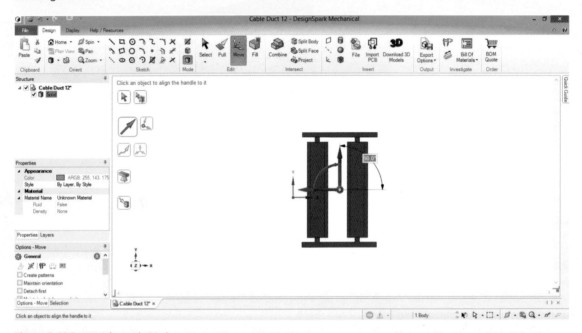

Figure 3-12 Rotate through 90 degrees

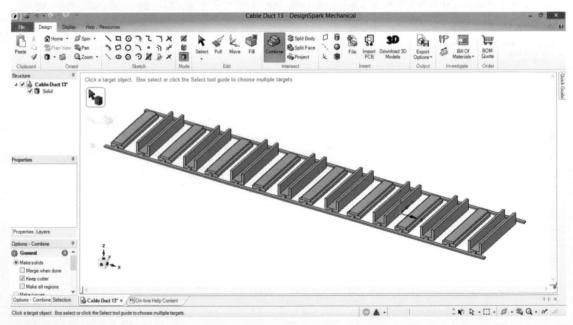

Figure 3-13 The completed long sprue

Station fencing

Our next example is a station fence, and for this we will use *Sketchup Make*, making the fence with the distinctive triangular-section arris rails that were used on the GWR and other railways.

First draw a paling, which we will make 4' 6" high using 2" x 1" timber. One of the nice features of *Sketchup* (and *DesignSpark*) is that you can use real-life measurements to do your drawing, then scale the printing to whatever modelling scale you want. Select the **Rectangle** tool, then click on the drawing origin (you can tell when you're there, because a little yellow circle will light up at the end of the mouse pointer arrow). Draw the mouse to

the right and down from the origin, until you have a rectangle. Don't click a second time – instead, type the measurements 2", 1", and press Enter. You will see these in the **Measurements** box at the bottom of the screen, provided you ticked **Measurements** on the **View > Toolbars** menu when you set up your default startup file (see Chapter 2). A 2" x 1" rectangle is very small, so zoom right in on the origin to see it (figure 3-14).

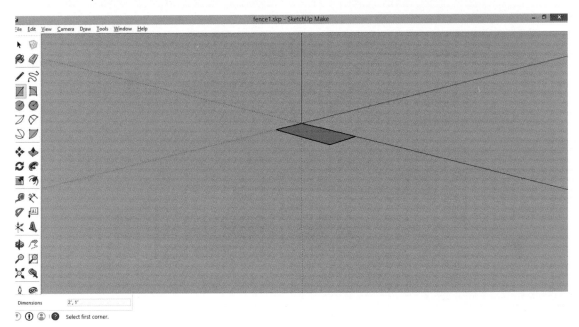

Figure 3-14 A 2in x 1in rectangle

Now, with the **Select** tool click on the surface of the rectangle – it will become peppered with blue dots. If you click too near one of the edges, the edge will turn blue, indicating that you've selected an edge only, not a surface. Use the **Push/Pull** tool to drag the surface a little way upwards and release the mouse. Type the measurement 4' 6", which will be the height to which we want to extend our paling, and again press **Enter** (figure 3-15).

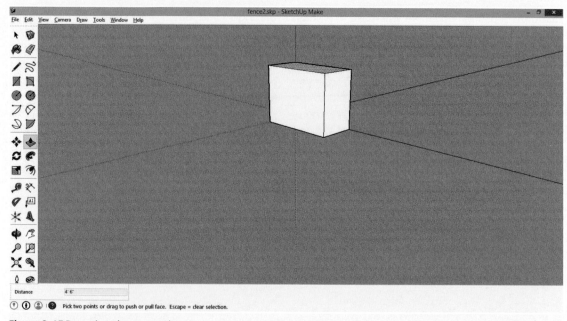

Figure 3-15 Dragging the rectangle

To see the whole paling, click on **Zoom Extents** at the bottom left of the toolbar, then zoom right in on the top of the post. With the **Pencil** tool, draw a line between the two mid-points of opposite sides of the rectangular top (see Figure 3-16). You will know when you're exactly at the mid-point, because a little blue circle will light up on the end of the **Pencil** tool. *Sketchup* calls this 'inferencing' and it can be very useful. Once you've drawn the line, select it and, using the **Move** tool, pull the line up 1" (figure 3-16).

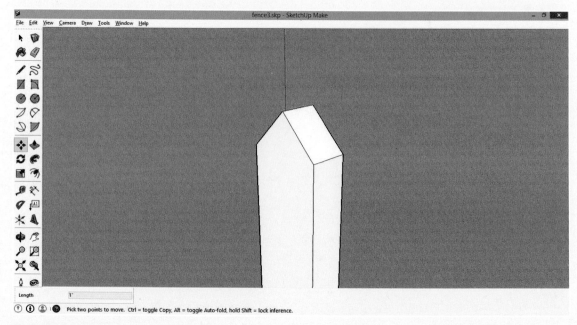

Figure 3-16 Forming the point on top

Use **Zoom Extents** again to see the whole paling, then select the complete solid by clicking **Edit > Select All**. Click the **Move** tool again, but this time press the **Ctrl** key once. A little plus sign will appear alongside the mouse pointer, indicating that we are going to make a copy rather than move the original. Drag the copy away from the original, taking care to keep to the x axis. Sketchup will tell you if you are on the axis when you drag – another example of inferencing. Leave the paling some random distance to the right, but type 4" into the **Measurement** box to make it exact and press **Enter** (figure 3-17).

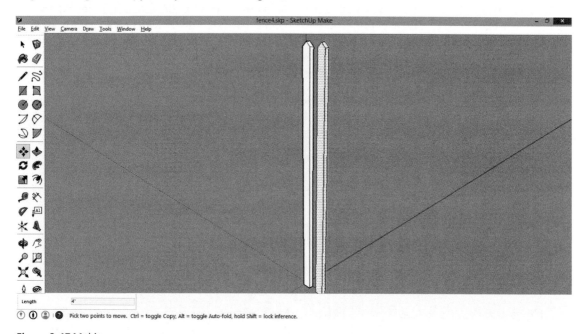

Figure 3-17 Making a copy

Immediately type 'x17' (meaning repeat 17 times) into the **Measurement** box and press **Enter** again, and you will have a full 6 feet of fence (figure 3-18).

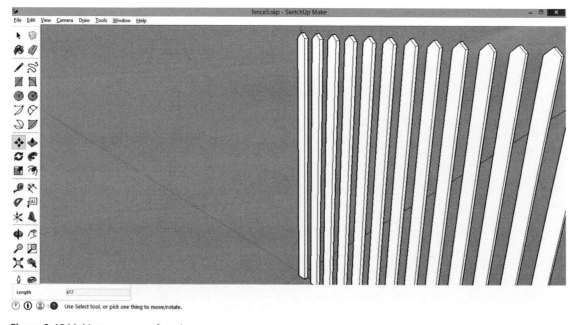

Figure 3-18 Making an array of copies

We now turn our attention to the distinctive triangular arris rail. This will be easier if we change from the isometric view to an end view. Bizarrely, if you want to change the view, you don't use the View menu! Instead, you click **Camera > Standard Views**. Click **Right** and we will have an end view from the right-hand end of our fence (as in Figure 3-20). It will make things easier if we also switch from a perspective view to a parallel projection, so click **Camera > Parallel Projection** also.

Select the **Polygon** tool, set the number of sides to 3 and make a couple of triangles to the right of the fence. Set the **Inscribed Radius** (in the **Measurement** box) to 2". For the next operation, we go back into isometric projection (**Camera > Standard Views > Iso**) and move around the back of the fence (click the **Orbit** tool and swing the fence around). Then click on the face of one of the triangles and, using the **Push/Pull** tool, draw it out to a length of 6' 6" (Figure 3-19). Repeat for the other triangle. Now switch back to a parallel projection from the right and move the arris rails until they just touch the uprights (Figure 3-20).

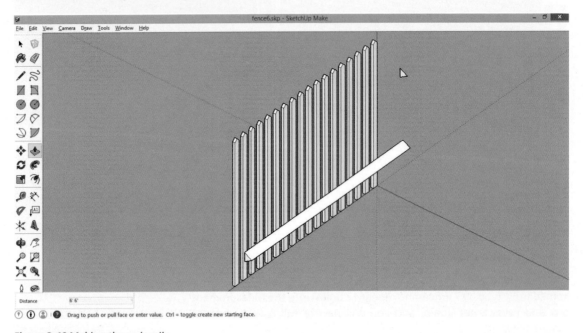

Figure 3-19 Making the arris rails

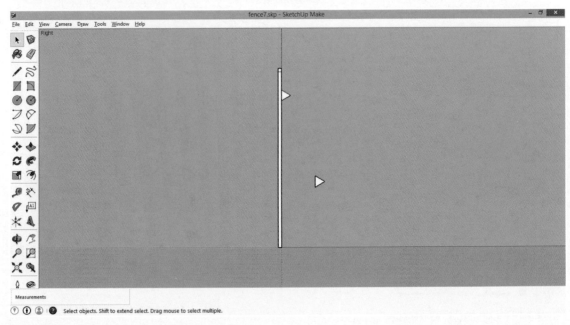

Figure 3-20 Move the arris rail to touch the fence

It is important when you move a complete object like the arris rail that you move all of it. To facilitate this, *Sketchup* uses the following convention: a single click on an edge or face will select just that edge or face. A double click on a face will select the face and its connected edges. A triple click on any face or edge of a solid object will select the whole object, including any invisible faces and edges. It is the triple click that you need when moving the rails as in Figure 3-20.

Next, switch to front view and move the arris rails laterally so that they are symmetric about the fencing (figure 3-21). We now need to group all of our faces, edges and vertices into a single entity. **Click Edit > Select All**, then **Edit > Make Group**.

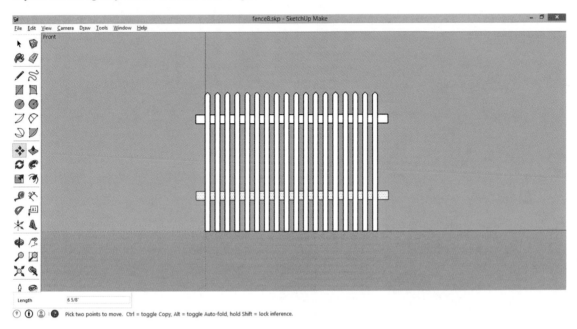

Figure 3-21 Adjust the arris rail positions

Our final component is the fence post, which we shall make 6' x 4½" x 4½". This is made in exactly the same way as the palings, so we need not go into the details of its construction. Make it just to the right of the fence (figure 3-22).

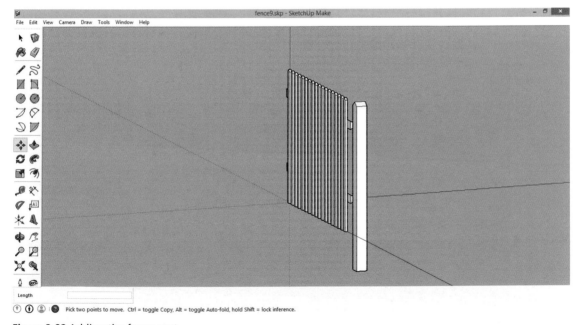

Figure 3-22 Adding the fence post

Finally, we need to cut two notches in the fence post to accommodate the arris rails. From a front view, draw two lines on the post in line with the top and bottom of the upper arris rail (figure 3-23). You will find *Sketchup*'s inferencing helpful here.

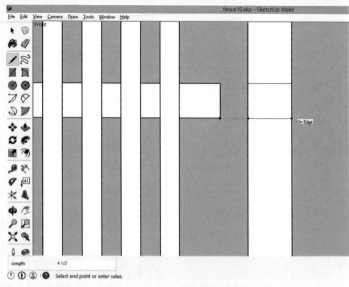

Figure 3-23 Drawing lines to match the arris rail

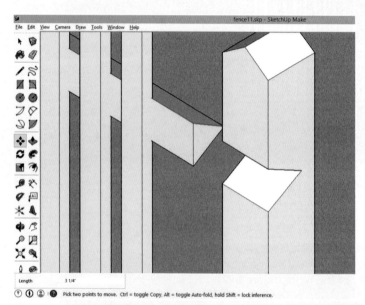

Figure 3-24 Making a notch

Then draw another line midway between the two lines you've just drawn, select it and use the **Move** tool to drag it into the post to make a notch (figure 3-24). Change the view to right to get the notch in line with the rail. Repeat for the lower arris rail.

It will make printing neater if we turn our fence post through 180° and align its rear face with the front faces of the palings. Do this with the **Rotate** tool (figure 3-25).

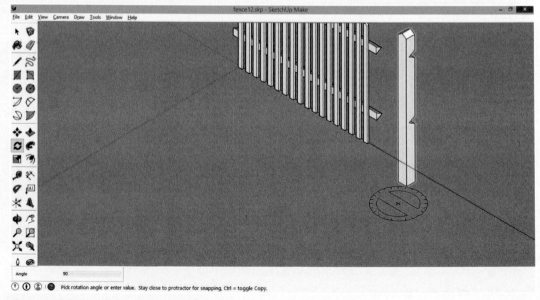

Figure 3-25 Rotate the post through 180°

We should now have a 3D printable entity. Before we can print our fence, however, we need it in stl file format. This is a problem, because only *Sketchup Pro* can export stl files – *Sketchup Make* (the free one we're using here) cannot. However, there are ways around this. One is to use *Meshlab*, a software package that has a truly impressive range of file formats from and into which it can convert. One of these formats is *Collada* (extension dae), and *Sketchup Make* is able to export in this format. Therefore, in *Sketchup* click **File > Export > 3D Model** and make the file type Collada.

Now open *Meshlab*, click **File > New Empty Project**, then **File > Import Mesh**. Browse around to find the Collada file you exported from *Sketchup* and open it. While you have it in *Meshlab*, have a look at it; just like *Sketchup*, *Meshlab* has a curious way of changing the view. Again, you don't click the **View** menu item! This time you click **Windows > View From**. Select the **View Camera** and pan around, making sure things look OK. While we're here, we might as well do some checking on our mesh. Click **Render > Show non-manifold edges and vertices**. As you can see (figure 3-26), there are no errors, so we can go ahead and click **File > Export Mesh** and select stl as the file type. We now have another file ready to print.

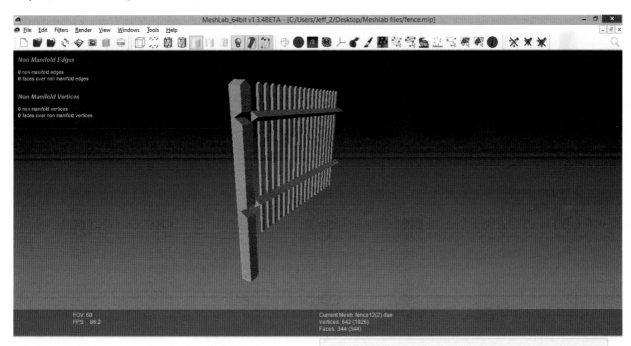

Figure 3-26 The fence in *Meshlab*

Sleeper stacks

Our previous examples have used CAD tools where the objects are created using click and drag graphical interfaces; these are fine, but sometimes you might find that other tools are better suited. For this example we will produce a stack of sleepers using *OpenSCAD*. This isn't a stack of one or two sleepers but a pile of more than 180 of them! These were used as part of a project to build a model of a sleeper works.

We could just have easily used the same tools we used for the previous examples, but placing 180 sleepers individually doesn't sound like a lot of fun, even using cut and paste. Using *OpenSCAD* makes this a fairly simple job and doesn't require the use of a mouse. Anyone who has done any computer programming will get the hang of this pretty quickly, but we'll start with something basic.

To create a single sleeper we can use a single line of *OpenSCAD* code. Type into the *OpenSCAD* text editor the line of code illustrated. We are using the 'cube' function, which is a bit of a misnomer as we are specifying different width, length and height values, thus creating a cuboid or rectangular prism. The dimensions are specified in millimetres and are the size of a standard UK wooden sleeper. Notice how the size parameters are specified inside square brackets, '[' and ']'. This is defining a vector of three items. Parameters to a function, in this case cube, are always specified between parentheses, so we end up with something looking a bit odd with brackets of all kinds scattered about. It's logical to us programmers, honest! Press **F6** and zoom appropriately (or click on the '**View All**' icon below the viewing area), and *OpenSCAD* will render our sleeper to look something like this (figure 3-27).

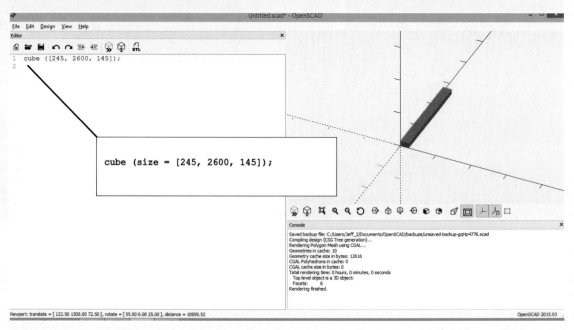

Figure 3-27 A single sleeper

OpenSCAD allows us to create a 'module' that is akin to a function or subroutine call. It's a convenient way of encapsulating a bit of coding so that we can simplify things elsewhere. In this case we create a module that creates a single sleeper, as shown (figure 3-28).

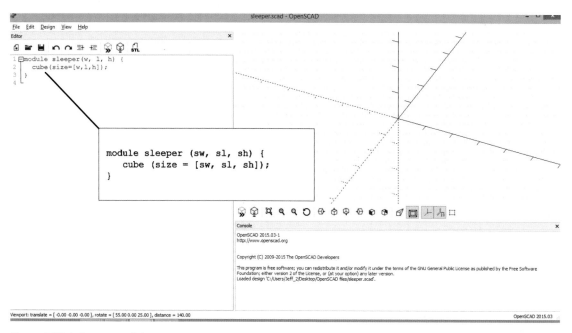

```
module sleeper (sw, sl, sh) {
    cube (size = [sw, sl, sh]);
}
```

Figure 3-28 A sleeper module

This is a pretty trivial module, but if we save it to a separate file we can use it later. The desired width, length and height of the sleeper are passed in as parameters and used for a call to the cube function.

It's therefore pretty simple to create a single sleeper, but how do we go about creating our stack?

We will start our main sleeper stack drawing by defining a few variables that describe the size of sleeper we wish to use, how many layers there are in the stack, how many sleepers are side by side in each layer, and the gap between them. The first dozen or so lines of figure 3-29 do this .

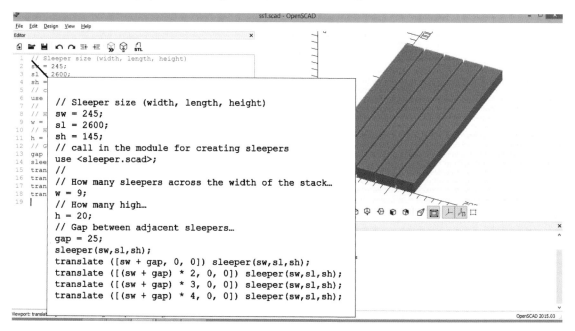

```
// Sleeper size (width, length, height)
sw = 245;
sl = 2600;
sh = 145;
// call in the module for creating sleepers
use <sleeper.scad>;
//
// How many sleepers across the width of the stack…
w = 9;
// How many high…
h = 20;
// Gap between adjacent sleepers…
gap = 25;
sleeper(sw,sl,sh);
translate ([sw + gap, 0, 0]) sleeper(sw,sl,sh);
translate ([(sw + gap) * 2, 0, 0]) sleeper(sw,sl,sh);
translate ([(sw + gap) * 3, 0, 0]) sleeper(sw,sl,sh);
translate ([(sw + gap) * 4, 0, 0]) sleeper(sw,sl,sh);
```

Figure 3-29 Multiple sleepers

For the programmers among us, this all looks fairly familiar. For those not used to programming languages, it probably looks a bit obscure. Each statement is terminated by a semicolon for reasons that are lost in history. The use of two slashes – '//' – denotes that everything following it to the end of the line is a comment and is ignored by *OpenSCAD*. The variable names – sw, sl, sh, w, h and gap – are simply convenient names chosen by the author.

The last five lines of Figure 3-29 draws five sleepers: we simply call the 'sleeper' module five times. This creates five sleepers placed alongside each other with a small gap. You can see from the code snippet that a bit more programming weirdness has crept in! The first line is pretty much self-explanatory – we call the sleeper function with the width, length and depth of the sleeper we wish to create. By default the new object will be created at the origin of the drawing surface. To place an object somewhere else we use the translate function. This takes a vector of three arguments contained in square brackets, '[' and ']', which are the x, y and z points at which we want to draw. It's slightly odd that we do the translate call first before creating the sleeper but, if we think of it as translating the drawing origin rather than the object, it has a certain logic.

So now we have multiple sleepers, but doing it this way we will have a lot of repetitive lines in order to arrange 180 of them. Luckily *OpenSCAD* gives us the ability to do this in a much more elegant and concise manner – we need a 'for' loop (figure 3-30).

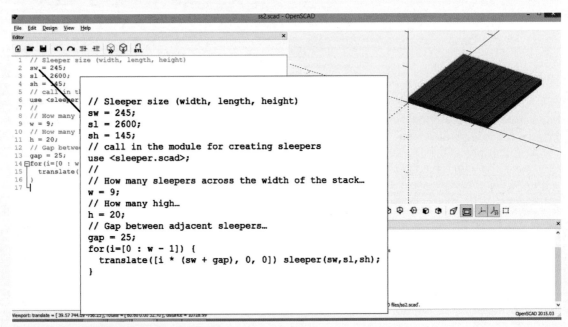

```
// Sleeper size (width, length, height)
sw = 245;
sl = 2600;
sh = 145;
// call in the module for creating sleepers
use <sleeper.scad>;
//
// How many sleepers across the width of the stack…
w = 9;
// How many high…
h = 20;
// Gap between adjacent sleepers…
gap = 25;
for(i=[0 : w - 1]) {
    translate([i * (sw + gap), 0, 0]) sleeper(sw,sl,sh);
}
```

Figure 3-30 A 'for' loop

Here we have a proper bit of computer programming, and in the last three lines we have created a complete layer of nine sleepers. Not only that, if you change the definition of variable w, the width of the stack, it will automagically create the right number of sleepers! As in the previous example, the proper work is done using translate to change the position of the drawing origin, then the sleeper function, to create a sleeper. The new feature is the first of these lines: the 'for' statement. This defines a section of code that is executed multiple times. In this case we define a new variable – i – and tell the program to execute the code within the curly braces, '{' and '}', for values of i from 0 to w-1. As w

is defined as 9, we will execute the code nine times, with i being set to 0, 1, 2 ... up to 8. In the translate function call we use the value of i to determine where on the x axis to draw each sleeper. Basically we multiply the width of a sleeper plus the gap between sleepers by i.

If you are still following this, well done! This, then, easily gives us a layer of sleepers, but we need to create several layers in a criss-cross fashion. To do this we will need to rotate every other layer through 90 degrees. To make things a little simpler, we will first rejig our sleeper module to package our 'for' loop. This gives us a module we will call sleeper_layer (Figure 3-31).

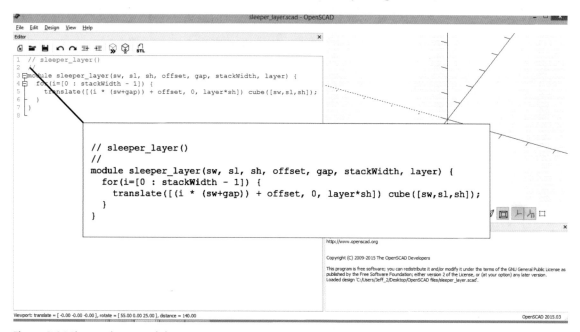

Figure 3-31 Sleeper_layer module

Unless you really want to, don't spend too much time analysing this code. Trust me, it lays out a layer of sleepers evenly spaced. For the pedantic you will see that the translate call now includes a fixed offset in the x direction to allow for the situation where the width of the number of sleepers we are building into the stack comes out at less than the length of a sleeper. This allows us to centre the layers on each other. Also, the z axis translation takes into account the fact that each layer is placed on top of the previous one.

Back in our main sleeper stack code, we now type in the code illustrated (figure 3-32). The definitions at the start are unchanged apart from the addition of the offset variable. In the guts of things you find another 'for' loop, which steps through creating each layer of sleepers using our sleeper_layer module. We treat odd numbered layers differently by rotating them through 90 degrees, but then unfortunately we also have to move the whole layer with a translate function to line it up again with the even layers. We determine that we are on an odd layer by using the built-in modulo operator (%) in the line i = j % 2, which gives us the remainder of dividing the level number by 2. If i is 1, then it must be an odd layer. By the way, do not worry if, when you press the '**Render**' button, or **F6**, nothing happens for a while. There is a lot of maths in the code, and it might take several minutes depending on the speed of your computer's processor. You might also find that you need to click the '**View All**' icon (a magnifying glass with four arrows) before any of the image is within the viewing window.

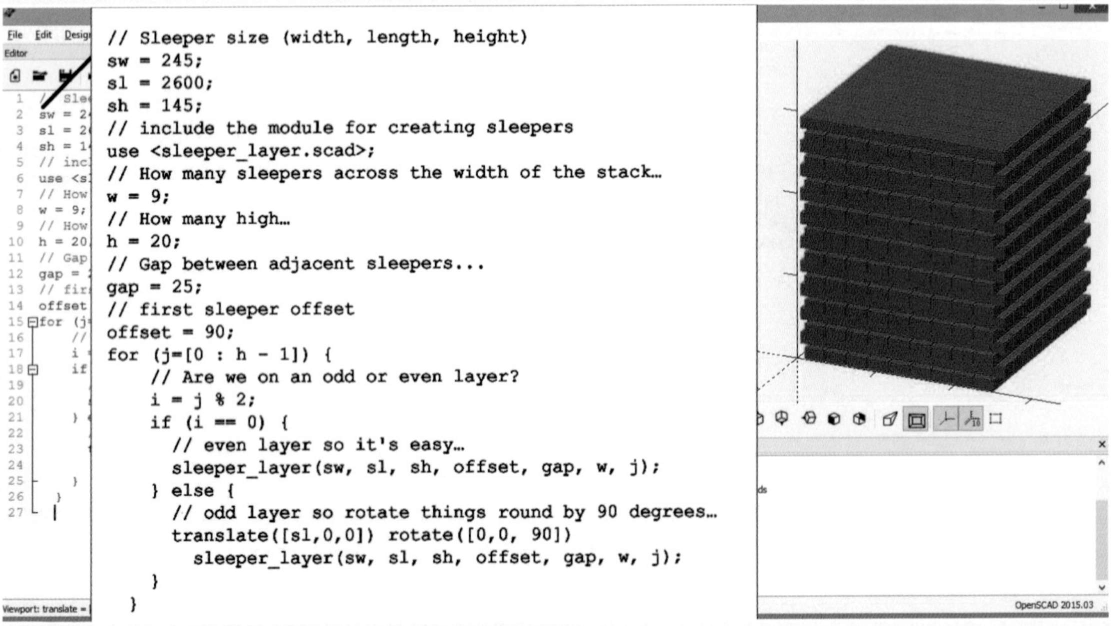

```
// Sleeper size (width, length, height)
sw = 245;
sl = 2600;
sh = 145;
// include the module for creating sleepers
use <sleeper_layer.scad>;
// How many sleepers across the width of the stack…
w = 9;
// How many high…
h = 20;
// Gap between adjacent sleepers...
gap = 25;
// first sleeper offset
offset = 90;
for (j=[0 : h - 1]) {
    // Are we on an odd or even layer?
    i = j % 2;
    if (i == 0) {
        // even layer so it's easy…
        sleeper_layer(sw, sl, sh, offset, gap, w, j);
    } else {
        // odd layer so rotate things round by 90 degrees…
        translate([sl,0,0]) rotate([0,0, 90])
            sleeper_layer(sw, sl, sh, offset, gap, w, j);
    }
}
```

Figure 3-32 A complete sleeper stack

The sleeper stack shown in Figure 3-32 will use an awful lot of plastic, most of which will be unseen inside the model. It will also take a long time to print. Let us therefore hollow it out, and Figure 3-33 shows the code to do this (the first few lines of code, i.e. the variable definitions, etc, are as before).

Just above the 'for' loop is a call to the difference function, which subtracts one 3D shape from another, and in this case right at the bottom of the code you will see that we position and create a cube. By subtracting this cube from the sleeper stack we end up with the hollow shape.

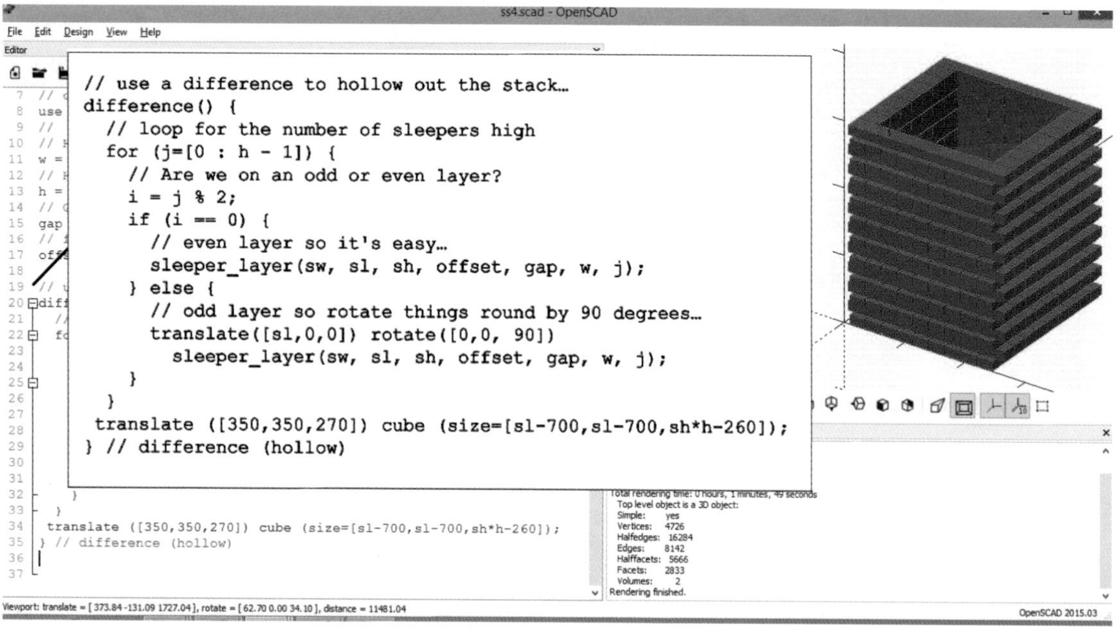
ss4.scad - OpenSCAD
// use a difference to hollow out the stack...
difference() {
// loop for the number of sleepers high
for (j=[0 : h - 1]) {
// Are we on an odd or even layer?
i = j % 2;
if (i == 0) {
// even layer so it's easy...
sleeper_layer(sw, sl, sh, offset, gap, w, j);
} else {
// odd layer so rotate things round by 90 degrees...
translate([sl,0,0]) rotate([0,0, 90])
sleeper_layer(sw, sl, sh, offset, gap, w, j);
}
}
translate ([350,350,270]) cube (size=[sl-700,sl-700,sh*h-260]);
} // difference (hollow)
Rendering finished.
OpenSCAD 2015.03

Figure 3-33 A hollow sleeper stack

We programmers do this for fun, but it may well seem painful to normal folks, who will be seen running and screaming back to their favourite drag-and-drop CAD program, but there is a final twist! Looking at Figure 3-33 it all looks too regular for a stack of sleepers built by human beings. In fact, it is so regular that when printed it looks artificial – we need some randomness. If we had built this using drag and drop, we would have had to go into the model and nudge individual sleepers around, but as we are using *OpenSCAD* it's really easy, by putting a small modification into our sleeper_layer module.

In the earlier definition of the sleeper_layer module we had a call to the translate function, and this determines the position of each sleeper in the layer. *OpenSCAD* has a random number generation function – rands – which can return a vector of random values within a predetermined range. We can add a small randomly generated offset to both the x and y axis positions of each sleeper by modifying the sleeper_layer module as illustrated in figure 3-34. The bit we have added is a call to the rands function requesting a single value randomly selected in the range 0 to 60. The rather obscure '[0]' indicates that we then extract the zeroth element (the first one in the vector) and use this. It's pretty ugly, but it works and we do it for both the x and y positions. The only modification required to our main code is to change the references to the sleeper_layer module to refer to rand_sleeper_layer instead.

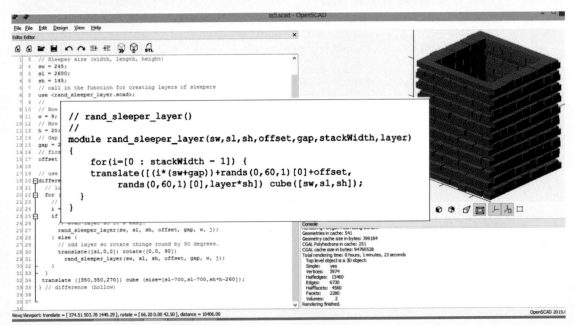

Figure 3-34 Adding some randomness

Finally, a sloping 'roof' structure is created separately to allow it to be printed in a different orientation to avoid unsightly layers in the sloping bits, and the code for this is illustrated in figure 3-35. If you have followed things up to this point, you should find this code fairly straightforward.

```
sleeper_stack_roof.scad - OpenSCAD
File  Edit  Design  View  Help
Editor                                                    x
  1  // Cr      // Create a sloping cover for a sleeper stack
  2  use <      use <sleeper.scad>;
  3  //         //
  4  // Sl      // Sleeper size (width, length, height)
  5  sw =        sw = 245;
  6  sl =        sl = 2600;
  7  sh =        sh = 145;
  8  //          //
  9  // Ho       // How many sleepers across the width of the stack...
 10  w = 9       w = 9;
 11  //          //
 12  // Cr       // Create the sloping top as a separate object...
 13  //          //
 14  // ro       // rotate cover so top layer horizontal so it prints better...
 15 ⊟rotat      rotate ([0, 356.5, 0]) {
 16    tra        translate([0, 0, 0]) sleeper(sw,sl,sh);
 17    tra        translate([0 + sw + 20, 0, 0]) sleeper(sw,sl,sh);
 18    tra        translate([(sw / 2), 0, sh]) sleeper(sw,sl,sh);
 19    tra        translate([(sl - sw), 0, 0]) sleeper(sw,sl,sh);
 20 ⊟  tra        translate([0, 0, (sh * 2)]) rotate([0,3.5,0]) {
 21 ⊟     f         for(i=[0 : 9]) {
 22                   translate([-20, (i * (sw +20)) + sw, 0])
 23  ⊦                   rotate([0,0,270]) sleeper(sw,sl,sh);
 24  ⊦  }            }
 25  }            }
 26            }
            }
Viewport: translate = [ 1020.06 1027.55 1.30 ], rotate = [ 55.00 0.00 25.00 ], distance = 7388.11         OpenSCAD 2015.03
```

Figure 3-35 A sloping roof

The final model was exported as an stl file and scaled for printing in 4mm/1ft scale. Figure 3-36 shows several of the models printed and painted. The prototype of this model was created by a club member using cut-down coffee stirrers, and it took him many hours of work to get an acceptable result. Creating this model in *OpenSCAD* took a couple of hours and the printer can create as many as you like with little effort. Oh, and if you want some variety you just re-render it in *OpenSCAD* and re-export, and the **rands** function will give you a slightly different model every time!

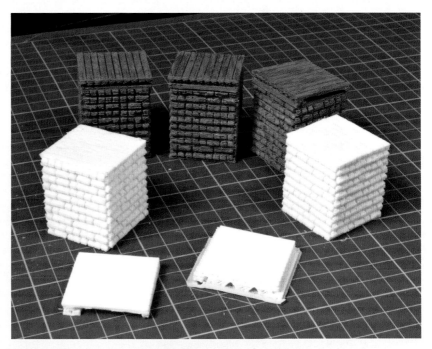

Figure 3-36 Printed and painted sleeper stacks

Rolling stock

In this chapter we will demonstrate some further 3D modelling techniques, including 'tracing' a 2D drawing from a background image, the use of layers, rotating objects and using mirror imaging to build symmetrical objects. We will also look at using multiple CAD programs in conjunction to create a model.

Buffer beam

In this example we will create a typical wagon buffer beam, together with a pair of buffer stocks and a slot for the coupling hook. The buffers themselves and the coupling hook/chain are probably best made by conventional means out of metal and suitably sprung, but we will design the buffer beam itself using *Sketchup Make,* then convert it into stl format using *Meshlab.*

A typical buffer beam is 8 feet by 1 foot, with the buffers 5' 8" apart. These dimensions vary, so check a drawing first. Load *Sketchup Make* and begin by drawing a rectangle; start at the origin and draw an arbitrary rectangle, then type in 8', 1' in the dimensions box at the bottom of the screen. The next few steps are best done in plan view, so click **Camera > Parallel Projection** then **Camera > Standard Views > Top**. Draw some guidelines on the rectangle by selecting the Tape Measure tool. If the tape measure cursor has a little '+' sign, you are in **Guideline** mode. If it doesn't, press **Ctrl**, which toggles between **Guideline** and **Measurement** modes.

Click on an edge parallel to the guideline you want to draw, and drag in the desired general direction, then place the guideline precisely by typing into the dimensions box. Draw lines parallel to the buffer beam sides at 1' 2" in from each edge and one in the centre, then a single line parallel to the buffer beam top along its centre-line. Using the **Circle** tool, draw 2" radius circles centred on the intersections of the buffer locating guidelines. With the **Select** tool, click in the area within the circle (*not* its edge) and delete it. This will make the holes through the buffer beam for the buffers (see figure 4-1).

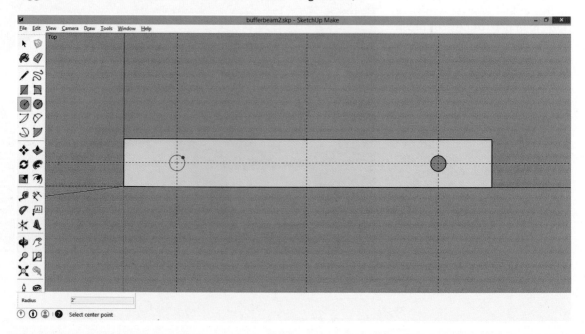

Figure 4-1 The buffer beam rectangle

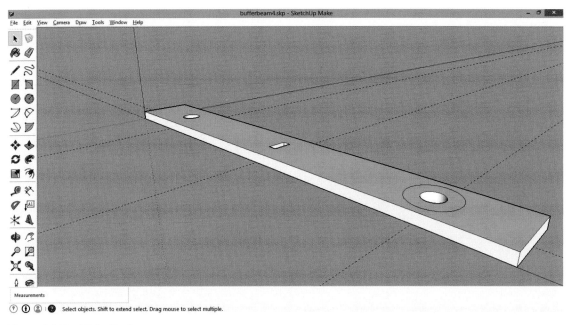

Figure 4-2 The 3D buffer beam

Draw a small rectangle in the centre of the beam for the coupling hook slot, and again delete that. Zoom in to get this accurately placed in the centre of the beam. Switch back to Isometric view and, with the **Push/Pull** tool, pull up the surface of the beam to a height of 2" (Figure 4-2). This may seem excessive but, as we shall see later, there is a limit to how thin you can print things without losing rigidity. At 4mm/1ft a buffer beam 2" thick would scale down to less than 0.7mm, and this is probably as small as we would like to get. More of this later.

Next we want to draw a couple of concentric circles around the buffer holes. This is best done in top view (**Camera > Standard Views > Top**). Click in the centre of the hole and draw a circle of 4½" radius. Then switch back to Iso view (Figure 4-2) and, using the **Push/Pull** tool, extrude this 2" – this is the flange of the buffer holder. Back in top view, draw another circle on this extruded section, this time of 3½" radius and extrude this 5" (these measurements are typical – check with a detailed drawing if you want to model a specific buffer). See figure 4-3.

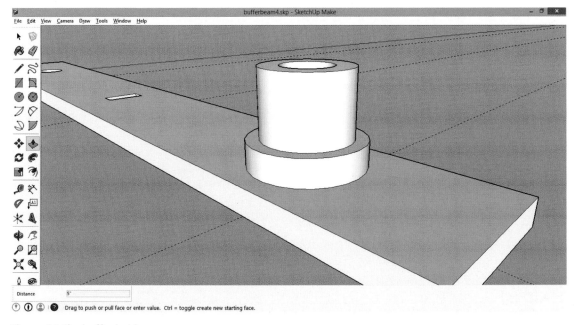

Figure 4-3 The buffer holder

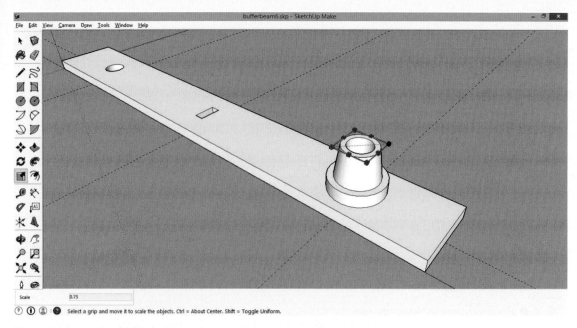

Figure 4-4 A tapering buffer holder

Let us suppose that the buffer stocks we are modelling are tapered rather than parallel, which will demonstrate a rather neat feature of *Sketchup*. Select the circumference of the uppermost circle, then click the **Scale** tool. You will notice that a box appears around the edge with a number of green cubes; these are scaling grips, which can be used to scale the circle in individual directions. However, if we press the **Ctrl** key and use one of the 'corner' grips this will give us uniform scaling, either according to the mouse movement or by typing the scale change we want (figure 4.4).

We then repeat the process at the other end of the buffer beam. We did try making half a buffer beam and making a mirror image to save effort, but to join the two halves together without manifold errors proved extremely difficult. One suspects that the Sketchup **Join** tool would have helped here, but this is only available with *Sketchup Pro*! The final job is to make the plate around the slot for the coupling hook. These came in a variety of shapes, so again check your prototype. We will make ours square.

All that remains is to click **Edit > Select All**, then **Edit > Make Group**, and we can export our buffer beam into Meshlab for creating an stl file in exactly the same way as we did with our fence in the previous chapter.

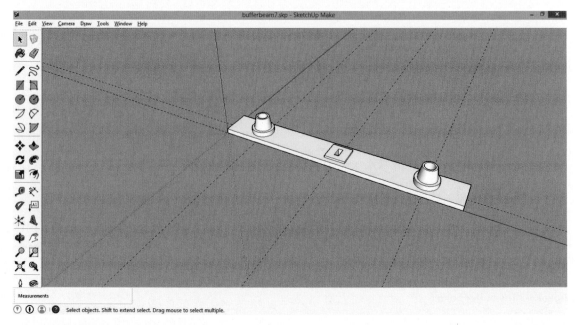

Figure 4-5 The completed buffer beam

A well wagon in 7mm

For this example we will build a Ministry of Supply 'Warwell' 50-ton bogie well wagon. The reader may well not have any need for such a wagon, but the principles of its construction – tracing a 2D drawing, converting to 3D and putting the 3D components together – are widely applicable.

One of the beauties of using free CAD software is that you can have lots of different CAD programs on your computer, then mix and match them according to which is best for a given job. This project is a case in point. We will create a series of 2D profiles using *DraftSight*, then use *OpenSCAD* to extrude these into three-dimensional objects.

We found a Ministry of Supply General Arrangement drawing on the excellent Rail Album website (see Appendix 1). The drawing image was downloaded in jpeg format, then loaded as a background image and 'traced' using our 2D CAD program.

We start by loading *DraftSight* and getting ourselves into imperial units. **Click Tools > Options > Drawing Settings**, then click '**Architectural**' – this will get you feet and inches. Having obtained our GA drawing as a jpeg file, we loaded it into *DraftSight* by clicking **Insert > Reference Image**. Make the insertion point the origin x=0, y=0, and make the scale something big, e.g. 100. If you leave the scale at the default (1) the image may well be miniscule, possibly too small to see (figure 4.6).

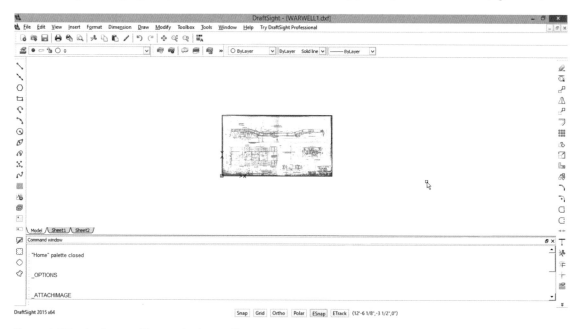

Figure 4-6 The background image. *Background images 4-6 to 4-12 from Rail Album website (http://www.railalbum. co.uk) by kind permission of Greg Martin*

The length over buffers of these wagons was 47', so we draw a line from origin to x=47'. The easiest way to do this is to click the **Line** tool and type in the coordinates (figure 4-7).

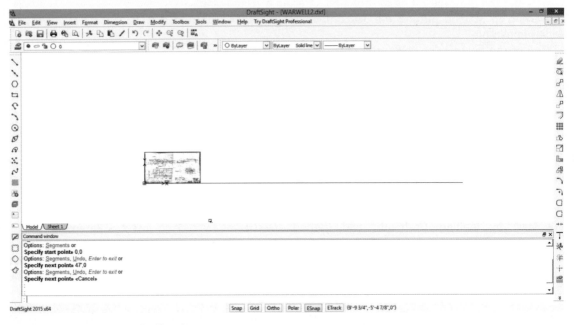

Figure 4-7 The 'length over buffers' line

We now need to get the image the right size. Select it by left-clicking near one of its edges, then using **Modify > Move** and the blue 'stretching' squares, adjust the size and position of the image so that the outside of the buffers coincide with the ends of our line (figure 4-8).

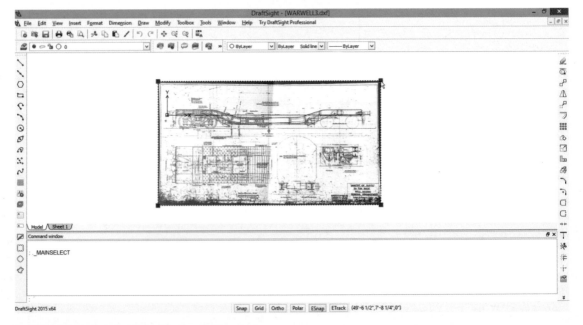

Figure 4-8 Rescaling and repositioning the image

We only need to draw half of the wagon, since the other half will be a mirror image of it. So left click the line to select it, then right click to bring up its context menu and select **Properties**. Change the line length to 23' 6" (figure 4-9), to denote the extent of our drawing.

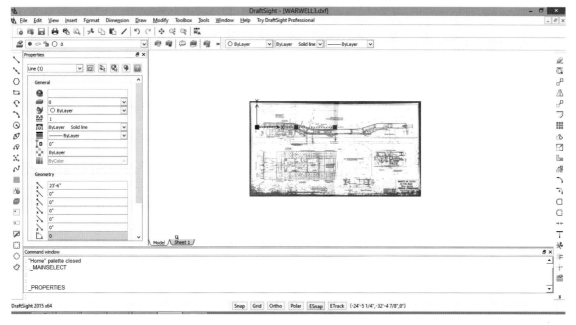

Figure 4-9 Halving the length of the line

Next we trace around the outline of the left half of the wagon body, using the **Line** tool. To make sure the lines are perfectly horizontal (or vertical), hold down the **Shift** key where appropriate. Notice that we have not drawn the lines around the curves on the upper and lower ends of the well wagon's 'slope'; press the **Esc** key here and start a new line on the sloping part of the well.

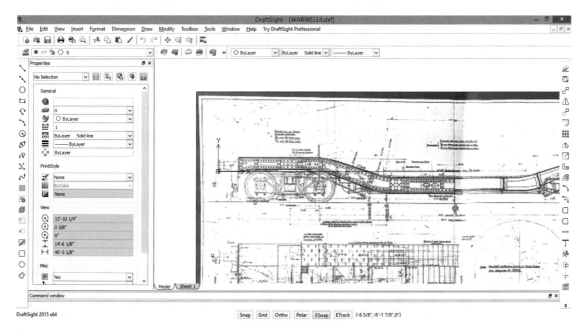

Figure 4-10 The wagon outline – straight lines only

Our 23' 6" line has now served its purpose, so we can delete it. Having done so, we can now move everything, including the background image, into the positive quadrant – that is to say, where all x and y coordinates are positive. The reason for this is that *OpenSCAD* (version 2015.03-1) has problems with certain rotation operations when things go into the negative, as we discovered from bitter experience! *OpenSCAD* is not alone in this, and it is generally a good idea to keep things in the all-positive quadrant (or octant in 3D) wherever possible. So **Edit > Select All**, then **Modify > Move** and select the top left corner as the 'from' point and type 1', 4' as the destination (figure 4-11).

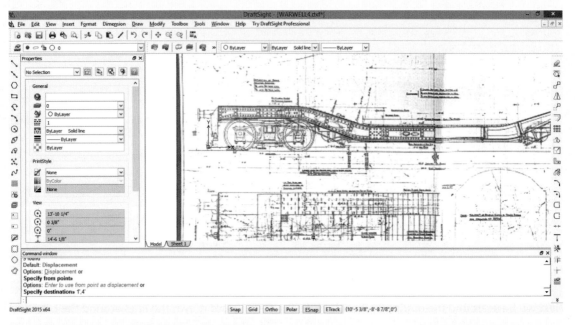

Figure 4-11 Move the image into the positive quadrant

We now use the **Modify > Fillet** tool to draw curves, which are tangential to the sloping lines of our well. You will have to experiment with the radius of these: type 'R' and enter a trial radius, and if it doesn't fit the background image click **Edit > Undo** and try again. We found that 6' for the larger curves and 4' for the smaller ones seemed to work (figure 4-12).

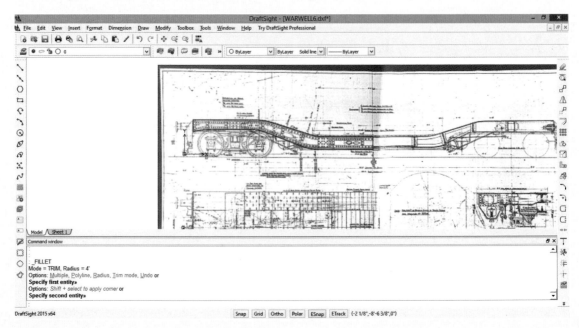

Figure 4-12 The wagon outline with fillet curves added

Once you are satisfied with the fillet curves, hide the background image by putting it onto a different layer. Click **Format > Layer** to bring up the layer manager, then click the **New** icon. Give the layer a name such as 'layer 1' and click OK. Then select the image by clicking near an edge and bring up its properties. Change its layer from 0 (the default) to 'layer 1'. Then click **Format > Layer Tools > Hide Layer** and click on the image: it will disappear. We can bring it back at any time by clicking **Format > Layer Tools > Show All Layers**.

We now need to turn our two-dimensional outline into a three-dimensional model. We do this using a rather neat feature of *OpenSCAD*, namely importing a 2D dxf file and extruding it to form a 3D object. So save the wagon outline in Figure 4-12 to whatever directory we have set up for our *OpenSCAD* files

under the filename OUTLINE1. Then we start up *OpenSCAD*, import the file and extrude it. When *DraftSight* saves an 'imperial' file it does so in inches, so our extrusion height should also be in these units; we will use 6" as the height to extrude. This may seem excessive, and it is indeed wildly out of scale, but when we print it at 7mm to the foot it will only be just over 3mm. In *OpenSCAD* type the single line of code illustrated in the inset to figure 4-13. This tells *OpenSCAD* to extrude to a height of 6" the result of importing the named dxf file. The result is a three-dimensional solid. Notice that *OpenSCAD* gives us a warning that it does not support background images. Thus we could not have used *OpenSCAD* to trace the 2D image, although the program does have a basic 2D subsystem enabling you to draw rectangles, ellipses, polygons, etc.

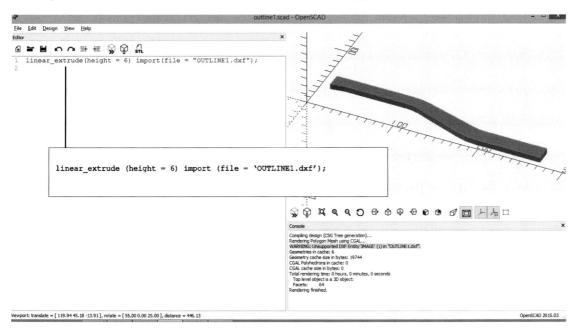

Figure 4-13 The 2D wagon side extruded

Back in *DraftSight*, we now need to draw a similar shape to OUTLINE1, but with a slightly reduced width. To do this, we draw lines parallel to the straight lines of OUTLINE1, but 2" in from them. To start with, draw a line perpendicular to the first horizontal line. Start it some distance below the horizontal line and hover around the line at a point where it joins at right angles. When *DraftSight* puts

up the word 'Perpendicular', click to end the line. We then set its length to 2" by clicking **Modify > Change Length** on the menu bar, then in the command window at the bottom of the screen we type 'T' for Total Length and set the length to 2", and finally click the entity whose length we want to change, i.e. the short vertical line we just drew as in figure 4-14.

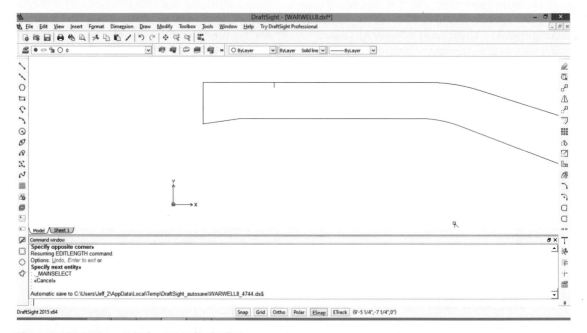

Figure 4-14 Drawing a 2-inch perpendicular line

Then, using the end-point of this line as our start point, we draw another, pressing the **Shift** key to ensure that it is horizontal and therefore parallel to our first line. Repeat this for each of the horizontal lines as in figure 4-15.

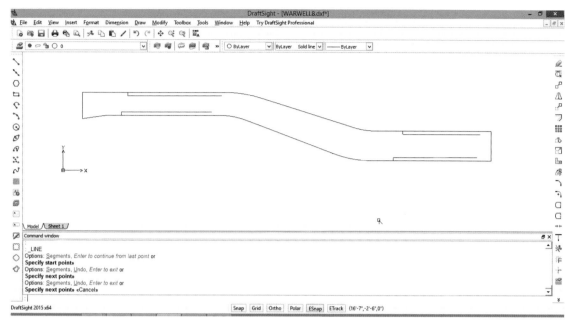

Figure 4-15 Drawing horizontal parallel lines

To draw lines parallel to the sloping edges of the well, we employ a slightly different technique. Again draw 2" perpendiculars as before, then start a new line from the end of that line. Hover the mouse over the line we want to draw parallel to, until the word 'Parallel' appears (but don't click here!). Then click around where you want the parallel line to end (figure 4-16).

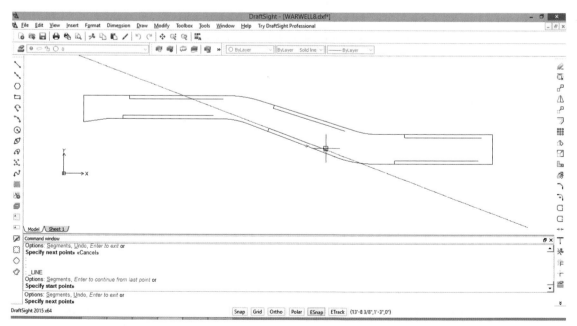

Figure 4-16 Parallel 'sloping' lines

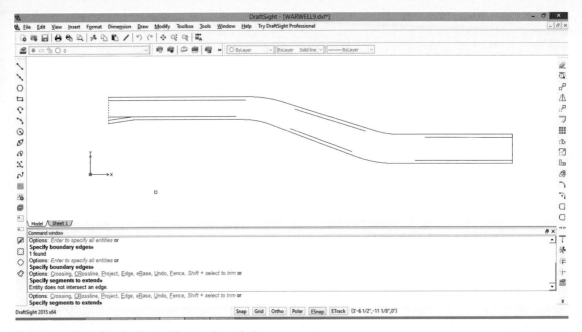

Figure 4-17 Extending horizontal lines to boundaries

It has to be said that there are slicker ways to draw parallel lines. *LibreCAD*, for example lets you set a distance then simply click on a line (or lines) to draw one parallel at the set distance away. However, *DraftSight* is handier then *LibreCAD* for certain other things – you pays your money (or not!) and you takes your choice! We now delete all the short lines and, using **Modify > Extend**, click a boundary edge, then press **Enter** and click the line(s) we wish to extend to that boundary as in figure 4-17. Note that you must extend the horizontal line to the left-hand edge of the outline before you extend the short sloping line up to it, because if the projected extension misses the boundary line *DraftSight* refuses to extend it. You then need to use **Modify > Trim** on the horizontal line, using the short sloping line as your cutting edge. Annoyingly, there is a 'corner trim' feature offered on the **Modify** menu, which is exactly what we need here, but it is only available with *DraftSight Professional*!

Join the remaining gaps with fillets, as before, remembering this time that, to be concentric, the radii of the curves must be 2" smaller or larger depending on whether this is inside or outside the original curve (figure 4-18).

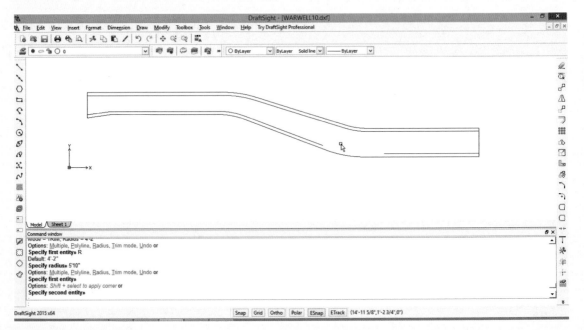

Figure 4-18 Add fillet curves

We now delete all the original lines of OUTLINE1, and draw new end lines (hover over the ends of the horizontal lines until the words 'End Point' appear) and save the file as OUTLINE2.dxf (figure 4-19).

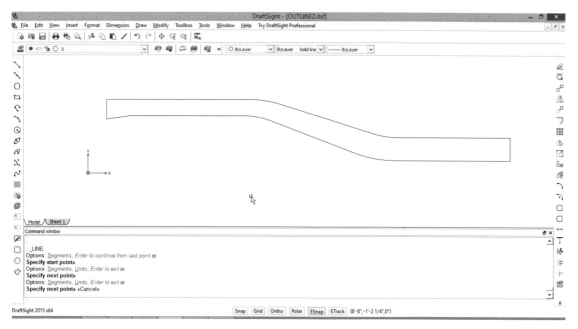

Figure 4-19 OUTLINE2.dxf

Now we see just how powerful *OpenSCAD* is. In just three lines of code, we import and extrude OUTLINE2.dxf and subtract it from OUTLINE1.dxf to give us (the left-hand part of) our wagon side. In figure 4-20 we use the **Difference** function to do the subtraction of the OUTLINE2 object (translated 3" in the z direction) from the OUTLINE1 object to give us the girder-like side illustrated in the figure.

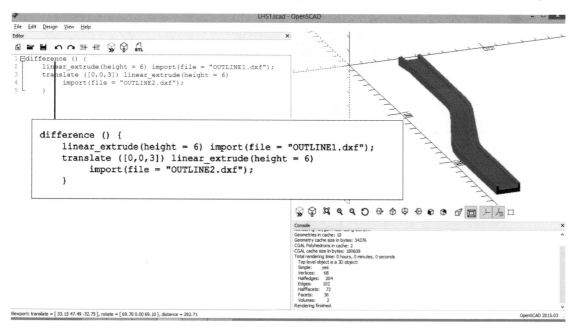

```
difference () {
    linear_extrude(height = 6) import(file = "OUTLINE1.dxf");
    translate ([0,0,3]) linear_extrude(height = 6)
        import(file = "OUTLINE2.dxf");
    }
```

Figure 4-20 Subtracting OUTLINE2 from OUTLINE1

4

Our next job is to add the triangular bracing pieces below the top lip of the girder. We could do this by drawing a triangle and extruding it, then moving it into place and repeating for each of the brackets. However, *OpenSCAD* gives us an alternative option. This is a representation of the shape we need at its absolute simplest. We have six vertices labelled 0 to 5, and nine edges defining the boundaries of two triangular and three rectangular faces. When a shape is as basic as this it is often easier to set it up as a polyhedron rather than drawing it in 2D and extruding, and the code illustrated in figure 4-21 shows how we would define the shape. The vertices (which *OpenSCAD* calls 'points') are defined by their x, y and z coordinates. The faces are defined by listing the corners that form them in *clockwise* order, when viewed from the outside of the solid body.

However, it would be tedious to work out the coordinates of each vertex in each copy of the triangular bracket object we need. Therefore we will create a *module* to make these brackets and place them in position, just as we created the sleeper_layer module in the previous chapter. We will make the module completely general so that it can be re-used in other projects: the shape, size, position and orientation of the required bracket can be passed as parameters. In figure 4-22 the height, width and depth form the first three parameters, then next come the x, y and z coordinates at which the origin of the bracket (point '0' in Figure 4-21) is to be placed, and finally the angle at which the bracket is to be drawn, measured anticlockwise from upright. The code within the module is fairly straightforward – we translate and rotate a polyhedron according to the parameters passed to the module.

```
polyhedron(
points=[[0,0,0],[1,0,0],[1,6,0],[0,6,0],[0,6,2],[1,6,2]],
faces=[[0,3,4],[1,5,2],[0,4,5,1],[3,2,5,4],[0,1,2,3]]
);
```

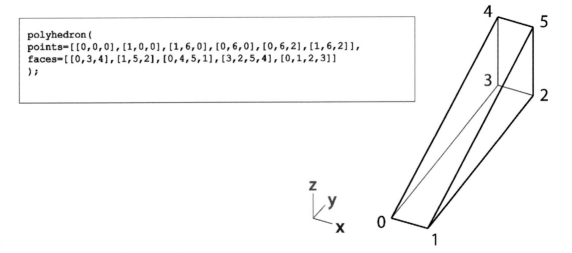

Figure 4-21 Bracket defined as a polyhedron

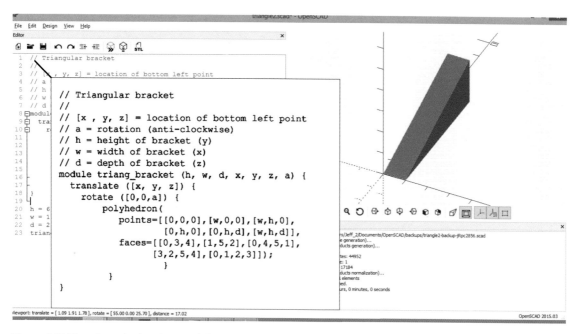

Figure 4-22 The triangular bracket module

We can find the positions for the brackets by going back to our original OUTLINE1 drawing in *DraftSight* and clicking **Format > Layer Tools > Show all layers** to bring it back (figure 4-23). That done, we can measure the location of brackets simply by hovering the mouse cursor over their bottom left corners and reading the mouse location on the bottom right of the screen. In tiny writing, we can see that the mouse position as it hovers over the first bracket's origin is x = 2' 7", y = 3' 0", or, as we are working in inches, 31", 36".

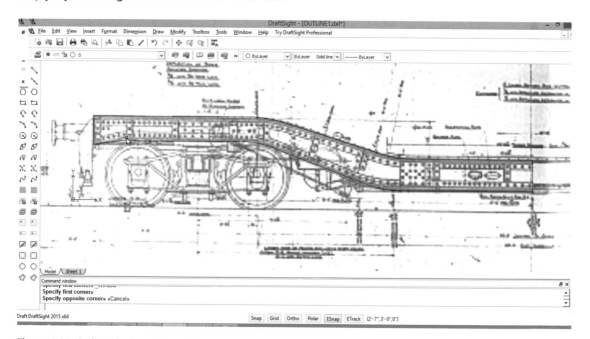

Figure 4-23 Finding the bracket positions

As shown in figure 4-24, we have positioned this bracket on the side of the wagon by means of a call to the triang_bracket module. Notice that in addition to the 31", 36" x and y positions, we have lifted the bracket upwards 3" in the z direction. If this were not done, it would be buried inside the main structure.

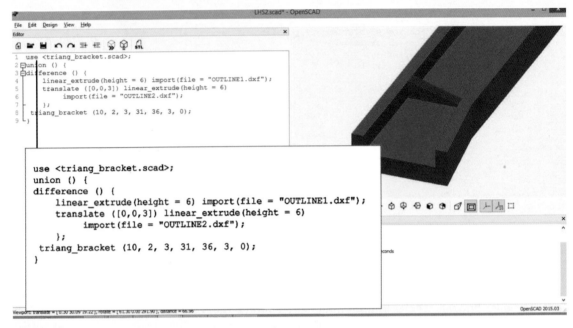

```
use <triang_bracket.scad>;
union () {
difference () {
    linear_extrude(height = 6) import(file = "OUTLINE1.dxf");
    translate ([0,0,3]) linear_extrude(height = 6)
        import(file = "OUTLINE2.dxf");
    };
  triang_bracket (10, 2, 3, 31, 36, 3, 0);
}
```

Figure 4-24 The first bracket in position

In addition to triangular brackets, inspection of photographs shows that there are also two rectangular ones that extend the width of the side. To construct these we employ a very simple module, analogous to triang_bracket but using a simple cube instead of the polyhedron of Figure 4-21. The code for this is illustrated in figure 4-25.

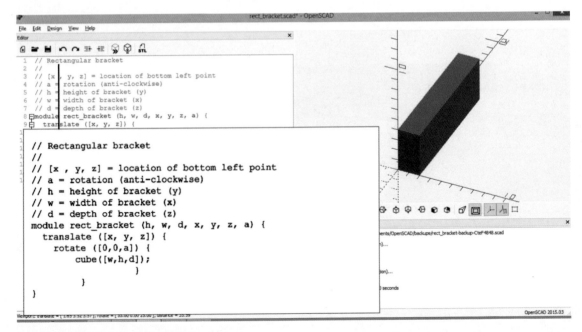

```
// Rectangular bracket
//
// [x , y, z] = location of bottom left point
// a = rotation (anti-clockwise)
// h = height of bracket (y)
// w = width of bracket (x)
// d = depth of bracket (z)
module rect_bracket (h, w, d, x, y, z, a) {
  translate ([x, y, z]) {
    rotate ([0,0,a]) {
        cube([w,h,d]);
                }
        }
}
```

Figure 4-25 The rectangular bracket module

In figure 4-26 we have placed all of the triangular brackets and a couple of rectangular ones according to the positions measured on our drawing (Figure 4-23). This completes the left half of our wagon side, which we can export as 'LHSide.stl' by clicking the 'stl' icon above the editor window.

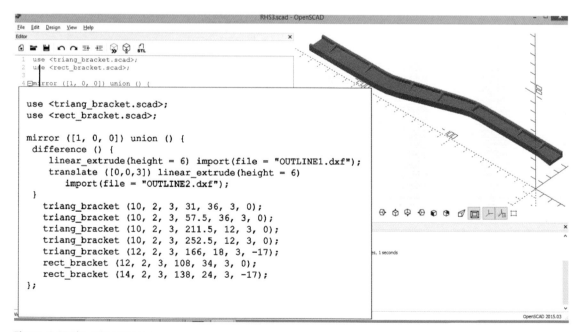

```
use <triang_bracket.scad>;
use <rect_bracket.scad>;

union () {
 difference () {
   linear_extrude(height = 6) import(file = "OUTLINE1.dxf");
   translate ([0,0,3]) linear_extrude(height = 6)
     import(file = "OUTLINE2.dxf");
 }
   triang_bracket (10, 2, 3, 31, 36, 3, 0);
   triang_bracket (10, 2, 3, 57.5, 36, 3, 0);
   triang_bracket (10, 2, 3, 211.5, 12, 3, 0);
   triang_bracket (10, 2, 3, 252.5, 12, 3, 0);
   triang_bracket (12, 2, 3, 166, 18, 3, -17);
   rect_bracket (12, 2, 3, 108, 34, 3, 0);
   rect_bracket (14, 2, 3, 138, 24, 3, -17);
};
```

Figure 4-26 All the brackets in place

We now employ the *OpenSCAD* **mirror** function, which you will see at the beginning of the code in figure 4-27. It means 'carry out all the following, then make a mirror image of the final result'. The argument to the mirror function is a vector, here [1, 0, 0], which is the normal vector to the plane of the mirror (a bit like the facet normals discussed in Chapter 1). In this case, the normal is along the x-axis, so the mirror is in the yz plane. We export this as 'RHSide.stl'. If the wagon was shorter, we could make a union between this and the left-hand side, but as our print bed is only 200mm long we shall have to print the two halves separately.

```
use <triang_bracket.scad>;
use <rect_bracket.scad>;

mirror ([1, 0, 0]) union () {
 difference () {
   linear_extrude(height = 6) import(file = "OUTLINE1.dxf");
   translate ([0,0,3]) linear_extrude(height = 6)
     import(file = "OUTLINE2.dxf");
 }
   triang_bracket (10, 2, 3, 31, 36, 3, 0);
   triang_bracket (10, 2, 3, 57.5, 36, 3, 0);
   triang_bracket (10, 2, 3, 211.5, 12, 3, 0);
   triang_bracket (10, 2, 3, 252.5, 12, 3, 0);
   triang_bracket (12, 2, 3, 166, 18, 3, -17);
   rect_bracket (12, 2, 3, 108, 34, 3, 0);
   rect_bracket (14, 2, 3, 138, 24, 3, -17);
};
```

Figure 4-27 The mirror image

Turning now to the floor of the wagon, this is made in a similar fashion. Returning to *DraftSight*, we re-open our OUTLINE1 drawing file and delete all but the 'top' of the outline (figure 4-28). Save this as OUTLINE3.

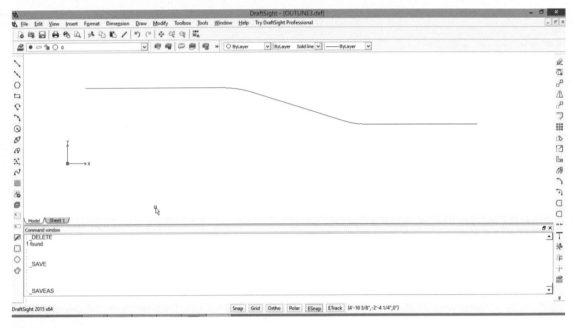

Figure 4-28 The floor surface profile

We now make a copy of this profile 6 inches below it, and the easiest way to do this is to make a pattern. Click **Edit > Select All**, then **Modify > Pattern**. In the pattern dialog set vertical copies to 2, horizontal copies to 1, vertical spacing to -6 and horizontal spacing to 0. Join the leftmost end points with a line (figure 4.29).

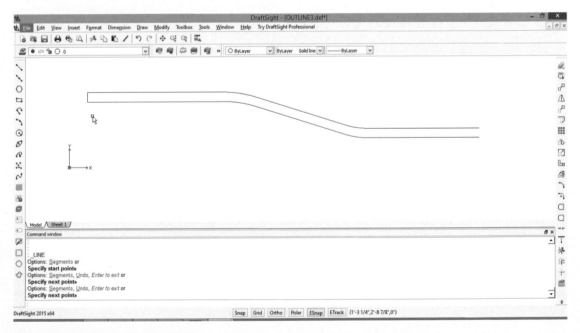

Figure 4-29 The floor underside added

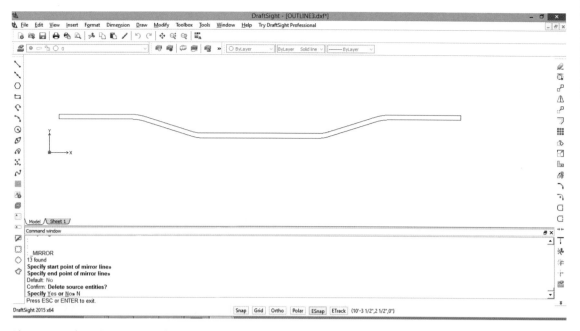

Figure 4-30 The mirror image added

We now make a mirror image copy of this half-floor. Select everything again and click **Modify > Mirror**. Click the two rightmost end points to define the mirror line and respond 'No' to the question 'Delete source entities?'. See figure 4-30. Save this as OUTLINE3.dxf.

We can now complete the floor in *OpenSCAD*. The floor length and width, as measured from the GA drawing, are 43' 0" and 8' 5" respectively, and the central 'gap' in the floor is 16' 6" by 4' 0" approximately. The constants fl, fw, gl and gw are set up to represent these dimensions in inches (remembering that 2 x 6" of the floor width will be taken up by the side members). We then use a cube with the dimensions of the gap to cut a hole in the floor. If you followed the *OpenSCAD* code to make the sleeper stack in the previous chapter, then this should present no problem (figure 4-31). One thing may not be immediately clear: remember that we moved the floor profile so that it was all in the positive quadrant in Figure 4-11? This is why we add 12" to the translation of the cut-out cube's calculated x coordinate. We don't need to bother about the y coordinate as we've made the cube very tall (100") in the y direction.

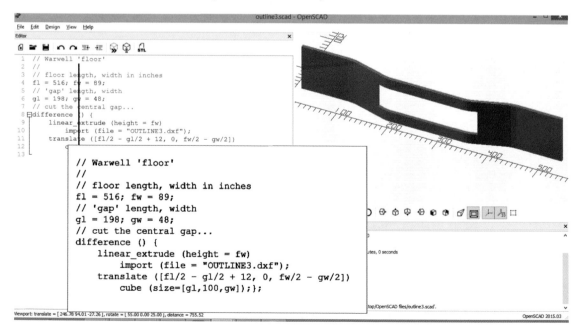

```
// Warwell 'floor'
//
// floor length, width in inches
fl = 516; fw = 89;
// 'gap' length, width
gl = 198; gw = 48;
// cut the central gap...
difference () {
    linear_extrude (height = fw)
        import (file = "OUTLINE3.dxf");
    translate ([fl/2 - gl/2 + 12, 0, fw/2 - gw/2])
        cube (size=[gl,100,gw]);};
```

Figure 4-31 The floor in 3D

The floor is too long to print as it stands, so we need to cut it into sections. However, we should not divide it into two equal halves, as this would mean that both the sides and the floor would have butt joints in line at the centre of the model, which would constitute a (probably fatal) weak point. Instead, we shall cut it into three sections. To make the outer sections, use the intersection of the floor with a cube positioned at its left- and right-hand ends. To make the central section we employ the **difference** operator to remove both of these sections from the floor.

In Figure 4-32, we take the intersection of the floor with a cube located at the origin. We export this left section as an stl file – let's call it Floor_L.stl. Then, by simply translating our cube to the right, we create the right-hand section, as in Figure 4-33, and export this as Floor_R.stl.

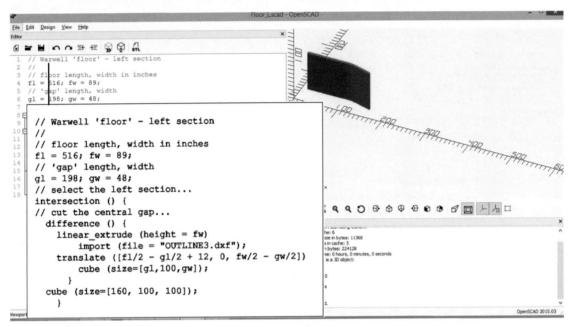

```
// Warwell 'floor' - left section
//
// floor length, width in inches
fl = 516; fw = 89;
// 'gap' length, width
gl = 198; gw = 48;
// select the left section...
intersection () {
// cut the central gap...
  difference () {
    linear_extrude (height = fw)
        import (file = "OUTLINE3.dxf");
    translate ([fl/2 - gl/2 + 12, 0, fw/2 - gw/2])
        cube (size=[gl,100,gw]);
    }
  cube (size=[160, 100, 100]);
    }
```

Figure 4-32 The left-hand section of floor

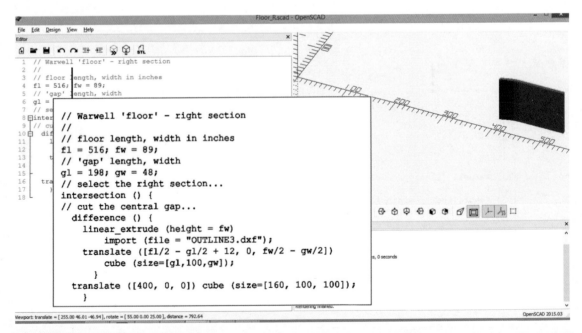

```
// Warwell 'floor' - right section
//
// floor length, width in inches
fl = 516; fw = 89;
// 'gap' length, width
gl = 198; gw = 48;
// select the right section...
intersection () {
// cut the central gap...
  difference () {
    linear_extrude (height = fw)
        import (file = "OUTLINE3.dxf");
    translate ([fl/2 - gl/2 + 12, 0, fw/2 - gw/2])
        cube (size=[gl,100,gw]);
    }
  translate ([400, 0, 0]) cube (size=[160, 100, 100]);
    }
```

Figure 4-33 The right-hand section of floor

Finally, we employ both the cube at the origin and the translated cube with the **difference** operator to form the central section, which we export as Floor_C.stl, as in Figure 4-34.

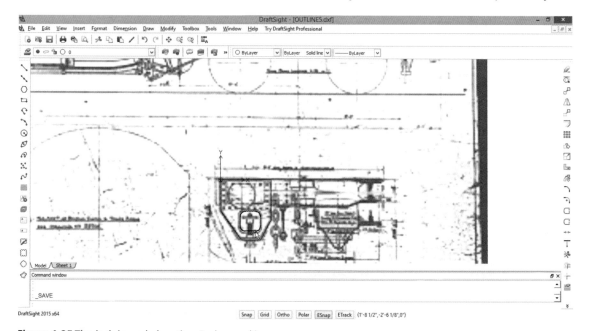

```
// Warwell 'floor' - central section
//
// floor length, width in inches
fl = 516; fw = 89;
// 'gap' length, width
gl = 198; gw = 48;
// cut out the left and right sections...
difference () {
// cut the central gap...
  difference () {
    linear_extrude (height = fw)
        import (file = "OUTLINE3.dxf");
    translate ([fl/2 - gl/2 + 12, 0, fw/2 - gw/2])
        cube (size=[gl,100,gw]);
    }
  cube (size=[160, 100, 100]);
  translate ([400, 0, 0]) cube (size=[160, 100, 100]);
    }
```

Figure 4-34 The central section of floor

We now need to give our wagon some buffers. We could use the method described already to make buffer beams in *Sketchup Make*, adjusting the dimensions to match our drawing. However, there is one additional feature of these buffer beams that is quite distinctive – the jacks. These can be seen in side elevation in Figure 4-10, and in end elevation in figure 4-35. They were used to steady the wagon when tanks were being loaded, but many had them removed in the post-war years.

Figure 4-35 The jack in end elevation *Background image: Rail Album website (http://www.railalbum.co.uk) by kind permission of Greg Martin.*

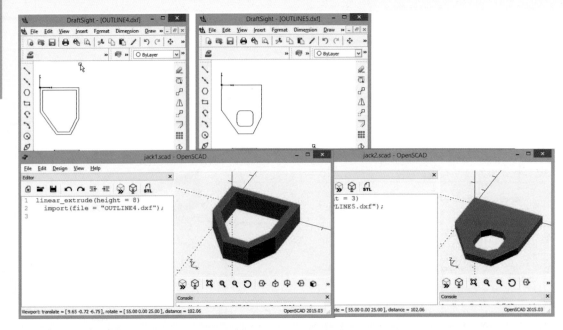

Figure 4-36 The traced outlines and extrusions for the jacks

We won't go through the construction of these jacks step-by-step, since in principle they are the same as the steps involved in constructing the wagon sides and floor. Essentially, we trace around the outline of the jack and this time create two separate outlines, OUTLINE4 and OUTLINE5, which we then import into OpenSCAD and extrude. Figure 4-36 is a composite screenshot illustrating the general idea.

Using these outlines and a couple of cylinders for the buffer stock, we can create a complete jack, and employ a suitably positioned cube to create the bevel at the top of the jack frame (figure 4-37). We decided that the jack screw would be best represented by a real 8BA screw. We now make the mirror image jack for the opposite side of the buffer beam using the mirror transformation, which is included in the code (see figure 4-37 inset), but commented out. Incidentally, the '$fn' variable defines the number of fragments used to draw cylinders and spheres. The larger it is, the smoother the surface appears, but the longer the model takes to render.

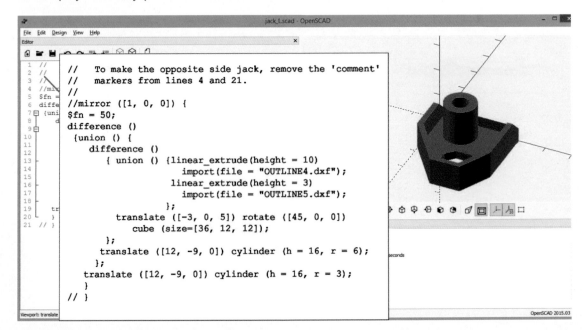

Figure 4-37 The combined jack and buffer stock

Finally, we combine a left- and right-hand version of the jack/buffer stock with a suitably sized cube to make the complete buffer beam (figure 4-38).

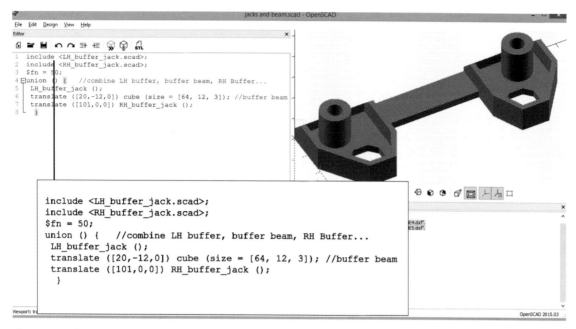

```
include <LH_buffer_jack.scad>;
include <RH_buffer_jack.scad>;
$fn = 50;
union () {    //combine LH buffer, buffer beam, RH Buffer...
 LH_buffer_jack ();
 translate ([20,-12,0]) cube (size = [64, 12, 3]); //buffer beam
 translate ([101,0,0]) RH_buffer_jack ();
  }
```

Figure 4-38 The completed buffer beam

It was decided not to attempt to 3D print the bogies – partly because the author happened to have some white-metal diamond-frame bogies to hand, and partly because we thought it was unlikely that these could be successfully printed. In this, we may well have been wrong, as the following project will show. Figure 4-39 illustrates the full set of parts 3D-printed in grey PLA plastic.

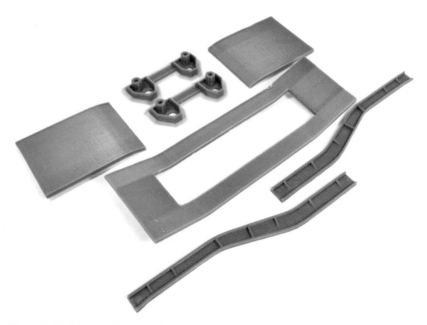

Figure 4-39 The complete set of parts

Midland Railway open wagon

The next example is a Midland Railway seven-plank 12-ton open wagon. We will build it in 7mm/1ft scale, then try to print in a smaller scale.

The model was created in *DesignSpark Mechanical* as a kit of parts: the underframe, sides, ends, floor, axlebox assemblies and brake gear were built as components, then printed separately. This allows us to orient the parts for printing to get the necessary strength and print quality.

We start by creating an assembly that contains the axlebox, hornblock, 'W' iron and springs. The basis of the 'W' irons is basically a set of rectangular boxes arranged appropriately (figure 4-40). These components would be fairly thin in the prototype but we have to make them just over a millimetre thick to allow us to reliably print them and for them to have adequate strength. The model has been arranged so that the back of the 'W' irons, in fact most of the model, will be flat on the print bed.

To this basic shape we can add a hornblock, axlebox and hornblock retaining strap (figure 4-41). You can see that so far we have only used various rectangular boxes apart from a couple of cylinders to represent the bolts holding the hornblock keeper plate; these cylinders project around 0.4 millimetre above the other part so that we get a few layers of printing. Some of the rectangular bits have had chamfers or bevels applied to give us a bit of shaping.

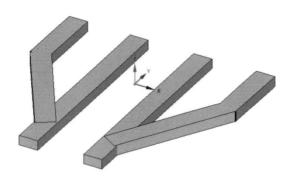

Figure 4-40 The 'W' irons

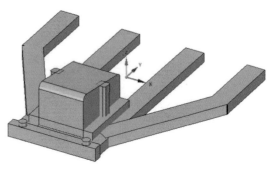

Figure 4-41 Adding the axlebox and hornblock

Now we tackle the leaf spring and its shackles. We can easily add a central spring anchor to the top of the axlebox – it is just another rectangle. To make the shackles we start by drawing a triangle with the Line drawing tool, then pull the surface into a 3D shape as we have done to produce the other rectangular boxes. We then apply a bevel to the lower edge to round it off. We can add another cylinder to represent the shackle pin, then copy and paste so that we have a pair, one at each end of the spring. This gives us something like figure 4-42.

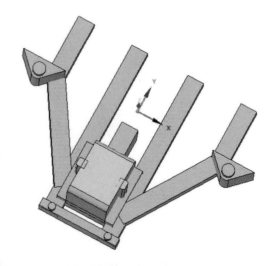

Figure 4-42 The spring shackles added

Some thought was put into how this piece of our model will be fixed to the rest of it. The top faces of the shackles will be glued to the underside of the wagon solebar with the top ends of the 'W' irons glued behind the solebar, much as in the prototype in fact, although the Midland Railway used bolts.

Now we need to model the leaf spring, which at first glance looks like a bit of a challenge. In fact, it's fairly easy, and we use the **3-point Arc** tool in *DesignSpark*. Working in top view, we draw a line from the left shackle to the right shackle, then drag the curve down till it runs through the spring anchor (figure 4-43). You'll probably need to have more than one go at this, as we did!

We now have what will be the top edge of the uppermost leaf of the spring. To make life a bit simpler we now hide all of the model apart from our newly drawn arc. In the left-hand 'Structure' pane you will see that each component and shape in the model has a tick box next to it. If you click these you can make various parts, or indeed the whole of the model, visible or invisible.

With only the new arc visible, we can now draw another 3-point arc about 0.4 millimetres below the first one. We now draw two straight lines, one at each end to cross the ends of the two arcs. Switch to the home view and into 3D mode and hopefully you now have a surface, and we can use the **Pull** tool to extrude the shape upwards by about 2 millimetres (figure 4-44).

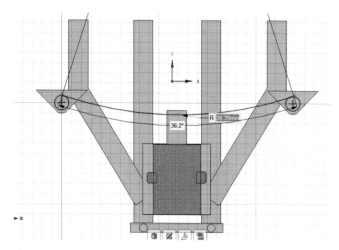

Figure 4-43 Creating the spring arc

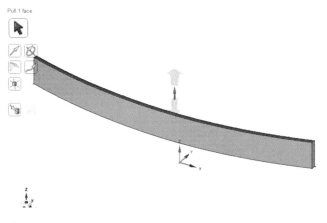

Figure 4-44 Pulling the first spring leaf

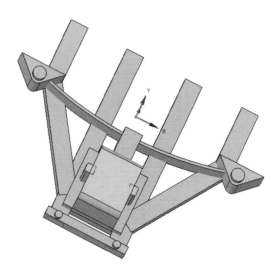

Figure 4-45 The first spring leaf in place

If we now check all the parts in the structure pane they will all be visible again, and we end up with figure 4-45. You may find that you have several small pieces left in the 'Curves' section of the 'Structure' panel. These are the remains of the arcs and lines you drew that were outside the shape we pulled, and they can be deleted.

All the tricky bits are now done and we have something that looks quite encouraging. To build up the rest of the leaf spring we copy and paste our first leaf and move the copy below the first. To reduce the length of the leaf we select each end in turn and move it inwards. Figure 4-46 shows the second leaf added. To ensure that we can see the individual leaves in our final print, we have set the leaf back a little. We can continue this copy, paste and modify process to build up the complete stack of leaves.

To complete our axlebox assembly we now need to cut a hole in the rear to allow us to fit a 'top hat' bearing. This is done as before by creating a 2.5-millimetre cylinder, positioning it, and using it as a cutter object with the **Combine** tool. Finally, we add a couple of small rectangular boxes on the front faces of the 'W' irons to act as locating lugs to allow us to accurately position these assemblies on our wagon solebars. Figures 4-47 and 4-48 show the final axlebox assembly.

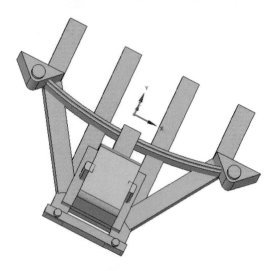

Figure 4-46 The second spring leaf in place

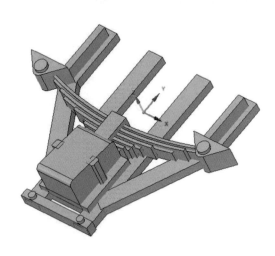

Figure 4-47 The completed axlebox assembly

Figure 4-49 shows a set of four straight from the printer complete with the brim still attached. The parts were printed in PLA without any support material. The finished article is far from perfect, but after some cleaning and painting it provides a passable representation of the prototype.

Figure 4-48 The axlebox assembly from the rear

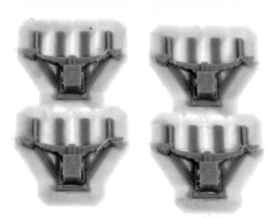

Figure 4-49 Printed axlebox assemblies

Next, we will tackle the underframe, which is not overly complex. We have not attempted to create an exact replica of the real wagon underframe but have drawn a simplified version that gives us adequate rigidity. Figure 4-50 shows it as we would wish it to be, and while it looks quite complex it was created using all the same techniques we have used before, so there is no real need to elaborate on them. The key to building something like this is to look at the prototype drawing and analyse how each of the many details would have been created, then to do something similar using the CAD tools, with maybe a little simplification.

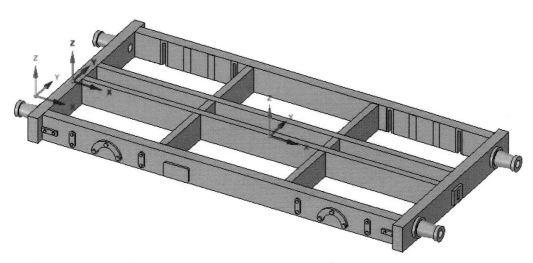

Figure 4-50 The wagon underframe

However, one aspect to highlight is the cut-outs in the rear of the solebar, which will accept the locating lugs we formed on the axlebox assemblies. To cut these out we imported our complete axlebox assembly into the underframe CAD file, then positioned four of them appropriately, using them as cutter objects to allow the **Combine** tool to remove the right bits from the solebars. Of course this gives us an exact-fit hole, which once printed will probably be too small, so the sides of the cut-outs can be eased out a bit by selecting each face and using the **Move** tool. If you get a cut operation wrong, there is a handy **Fill** tool in *DesignSpark Mechanical* that does exactly what it says!

The underframe looks great in the CAD program, but because we have a low-end printer we need to consider how best to orient the model for printing to get a good surface quality on the visible parts. It would be perfectly feasible to print the model exactly as it is, but this might lead to problems in rendering the circular section of the buffer casings, and we would get a grainy effect on the vertical surfaces of the solebars and buffer beams. This effect is shown by one of our early test prints (figure 4-51).

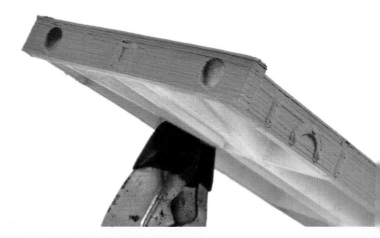

Figure 4-51 Graining in the printed result

While this effect does look a bit like wood grain, it is rather too pronounced to be acceptable, so to get round the problem we split the underframe into pieces for printing. We could have simply removed and reoriented the solebars and buffer beams, which would require them to be glued to the central frame section later on. We tried this but PLA plastic is quite difficult to glue and this would require the glue joints to be strong. Instead, the solebars and buffer beams were split down their lengths to leave a strong central frame and a set of facing pieces. The facings were rotated through 90 degrees so that the detailed visible surfaces were uppermost and the bits arranged for printing. Figure 4-52 shows our modified drawing. Keep a copy of the original drawing as it will be useful later. This gives us an improved print, but it isn't perfect and still needs some surface preparation to be acceptable. Figure 4-53 shows the underframe components on the printer build table.

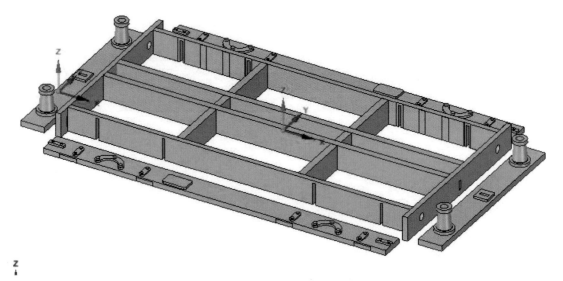

Figure 4-52 The modified underframe split for printing

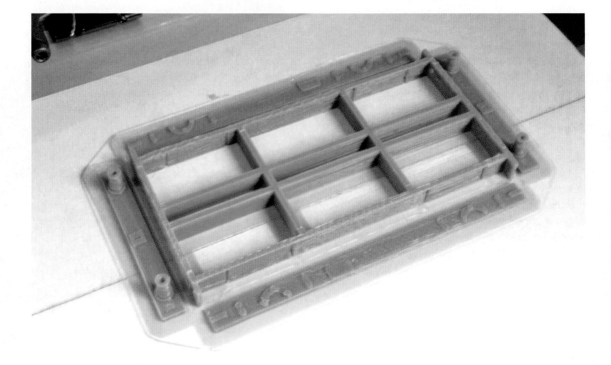

Figure 4-53 The underframe printed

Next we need a floor, sides and ends. For most wagons of this type the sides and ends are symmetrical, so you only need to create one side and one end, but this particular wagon has an end door so we need to create two separate ends. We can get away with only modelling one side as we can mirror it for the other side when we come to slice it. There are no particular problems in modelling the bodywork parts, so we won't go into great detail. We wanted to get the detail of the joins between the planks on both surfaces of the sides, and achieved this by modelling each of the planks individually with a chamfer on the corners, then arranged the seven planks around a solid core to maintain the strength of the final part. This detail can be seen in figure 4-54, which also shows how the various bits of strapping, hinges and bolts are made up from simple shapes.

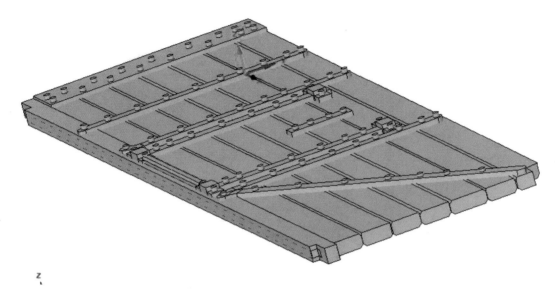

Figure 4-54 The wagon side

The floor is the simplest component, being merely a rectangular box with lines scribed into it to represent the plank and door joins. This was done by creating a thin rectangular box and using it as a cutter repeatedly with the **Combine** tool. The result can be seen in figure 4-55.

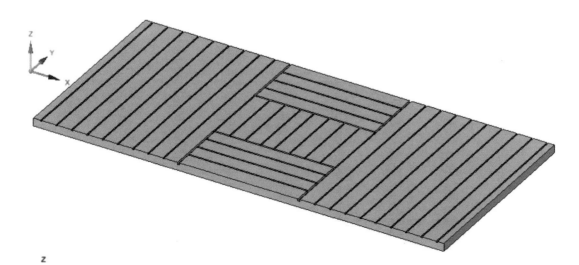

Figure 4-55 The wagon floor

We have now created CAD representations of nearly all our wagon pieces, but we need to make sure that they will all fit together. This is where keeping a copy of the intact underframe and any other components comes in handy. We create a complete model of the wagon by bringing in all the separate parts as components using the *DesignSpark* '**Insert geometry from file**' tool. Bear in mind that if we make modifications to any of these components they will be reflected in the original component's CAD file, which is very useful but you might want to take copies in case it all goes wrong!

Figure 4-56 shows the complete model of the open wagon with one side missing; we will create this by mirroring at the slicing phase. We have here two axlebox assemblies, underframe (in its original form), the ends, one side, the floor, and a crude representation of the brake gear. There are also a couple of cylinders giving us an idea of where the wheels will fit. We won't be printing the wheels and axles – that would be a step too far (at the moment)!

We haven't put the complete model together simply because it makes you feel good to see something like this, but we need to check the fit of the parts. By hiding parts of the model we can see where things are sitting; for instance, if we hide the end door and rotate and zoom in as in figure 4-57, we can see how the floor fits and how the side fits against the floor and solebar.

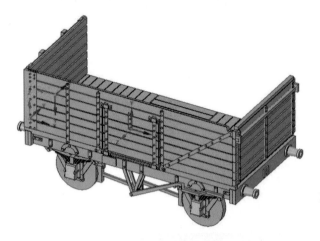

Figure 4-56 The almost complete wagon

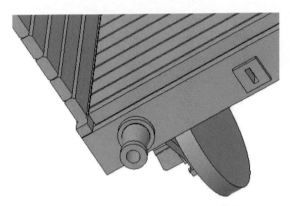

Figure 4-57 Checking the fit of the sides

One of the trickiest bits to get right on our model was the join between the end and the side. We tried mitre joins but that didn't work well, as the PLA tended to warp and give us odd angles that we couldn't get to fit. In the end we used a step joint, and is shown in figure 4-58 from above, with the end highlighted. Interestingly, this joint is quite sloppy! When printed on our FFF printer things didn't fit well at first, despite checking and making allowances, so we had to adjust the CAD model to suit the printer, where horizontal dimensions are less accurate than vertical.

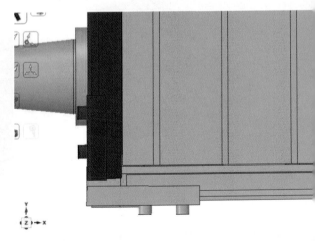

Figure 4-58 Checking the side corner joint

Once you have all the components suitably arranged, you will hopefully have spotted any problems and resolved them, adding any required construction aids such as tabs. Figure 4-59 shows a complete set of parts for the wagon as they come from the printer. This is the result of around 7 hours of printer time, with all the parts printed at 100 micron resolution in PLA. (A micron is one millionth of a metre, or one thousandth of a millimetre.)

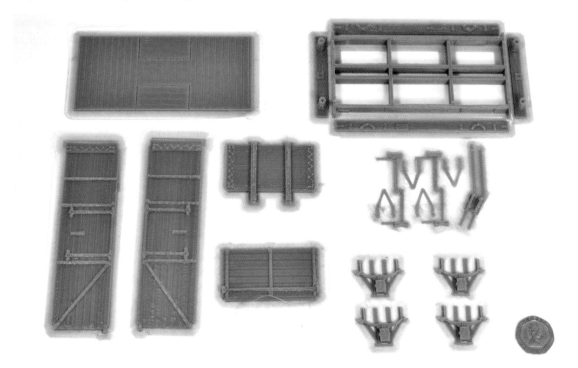

Figure 4-59 The printed wagon parts

The brims and odd stray bits of plastic filament can be removed fairly easily with a sharp craft knife and the parts finished with a fine file where necessary.

The model is designed to use a standard set of 3ft 1in wagon wheels, so the holes for the 'top hat' bearings in the back of the axlebox assemblies are opened out gently with a 2.5mm drill. The bearings can then be push-fitted, and the axlebox assemblies glued to the inside of the solebars, hopefully fitting nicely into the locating holes and carrying the wheelsets; we used good-quality thick cyanoacrylate ('superglue'). We then fixed the solebar and buffer beam facings, added the floor and built up the sides around it.

The whole model was given a coat of grey car primer from a rattle can. Some areas were rubbed down with a glass-fibre scratchy brush, and another coat of primer applied. Finally, a coat of wagon grey was applied by brush and the axlebox assemblies painted black. Figure 4-60 shows the completed wagon, with metal buffers and couplings added.

The buffer carriers have not rendered well and are fragile. Fitting commercial brass examples is probably a better bet.

Figure 4-60 The completed wagon

Changing scale

To really push our printing capabilities to the limit, we also tried printing the same wagon in 4mm scale. We decided to leave out the underframe parts and print just the wagon body, buffer beams and solebars as a single piece, and the CAD drawing for this is shown in Figure 4-61. The far side of the wagon is shown in blue; if you recall, we did not model this side of the wagon as it is a mirror image of the opposite side. This was not a problem when printing the wagon as a set of parts, but now, to print the body as a single piece, we need both sides, so we have imported the mirrored side as an stl file, and *DesignSpark Mechanical* has highlighted the fact that this is an imported component. As we are going to scale down this model for printing, we have filled in the holes in the buffer housings as they will not be printable as they are.

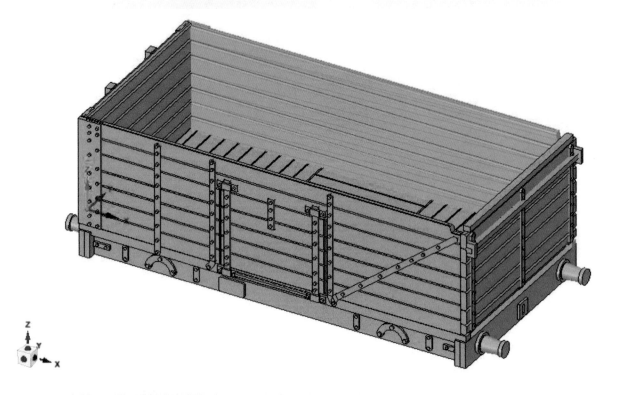

Figure 4-61 The CAD drawing for a 4mm print

The modified CAD file was exported as an stl file, loaded into netfabb and changed from a 7mm model to a 4mm one by scaling with a factor of 0.57 (⁴/₇ths). The model was sliced and printed on our low-cost FFF printer and submitted to a printing bureau for printing with a high-tech SLS process to give a comparison. (These technologies will be described in detail in Chapter 6.) For the bureau print we uploaded the stl model via the web and used the company's online tools to check the printability of the model and to make minor adjustments. Depending on which bureau you use, the tools and process will vary, so we will not attempt to describe this step in detail. A wide variety of materials were available to print in, ranging from plastics through ceramics into precious metals such as gold and platinum! Being frugal, we chose to print using a 150-micron SLS process with plastic, the cheapest option.

After a week or so the model duly arrived from the bureau by post and Figure 4-62 shows it on the right, alongside our home-printed version. The SLS print has rendered the detail of the model quite well, even though the resolution is only 150 microns. There is no support material to clear away as the printing process obviates the need for this.

Figure 4-62 Comparison of printed wagon bodies in 4mm

Our FFF version, printed at 100-micron resolution, has suffered from some strange side effects in the slicing, but has printed reasonably successfully apart from the buffers. We could possibly have improved the result by slightly increasing the filament extrusion rate. There was support material to clean away and below the floor is a lot of supporting plastic that would be quite difficult to remove. As with the 7mm model, we would probably be better off printing the solebar and buffer beams separately from the body and floor. Commercially available buffers would also be a better option for both models.

Using the bureau SLS facilities generally gives a finer model, especially if you want to print a complete structure. The only problem is the cost; in this case the single wagon body was in the region of £20, nearly 50% of this being postage and packaging. When we looked at printing the 7mm version via the bureau the costs became very high, so we did not pursue this.

5

Locomotives and fittings

In this chapter we will introduce some more advanced techniques including rotational extrusion, forming complex shapes by manipulation of individual vertices, and checking for and correcting manifold errors. We will also make our first venture into the slightly quirky world of *Blender*!

Drawing a chimney

Undoubtedly the chimney of a steam locomotive presents a challenge. The problem is the flared base of the chimney, which has to match up with the round top of the smokebox. We shall use *Blender* to demonstrate one way of doing this, based on that described by Paul Hobbs in his excellent tutorial (see Appendix 1). The general plan is to draw a 2D profile of the chimney, then spin it through 90° to get a solid quarter chimney, which we then manipulate to fit onto a round smokebox top. Using a nice feature of *Blender*, we can mirror the manipulation of the quarter chimney in the x and y planes to give us a complete 3D chimney.

It will be useful to have a 2D background image of the chimney against which to draw the initial profile, so our first job is to load this. We took as our example the standard LMS chimney designed by Sir William Stanier for his 2-6-0 and 2-6-4T locomotives. A suitable drawing can be found in F. J. Roche's *Historic Locomotive Drawings in 4mm Scale*. The drawing is scanned and saved as a jpeg file.

We now open *Blender* and load the jpeg file as a background image. **Click View > Properties**, or

hit the **N** key. Scroll down to Background Images and click on the little right-pointing arrow, then click the **Add Image** button that will appear. Click **Open**, browse the file list to find your jpeg file, then select it with the left mouse button and click **Open Image**. The background image will now appear on our 3D view.

Adjust the size and location of the image so that the centre-line of the chimney lies on the z axis, and the top of the smokebox lies along the y axis, and the image is correctly scaled (figure 5-1). We have chosen one *Blender* unit to represent 6 inches, so we want the base of the chimney (actually 2ft 4in) to be 4.66 units wide. In this case the appropriate scale figure is 8.32 and the offsets are -0.77 and 1.75 units. You can see these numbers at the bottom of the **Add Image** section. Clicking the little arrows on either side of these numbers conveniently changes them in steps of 0.1 unit. If your scanned image is not quite horizontal you can rotate it slightly to make it so. Once the background image is correct, save the file using the **Save As** menu option. It is handy to call it something with a numerical suffix – in this case 'Stanier Chimney 1'.

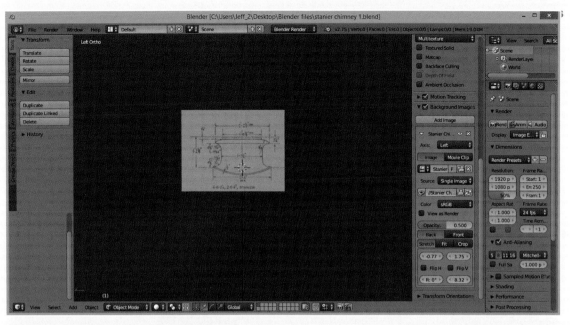

Figure 5-1 **Background image of the chimney.** *Background images 5-1 to 5-3 from* Historic Locomotive Drawings in 4mm Scale *by F. J. Roche (Ian Allan, 1976), reproduced with permission*

Next we want to create a 2D profile of the chimney. We can get rid of the numerical properties window by pressing the N key. Zoom in on the chimney (use the mouse wheel) then, with the 3D cursor at location (0,0,0) click the **Create** tab on the toolshelf and add a plane. With the plane selected (as it will be immediately after creation) down at the bottom of the screen, click on **Object** mode and switch to **Edit** mode (you can also do this using the Tab key shortcut). Then from the **Mesh** menu, select **Vertices > Merge > At Center**. This will merge all four vertices of the plane into a single vertex at (0,0,0). We now extrude this vertex into a line down below the

chimney base. Press the E key and move the mouse – notice how the vertex extrudes itself into an edge. Press the Z key to limit the extrusion to the z direction, and left click when the extruded edge is well below the bottom of the chimney (figure 5-2). Now extrude in the y direction until you are level with the extreme outer edge of the chimney base and left click again. Instead of pressing **Save** to save your file, press **Save As**, then click the + button to the right of the file name. This handy little feature of *Blender* will increase the numerical suffix by 1. This will enable you to go back to previous versions if you make a mess of things!

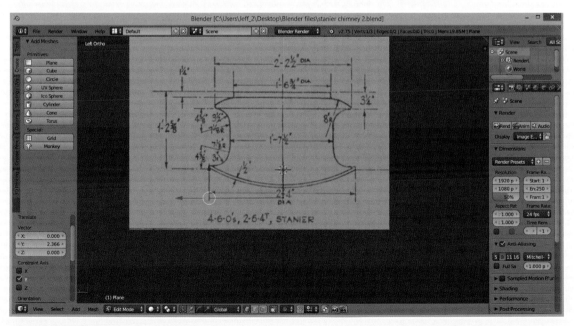

Figure 5-2 Extruding the chimney base

Press E again, then Z, to extrude up to the top of the chimney base. Continue round the chimney profile, pressing E to extrude and left-clicking where the extrusion is to end. Use the Y and Z keys to limit extrusion to the y and z directions where appropriate. Once you reach the top dead centre of the chimney, ensure that this vertex is directly above the first vertex at (0,0,0) by hitting the N key to bring up the properties window again and manually setting its x and y coordinates to zero (figure 5-3).

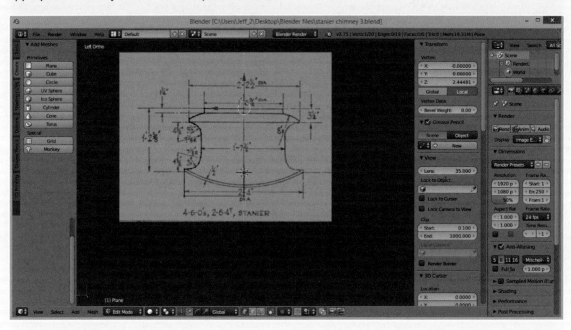

Figure 5-3 Extruding the chimney profile

Our final extrusion will be from this point to the first vertex, so hit E followed by Z and extrude down to somewhere close to the origin point. With this vertex selected, additionally select the vertex at the origin (Shift and right click) and click **Mesh > Vertices > Merge > At Last**. This will merge the two vertices into a single vertex at the origin. Having obtained our chimney profile, we can now remove the background image, so scroll down the properties window to **Background Image** and click the X button to delete it (figure 5-4).

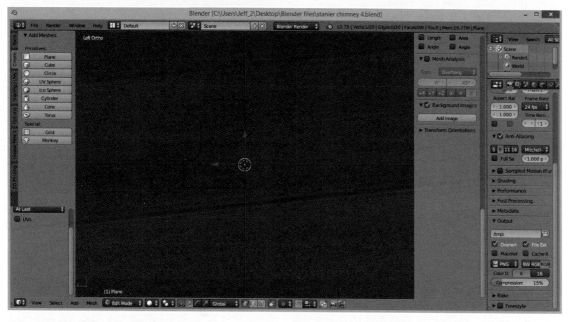

Figure 5-4 The final chimney profile

We now spin our profile to create a three-dimensional object. Select all the vertices by hitting A twice. *Blender* always spins around an axis normal to the screen, so click **View > Top**. On the **Toolshelf** at the left, click **Tools**, then, under **Mesh Tools**, **Spin**. Set steps to 6 and angle to 90° and hit **Enter**. The result should be something like figure 5-5.

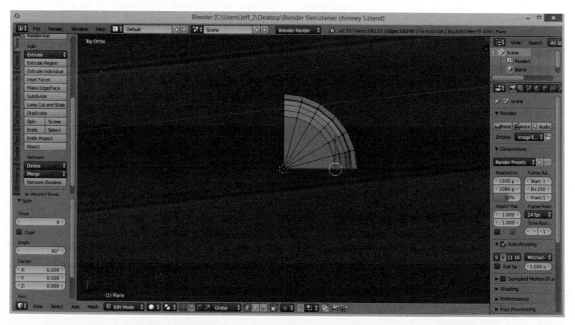

Figure 5-5 Top view of the quarter-chimney

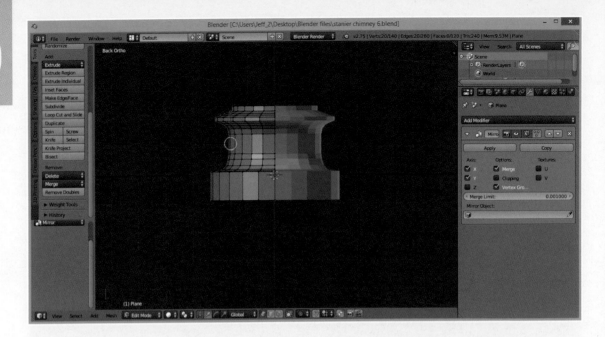

To see the three-dimensional surface we have created from a variety of angles, click the centre mouse button, or mouse wheel, and move the mouse around to get different views. We now need to create the other three quarters of the chimney. We do this by mirroring. Change to a back view by clicking **View > Back**, then, in the right-hand **Property Editor** window, click on the **Modifiers** icon (a little spanner). You might find that to see all the icons you need to widen the window by dragging its left-hand edge. Click **Add Modifier**, from the list of available modifiers select **Mirror**, and check both the X and Y checkboxes. Do *not* click **Apply** just yet – see figure 5-6. The **Mirror** modifier is different from the **Mirror** tool that we will use later in the chapter; there we will make a second copy of an object then use the mirror tool to reflect this object along

ABOVE *Figure 5-6* The mirrored chimney

the z axis, and the two objects remain completely separate. Here, the **Mirror modifier** makes mirror-image copies of the edges and vertices forming our quarter-chimney *within the same object*. By reflecting along both the x and y axes we make all four quarter-chimneys. However, because three of these are in effect reflections, any changes we make to edges and vertices of our original quarter-chimney will be reflected in the other three.

We now add a cylinder to represent the smokebox. Return to **Object** mode and click **Add > Mesh > Cylinder**. Change the cylinder radius to 5.25 (to correspond with the 5ft 3in smokebox diameter on Roche's drawing) and its depth to 6. Change its location on the z axis to -5.25 and rotate 90° in X as per figure 5-7.

Figure 5-7 Adding the smokebox

Now we get to the tricky part. Switch to back view and zoom in for this. Select the chimney with the right mouse button and go into **Edit** mode. Then right click the vertices around the bottom in turn and drag them down to just above the smokebox, hit Z to restrict dragging to the z direction and left click when the vertex is in position (figure 5-8. Notice how the mirrored vertices move also. This is why we didn't click Apply earlier – if we had done so, the mirrored parts would have been merged into a single entity and we would have four times the work to do!

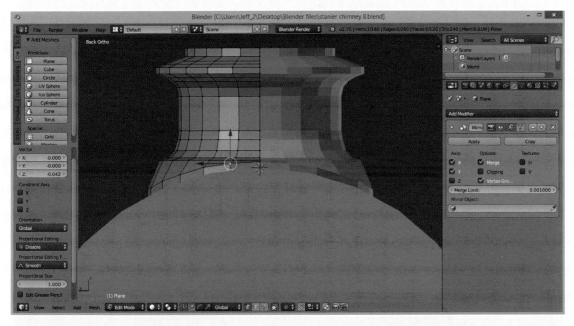

Figure 5-8 Dragging the vertices down

Having done the bottom row of vertices, drag the next row, and so on. We are trying to form the distinctive flare at the base of the chimney, as in Figure 5-9. Once you are happy with the chimney shape, switch back to Object mode, click **Apply** and the chimney will become a single solid object.

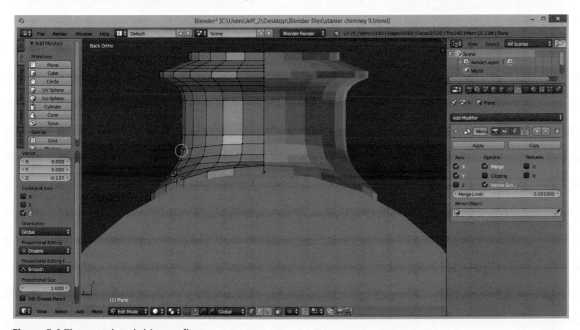

Figure 5-9 The completed chimney flare

We need to do a little housekeeping next, otherwise the next step won't work. Select the chimney (*right mouse button*) and click the **3D Printing Tools** tab on the **Toolshelf**. Click **Check All** and, as you can see in figure 5-10, there are numerous manifold errors arising from the mirroring we did earlier. When *Blender* makes a mirror image in, say, the x direction, it makes a copy of every vertex, keeping the y and z coordinates the same but reversing the sign of the x coordinate. However, for vertices in the yz plane, i.e. where x = 0, this means that we will end up with two vertices at the same location (since -0 = 0), but without a connection between them. This is the source of most of the manifold errors we see in figure 5-10.

To fix them, go into Edit mode, select all vertices (press A twice), then click **Mesh > Vertices > Remove Doubles**. This will merge all vertices that have the same coordinates, thus fixing most of our manifold errors. To see this, click **Check All** again and notice that most of the warnings have disappeared. There remain just a couple of non-manifold edges, and to see what these are we switch to **Wireframe** mode by hitting the Z key, then click on **Non Manifold Edge** in the error report. This will select and highlight the edge(s) in question. As you can see in figuer 5-11, the source of our problems is the original line we drew along the z axis. This now finds itself inside a solid body, i.e. the chimney. You can't have an edge inside a solid, so simply press Del and delete the offending edge(s). We now have a clean, watertight chimney. The remaining message, about overhanging faces, is just a warning that some of our faces may need propping up during the printing process. Don't worry about this – the slicing program will take care of it.

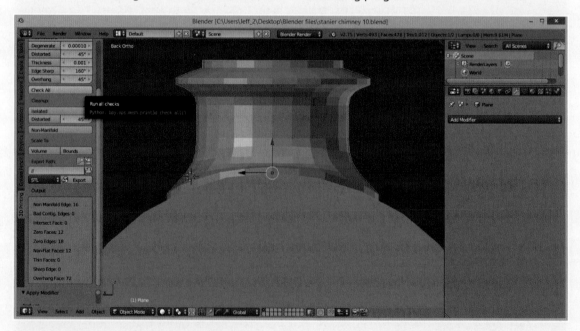

Figure 5-10 Manifold errors

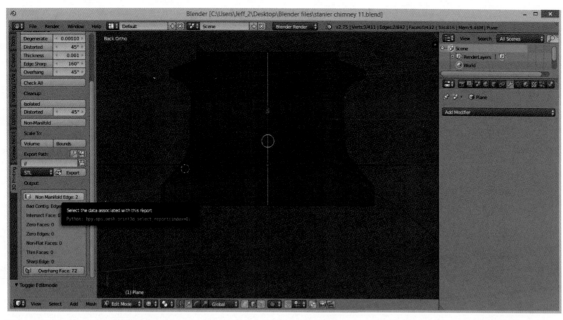

Figure 5-11 Non-manifold edge

We now want to get rid of the parts of the chimney that lie 'inside' the smokebox, and to do this we use another modifier. Go into Object mode and select the chimney with the right mouse button, then click **Add Modifier** again (figure 5-12). This time select the **Boolean** modifier; this carries out one of three operations: **Union**, which combines two objects into one; **Intersection**, which selects only those parts that lie within both objects; and

Difference, which selects the parts that lie within one object but not the other. This latter is the one we want, so click **Difference**, then click **Object** and select the cylinder representing the smokebox. Finally click **Apply**. Not much is immediately visible, but if we now select the smokebox cylinder (*right* mouse button, remember!) and delete it, we see that the base of the chimney that lay inside the smokebox has gone (figure 5-13).

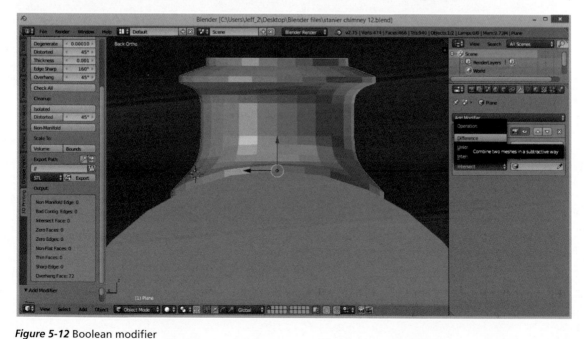

Figure 5-12 Boolean modifier

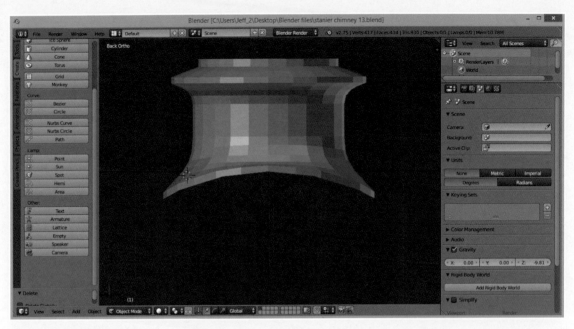

Figure 5-13 Surplus chimney base removed

The final job is to add the most important part of any chimney, which is the hole through its middle! To do this, we add another cylinder, this time at location 0,0,0 and with dimensions as shown in figure 5-14.

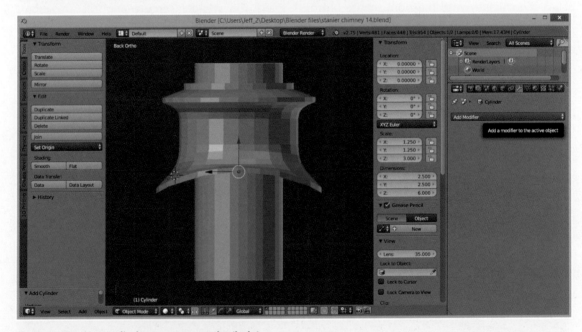

Figure 5-14 Using a cylinder to represent the 'hole'

Select the chimney, add another Boolean modifier, click **Difference** for the operation and Cylinder for the object, then **Apply**. Finally, delete the cylinder used to make the hole – the result is as shown. If you want a smoother finish than this, simply use more steps in the initial rotation (Figure 5-5) and use cylinders with a greater number of faces for the smokebox and the 'hole'.

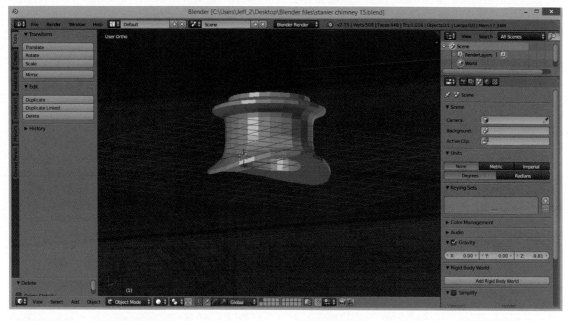

Figure 5-15 The finished chimney

Exhaust steam pipe

For our next example we will construct the exhaust steam pipe that appears on GWR 'King' and 'Castle' class locomotives. This presents some interesting geometry. Because the outside cylinders of these classes were set well back from the smokebox, the exhaust pipe had to come up through the running plate, then some distance forward before turning through a right-angle to enter the smokebox. This gave rise to a very distinctive feature, in contrast to most other steam locomotives, where the exhaust pipe simply came out of the cylinder and went in a straight line into the smokebox. Once again, we turn to F. J. Roche's book for a drawing (Figure 5.16).

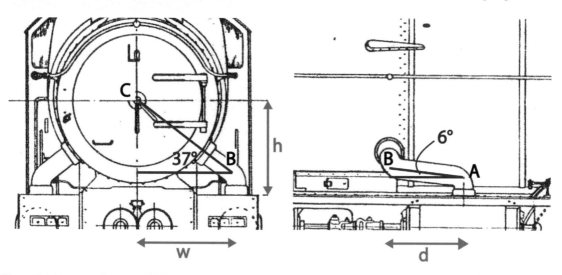

Figure 5-16 Steam exhaust pipe geometry.
From *Historic Locomotive Drawings in 4mm Scale by F. J. Roche*
(Ian Allan, 1976), reproduced with permission

5

As can be seen, the pipe comes up through the running plate, turns through (nearly) a right-angle, then runs forwards at a slight upwards angle before turning through another right-angle to enter the smokebox. In Figure 5-16 we have highlighted in red the two critical angles, namely the rise of the forwards-running part of the pipe and the angle at which it enters the smokebox. Both are measured from the horizontal. In addition, highlighted in blue are three key measurements. First, the horizontal distance d measured in the forwards direction, from the point at which the centre-line of the pipe emerges from the cylinder to the point at which it enters the smokebox. Second, the horizontal displacement w of the point at which the pipe emerges from the cylinder from the centre-line of the smokebox. Finally, the height h of the centre-line of the smokebox above the running plate.

From Roche's drawing, we find that the two critical angles are approximately 6° and 37°, and the key measurements are d = 32 inches, w = 42.5 inches and h = 41.7 inches. The pipe diameter is approximately 8 inches and the radius (to the centre-line) of the bends is 5 inches. Of course, these measurements are subject to a considerable margin of error. If you wanted a really accurate model, you should measure the prototype rather than a 4mm scale drawing. However, what we are interested in here is the method of creating the 3D

drawing rather than the actual measurements. Three key points are shown in Figure 5-16. These are 'A', the intersection of the projected centre-line of the pipe coming vertically up through the running plate with the centre-line of the forwards-sloping section; 'B', the intersection of the centre-line of the forwards-sloping section of the pipe with the centre-line of the section that enters the smokebox; and 'C' the intersection of the latter with the centre-line of the smokebox.

By simple geometry, we can use the tangents of 6° and 37° to find that point B is 32 times tan(6) = 3.4 inches higher than point A. Likewise, point C is 42.5 times tan(37) = 32 inches higher than point B, and therefore 35.4 inches higher than point A. Since point C is 41.7 inches above the running plate, point A must be at a height of 6.3 inches. This gives us all the measurements we need to locate points A, B and C in three-dimensional space. We shall create the model in *Blender* and, to make the arithmetic easy, we shall adopt a scale where one *Blender* unit equals 10 inches.

Start up *Blender* and set the view to front ortho. We are going to start with the bend at point B. Click **Add > Mesh > Circle** and, in the **Properties** window on the left, change Radius to 0.4, Fill Type to Ngon, set the X location to -0.5, and the x rotation to 90. Zoom in with the mouse wheel and you should have something like figure 5.17

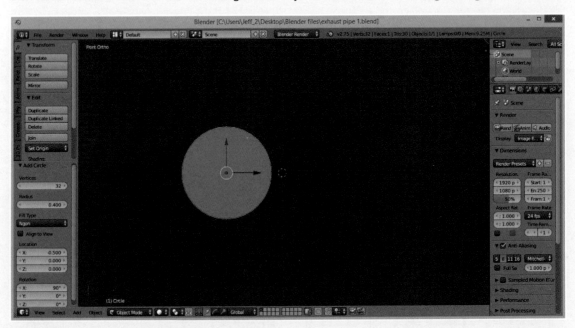

Figure 5-17 The starting circle

Now, with the new circle selected go into **Edit** mode. Change the view to top – our circle is now seen edge-on as a line. On the **Toolshelf** on the left, under the **Tools** tab find **Mesh Tools** and click **Spin**. The circle will immediately generate a pipe bend by extrusion around the origin. However, this is not the bend we want – *Blender* does a default spin of 90°, but we want a spin of -86.4°, so type this into the **Angle** box (figure 5-18). You might ask why -86.4°? When looked at from the top, the pipe before the bend runs forwards along the footplate, and after the bend it runs at right angles to join the smokebox, so 90° would seem to be the obvious angle to bend. However -86.4° is the angle that, when we rotate the pipe bend so that it points downward by 6° in one direction and upwards by 37° in the other, will ensure that the pipe enters the smokebox at right-angles. How do we know this? Well, the maths is not trivial, so it has been relegated to an appendix so as not to disturb our flow just now – those interested can read Appendix 2.

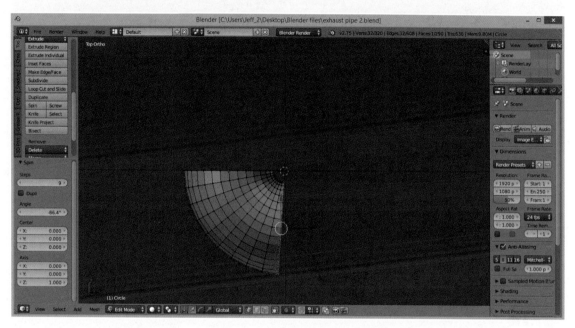

Figure 5-18 Spinning the pipe bend

It will greatly simplify matters to have the pipe run along the y axis, so we need to move point B, the intersection of the projected centre-lines of the two sections of straight pipe to the origin. At present, the origin is at the centre of curvature of our pipe bend, as in Figure 5-18. With a little simple geometry, we can place the origin at point B by moving everything 5 inches along the x axis and 4.7 inches along the y axis (figure 5-19). Note that 43.2° is half of the angle of the bend, and that the tangent of an angle is opposite over adjacent.

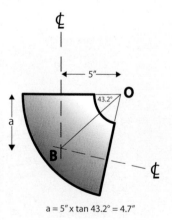

$$a = 5'' \times \tan 43.2° = 4.7''$$

Figure 5-19 Moving the origin to point B

5

To accomplish this, go back into **Object** mode and, with the pipe bend selected, click **Translate** on the **Toolshelf** on the left. Instead of trying to move the object with the mouse, type in 0.5 for the change in x, then press the Tab key. Type 0.47 for the change in y, press Tab again, then type 0 and press **Enter**. You can see these numbers on the bottom left of figure 5-20.

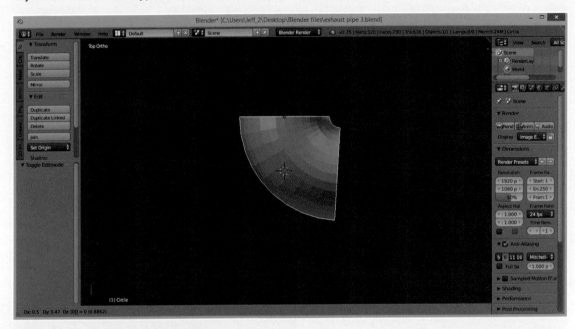

Figure 5-20 The pipe bend repositioned

For the following extrusion operations, it will be useful to see the faces of the pipe bend that we are going to extrude, so press the middle mouse button (or wheel) and move the mouse around till you get something like figure 5-21.

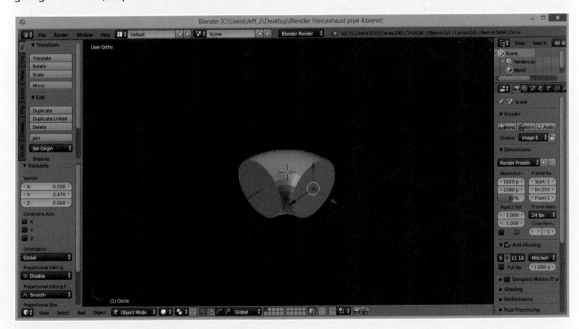

Figure 5-21 3D view of the bend

Now go back into **Edit** mode, press A to deselect whatever happens to be selected, and go into **Face Select** mode. At the bottom of the screen (figure 5-22)you will see three little cube icons. One of these has a vertex highlighted, another an edge, and the third a face. Click the **Face Select** cube, and you will see all the faces of our pipe bend displayed individually as in figure 5-22.

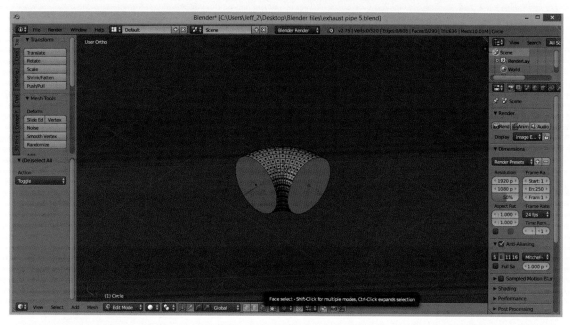

Figure 5-22 Face Select mode

With the right mouse button, click the right face of the pipe bend. Press E, for extrude, and notice that by moving the mouse you can extrude the selected faces in and out to create the straight section of pipe. However, rather than rely on the mouse, we shall type in the length we want to extrude. From the Roche drawing we measure the 'straight' length of pipe as 22 inches, so type in 2.2, as in Figure 5-23 (bottom left of screen). Now repeat the exercise for the other face of the bend, as in Figure 5-24. This time, the length of the extrusion is not critical, since we shall eventually trim it to fit the smokebox. For the time being, make it the same length as before (2.2 *Blender* units).

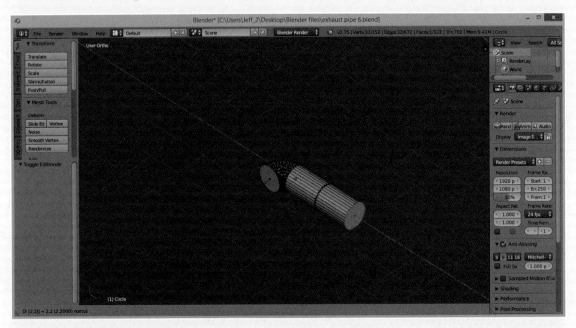

Figure 5-23 Extruding the first face

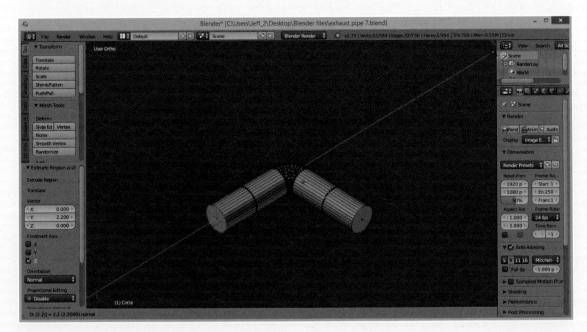

Figure 5-24 Extruding the other face

We now need to make two rotations such that one section of pipe points upwards at 37° and the other points downwards by 6°. You might think that it would be as easy as making a rotation around the y axis of 37° followed by one around the x axis of 6°. However, the latter rotation would actually increase the 37° very slightly. The effect is very slight in this case, but if you want your pipe to be spot-on, the first rotation should be one of 36.85°. If you're interested in the geometry of this, see *Appendix 3: Rotation around axes*. Switch to **Object** mode and change the view to front. With the pipe selected, click **Rotate**, type in -36.85 and press **Enter** (figure 5-25).

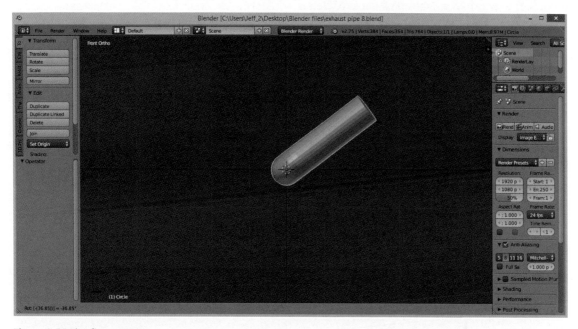

Figure 5-25 The first rotation

Before we make the second rotation, it will be convenient to make the second pipe bend. Change the view to back, change to **Edit** mode, press A if anything is selected already, then in **Face Select** mode select the end-on face of the pipe (figure 5-26).

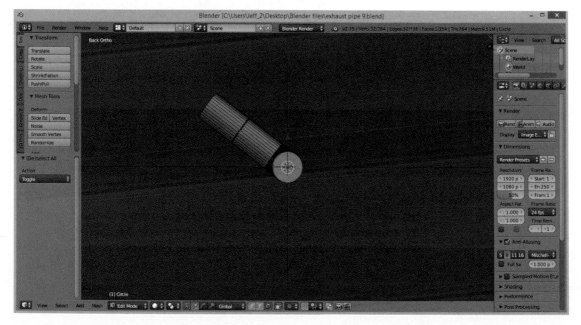

Figure 5-26 Select face

Click **Spin** on the **Toolshelf**. Do not worry if weird things happen – *Blender* makes some 'default' assumptions about what you want to do, and they aren't always right! Type in the correct values on the left, press **Enter** and things should come right. Set the angle of spin to -84° and the spin centre to x = 0, y = 2.67 and z = -0.5. We get these numbers as follows: the length of straight pipe we extruded is 22 inches, plus the distance 'a' from Figure 5-19, which was 4.7 inches, so that the face is 26.7 inches from the origin, = 2.67 Blender units. The radius of curvature we want is 5 inches, so the centre of spin is 0.5 units below the origin. After the spin is completed, your pipe should look like figure 5-27 when viewed from the left.

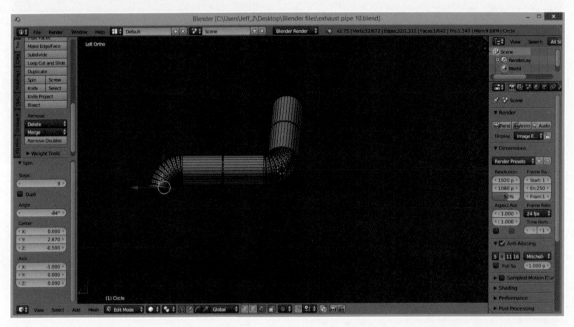

Figure 5-27 Spin the face to get the second bend

We are now ready to make the second rotation. Switch to **Object** mode, click **Rotate** on the **Toolshelf**, and type -6, then **Enter**. The result should be as shown in figure 5-28. Notice how the rotation has made the 'smokebox' part of the pipe point upwards as required.

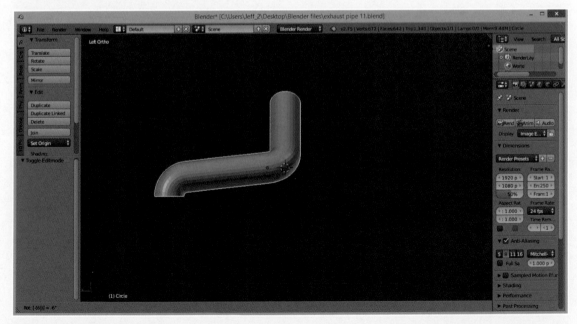

Figure 5-28 The second rotation

We now extrude the downwards-facing face of our pipe to meet the running plate. Recall that point A is 6.3 inches above the running plate. We employ similar geometry to that illustrated in Figure 5-19 to work out that the face is 5 x tan(42) = 4.5 inches lower, so we need to extrude it 1.8 inches to meet the running plate. Switch to a 3D view by pressing the centre mouse button/wheel. Go into **Edit** mode and, with the face selected, press E. Type 0.18 as the length of the extrusion and press **Enter**. The result should be as shown in figure 5-29.

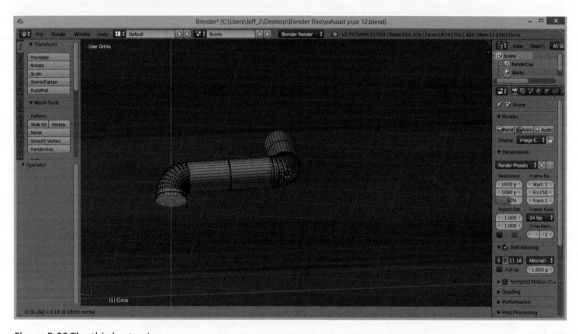

Figure 5-29 The third extrusion

We will now make the flanges at the pipe ends. Switch the view to left and enter **Object** mode. Click **Add > Mesh > Cylinder** and set the radius to 0.45 and the position on the z axis to -0.97 to ensure that it is exactly on the running plate. Click on the **Modifiers** button in the **Properties** window (the little spanner) and select the **Bevel modifier** (Figure 5-30) and apply it to our cylinder, which will round off the sharp edges. Set Segments to 3, Limit Method to Angle and click **Apply** (Figure 5-31)

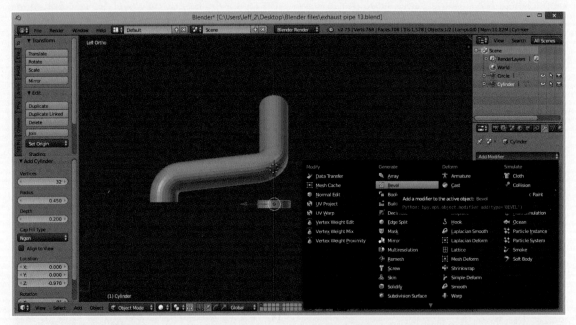

Figure 5-30 The first flange

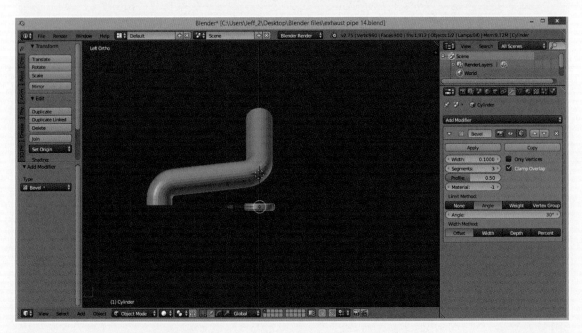

Figure 5-31 Applying the Bevel modifier

Next, move the flange in the y direction so that it is concentric with the bottom of the pipe. You can best do this by clicking **Translate**, then enter 0 for Dx, press **Tab** and enter 3.11 (a figure found by trial and error!) for Dy. You may have to tinker with this (figure 5-32).

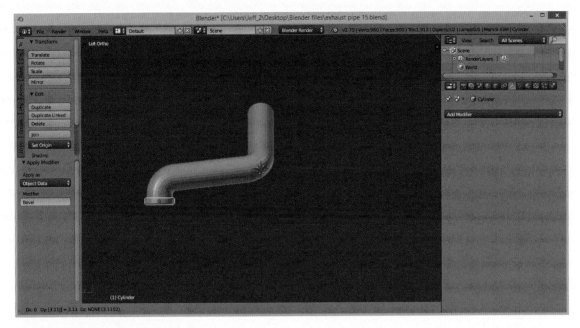

Figure 5-32 Move into position

Next we need to apply another modifier, this time a Boolean one. Right click on the pipe to select it, click **Add Modifier > Boolean**, for **Operation** select **Union**, and for **Object** select Cylinder (this is the bevelled cylinder we have just moved into position).

Click **Apply** and our pipe has been modified by adding the cylinder to form a single entity. The original cylinder is still there, but has now been duplicated as part of the pipe, so right click it and press **Delete**.

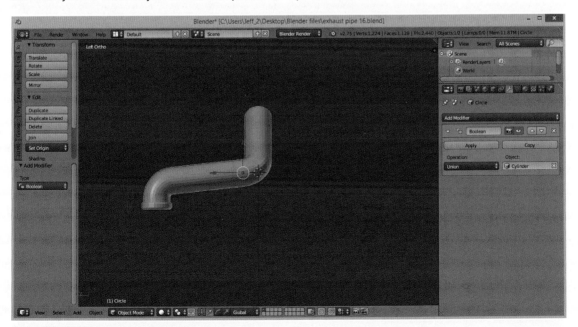

Figure 5-33 Union of the two objects

We now need to apply another Boolean modifier. You may have noticed that when we applied the Bevel modifier to our cylinder it bevelled not just the upper edge but the lower one as well. However, we want a nice flat base, so we need to slice off the lower part of the cylinder. To do this we create a cube (**Add > Mesh > Cube**) and Translate its centre from the origin to 0, 3, -1.97 (figure 5-34).

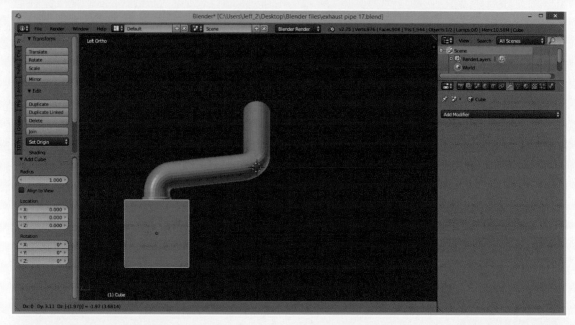

Figure 5-34 Positioning the cube

Select the pipe and click **Add Modifier > Boolean**. This time, for the **Operation** select **Difference**, and for the **Object** select Cube. Press **Apply** and nothing visible happens. However, concealed from view inside the cube *Blender* has deleted the parts that were common to both the cube and the pipe, as you will see when you delete the cube (figure 5.35).

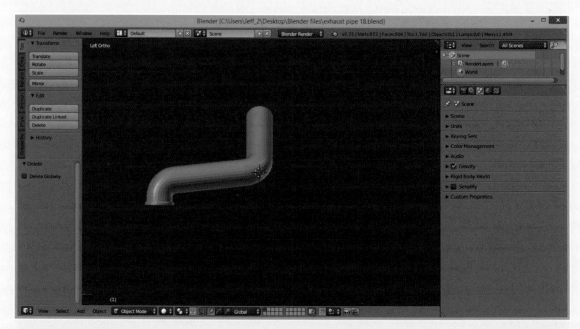

Figure 5-35 The flange trimmed square

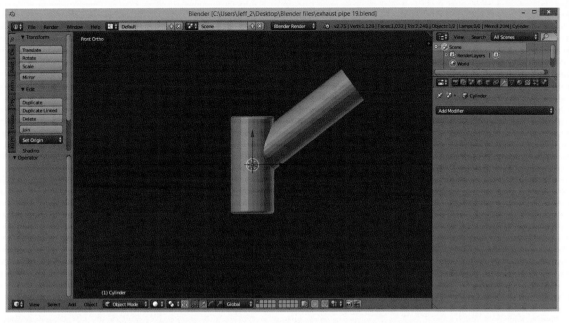

Figure 5-36 The second flange cylinder

We will now form the flange at the smokebox end of the exhaust pipe. Roche's drawing seems to show this as similar to the one we've just made. However, a well-known Maurice Earley photograph of No 6028 *King Henry II* taken in 1935 seems to show it as considerably longer. Again, we are concerned here with the principles of how to do things, not with numerical accuracy, so we will make a flange that looks roughly like the one in Earley's photograph. We switch the view to front and click **Add > Mesh > Cylinder** and set its radius to 0.45 and fill type Ngon. With the cylinder selected, click the **Modifiers** button (the little

spanner) and add another **Bevel** modifier, again setting segments to 3 and the limit method to angle, then click **Apply** (figure 5-36).

Don't worry about the fact that the cylinder appears to occupy the same space as our exhaust pipe – the two are still completely separate. Rotate the cylinder by 53° to make it parallel with the 'smokebox' section of the exhaust: click **Rotate**, type 53 and **Enter**. Then right click the cylinder and drag it, manoeuvring the mouse to get it into the position shown in figure 5-37, then left click. Zooming in will help here.

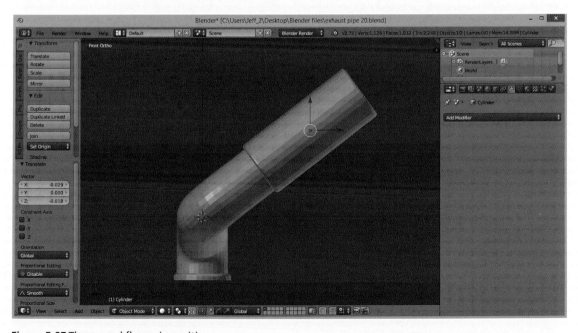

Figure 5-37 The second flange in position

Once you are happy with the position, select the main body of the exhaust pipe again, click **Add Modifier > Boolean**, and this time make the Operation **Union** and the Object Cylinder. Click **Apply**, then select the original cylinder and delete it – a copy of it will have been incorporated into the exhaust pipe.

Next, we need to trim off the surplus. This time, however, we want the resulting surface to be concave and to the same radius as the smokebox to ensure a neat fit. To achieve this, we construct a cylinder to represent the smokebox and apply a difference modifier as before. Roche's drawing shows the smokebox as 6 feet (72 inches) in

diameter, and we have already determined that its centre-line is 42.5 inches from point B (which is at the origin). Therefore we click **Add > Mesh > Cylinder** and this time, because it is a much bigger cylinder than before, we set vertices to 128, set radius to 3.6, X location to 4.25, and Z location to 3.2. Rotate 90° in X (Figure 5-38).

We now need to subtract the smokebox from the exhaust pipe, so right click the exhaust pipe and click **Add Modifier > Boolean**. This time we want to apply the **Difference** Operator, with the Object set to Cylinder. Click **Apply**, delete the 'smokebox' cylinder, and you will see that the end of our pipe is formed perfectly to fit (figure 5-39).

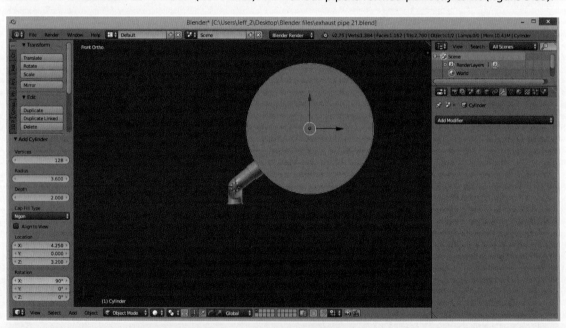

Figure 5-38 The smokebox added

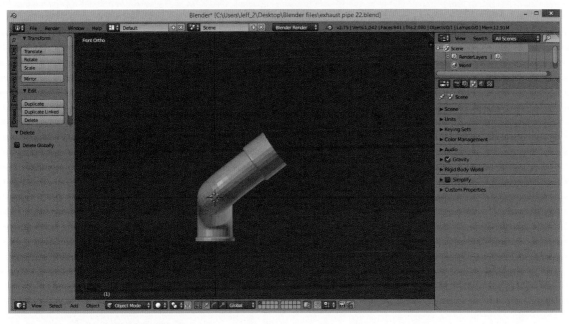

Figure 5-39 The smokebox removed

Our final task is to make a mirror-image copy of this pipe for the other side of the loco. To do this, change the view to left, right click the pipe and move it with the mouse until its base is just above the origin point (which is also where the 3D cursor should be). When it is in position, left click. To make our mirror image, we need to set an appropriate pivot point, the point about which the mirror image will be formed. At present the pivot point will be at the median point of our pipe, which is its default location, marked by the little yellow dot. To change it, click the **Pivot Point** button (showing two little circles) at the bottom of the screen and select **3D Cursor** as the pivot point. Notice that the white circle moves from the little yellow dot to the 3D cursor (figure 5-40).

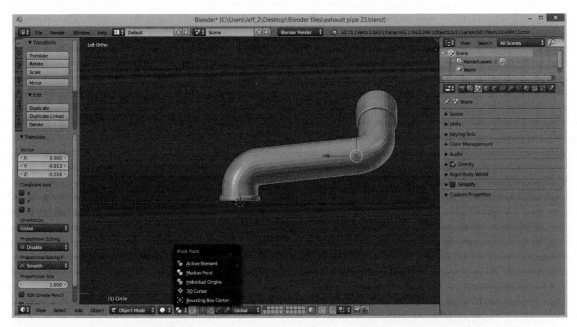

Figure 5-40 Setting the pivot point

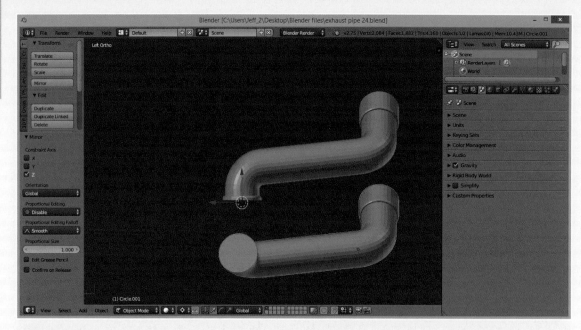

Figure 5-41 The mirror image

We now make a duplicate of the pipe. For this operation it is preferable to use the keyboard shortcut rather than clicking **Duplicate** on the Toolshelf. The reason for this is that as soon as you click **Duplicate**, the copy of the pipe will follow every movement of the mouse, even without any mouse buttons pressed. We want our copy to stay put, so press **Shift + D** then **Enter**. A duplicate pipe is now lying over our original. Click **Object > Mirror > Z Global**, then press Enter, and a mirror image is created reflected along the z axis (figure 5-41). You can see, however, that it is not what you might expect a mirror image to look like – there seem to be a couple of rotations needed. There is probably an explanation for this, but the authors don't know

what it is – it's just one of those quirks of *Blender* that you either accept or they make you cross!

If you want a more conventional orientation, select the lower pipe and change the pivot point from 3D cursor to Median Point. Then go into front view, click **Rotate** on the Toolshelf on the left and, with the mouse, turn the pipe round so that its base is at the bottom, then left click. Go into left view and again click **Rotate** and turn the pipe until the forward-rising lengths are parallel, and right click. Then go into top view and rotate until the forward lengths are one above the other. When viewed from the left, we now have Figure 5-42, which is a more conventional representation of a mirror image.

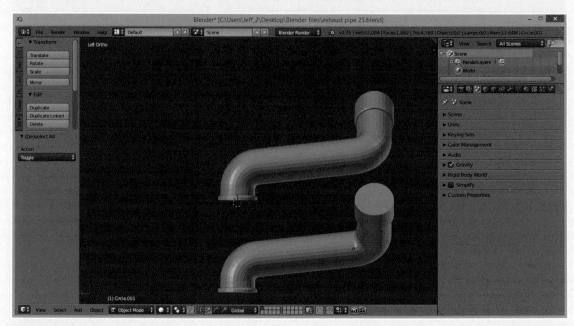

Figure 5-42 A matching pair!

Printing a fireless locomotive

Printing a complete locomotive might seem over-ambitious, and if the locomotive in question was a 'Britannia' or similar it probably would be. However, just to see if it is feasible, we decided to have a go at something a little smaller. We chose as an example a little 0-4-0F loco built by Andrew Barclay & Co. This loco was fireless: it had no firebox, no smokebox and no chimney. Instead, the loco's boiler was filled up from a stationary boiler with water and superheated steam, with which it could run for several hours at a stretch. These engines were used in places like munitions factories, where an escaping spark or glowing coal could set off a devastating explosion. So far as we are aware, no kit is available for these unusual little engines, so if you want one, you will need to print one yourself! We will print the body only; the frames, wheels, motion, etc, are probably best made in metal.

Because this is a much bigger task than our chimney and exhaust pipe examples, we will not describe every keystroke. Most of the principles have been demonstrated before, so we shall simply summarise the main steps in construction. We start with a background image, as we did in the chimney project. There are not many drawings available of these engines – that used in Figure 5-43 is derived from one in an excellent little book in the Oakwood Press 'Locomotion Papers' series (No 97 *Fireless Locomotives* by Allen Civil and Allan Baker). The drawing has been scaled so that 1 foot corresponds to one Blender unit and positioned so that the boiler centre-line lies along the y axis and its back centre-point lies at the origin. The latter does not feature on the original drawing – an assumption was made that it was the same as the front, which was copied, mirrored and pasted onto the original drawing. Set the axis from which the image is viewed as left, otherwise it will be presented when viewed from front, top, etc, and will cause confusion.

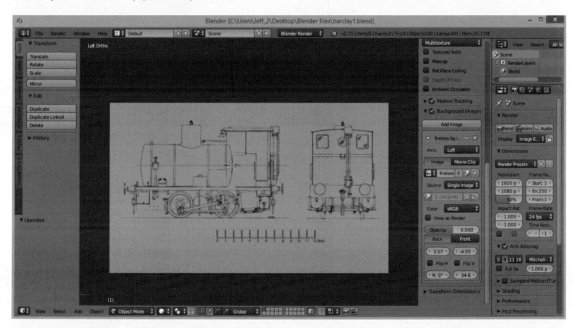

Figure 5-43 The background image of the fireless locomotive.
Figures 5-43 to 5-52 from *Fireless Locomotives* by Allen Civil and Allan Baker
(Oakwood Press, 1976), reproduced with permission

5

First, we make our boiler. As with the chimney, create a single vertex at the origin by adding a plane then merging its vertices. Extrude it around the boiler outline (Figure 5-44). To get the best accuracy, zoom right in on the vertex. You can follow it around using the mouse wheel in conjunction with Shift/Ctrl, or use Ctrl + NumPad keys. Make sure your final vertex is on the centre-line by manually setting its z coordinate to 0.

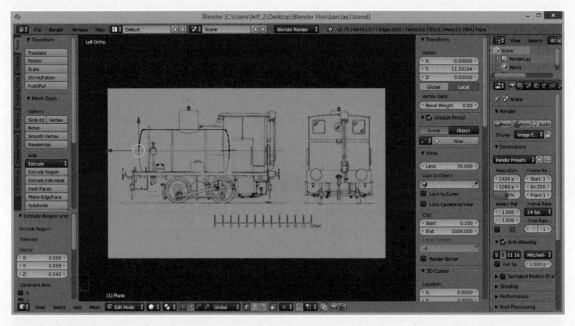

Figure 5-44 The boiler profile

Next, from front view, select all the vertices and spin 360° around the 3D cursor. Set segments to a large number – we used 64. After spinning, change the view back to left and you should have a boiler as in figure 5-45. Bring up the **3D Printing Tools** and click **Check All**. You will probably find a few manifold errors, as discussed in connection with the chimney above. Click **Mesh > Vertices > Remove Doubles**, then press **Clean Up Non-Manifold** and this should get rid of them.

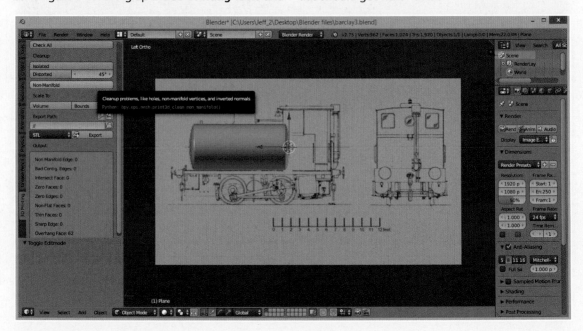

Figure 5-45 The boiler complete

Next, we make the dome in precisely the same way as we made the chimney earlier. It will help to move the boiler out of the way first, so do this with **Tools > Transform > Translate** and type in 0 **Tab** 12 **Tab** 0 **Enter**. That way, you will move the boiler exactly 12 feet left and can easily put it back in precisely the right place. Left click the top of the dome, add a plane mesh, then merge it to a single vertex. Trace the dome outline starting at the top and extruding vertically downwards, then out in the y direction (figure 5-46).

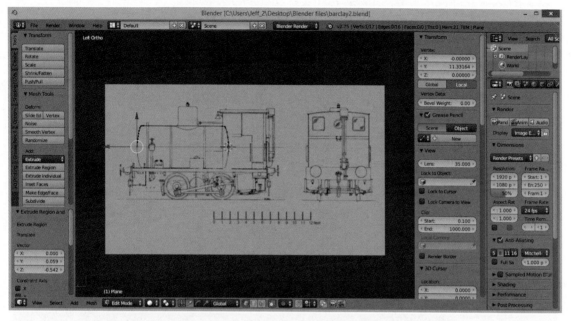

Figure 5-46 The dome outline

Then, just as we made the chimney, we spin the dome profile 90° and apply the **Mirror modifier** in the X and Y planes, but *do not* press **Apply** yet. With the left mouse button, grab and drag the vertices on the 'flare' of the dome down to meet the boiler (figure5-47). Once all the vertices are in position, click **Apply**.

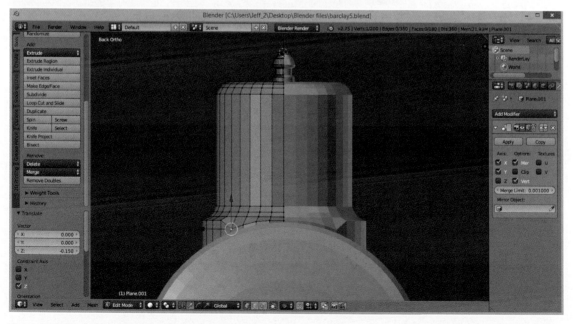

Figure 5-47 Drag the vertices to form the 'flare' of the dome

Put the boiler back in position (**Translate** 0, -12, 0) and merge it and the dome using the **Union Boolean modifier** (figure 5-48). Notice that we have renamed the dome and boiler from their previous designations of 'plane' and 'plane.001'. To do this right click their names in the **Outliner** window on the top right and select **Rename** from the pop-up menu. Remember also that we now have two domes: the original and the one merged with the boiler. You can get rid of the spare one by clicking its name in the scene list and pressing **Delete**. Alternatively, you could export it as an stl file in case you need a similar one again: **File > Export > STL**.

To make the footplate, we simply add a cube, press N to bring up the **Numerical Properties** window and adjust its size and position to match up with the drawing. Remember to right click and drag to select, then move it around with the mouse and left click when it is in position. To get its width right, rotate it 90° (**View > Top** for this) and size it using the rear view.

To make the cab front and back we form a single vertex as before, then trace around the profile, extruding the single vertex to form the edges. Then select all the vertices and click **Mesh > Faces > Fill** to fill in the gaps. Then in top view, extrude this in the x direction. We are going to attempt to print the locomotive in a single print, i.e. print the walls upright, so these need to be quite fat extrusions. You cannot 3D print the equivalent of a sheet of 20-thou nickel silver standing on edge! This will make the thickness of the cab sides well over scale, but this is one of the drawbacks of the plastic filament technology. Once again bring up the **3D Tools** and clean up non-manifold errors if any. If your extruded cab front/rear is dark in colour, this indicates that it contains some errors (figure 5-49).

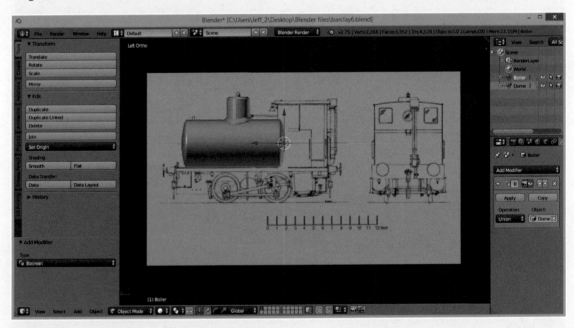

Figure 5-48 Boiler and dome merged

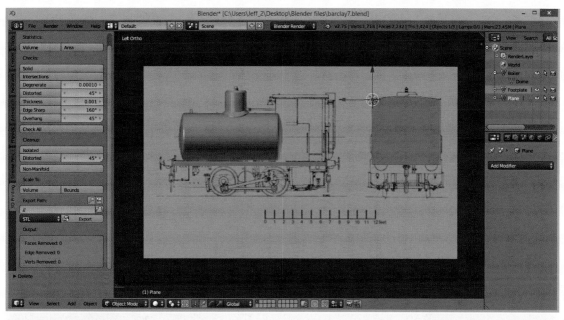

Figure 5-49 Footplate and cab front/back

To make the windows, we shall fabricate a special tool with which to punch them out. Add a cube and bring up its numerical properties (hit N). Adjust its Y and Z dimensions to match the hole we want to make, then Add **Modifier > Bevel** and **Apply** with the values shown, found by trial and error to give the best match to the window shape required, as in Figure 5-50.

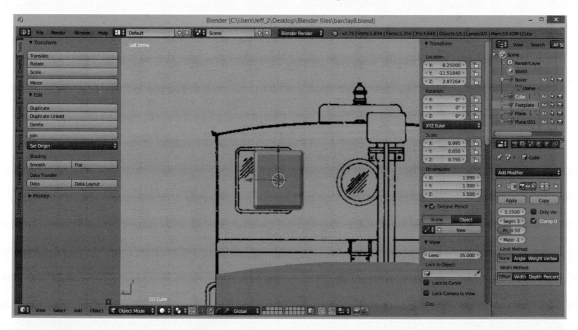

Figure 5-50 A 'hole punch' for the windows

To use the 'punch', move it into place such that it protrudes through the cab front/rear, then select the cab and apply a **Boolean Difference** modifier with the 'hole punch' as the object (figure 5-51). Before making the central window, using a suitably sized and positioned cylinder, make a copy of the cab rear and drag it out of the way to form the cab front. We have also now finished with the hole punches, so you can delete them.

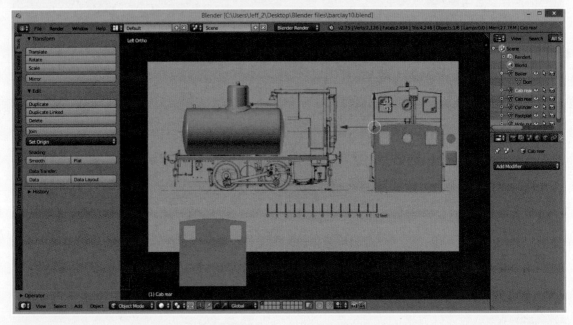

Figure 5-51 Punching windows in the cab front/rear

Make the cab sides exactly as the front/rear – hint: if you turn the left side through 180° round the z axis it becomes a right side) – as well as the cab floor and the boiler saddle. The drawing gives no indication of what the latter looks like, so we have just stuck a cube underneath the boiler and adjusted its dimensions to suit. The exhaust pipe that comes up the back of the cab is made in the usual way by spinning then extruding a circle, as we saw earlier. Figure 5-52 shows the main components.

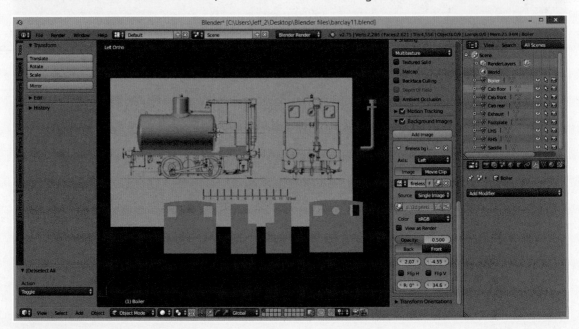

Figure 5-52 The main cab components

The buffer beams and cab roof we decided to print separately, as this would eliminate the need for a lot of supporting material. The next job was to assemble the main parts of the locomotive. It turned out that this was a big mistake, as will become clear shortly. However, we will include a description of the assembly process for completeness. You will find that this requires frequent switching of views and panning around with the middle mouse button depressed to get 3D views. Once you have a component in place, use the **Boolean Union** modifier to weld it to the boiler/dome assembly. Obviously you start with the saddle, then the footplate, cab floor and so on. You might find that the background image gets in the way a bit, so restrict this to a view you don't often use, such as 'bottom' (hit N, then scroll down to **Background Image** and set **Axis** to **Bottom**). Remember when making your unions that you will retain an 'un-unioned' copy of the union object, which you need to delete. You should end up with something resembling figure 5-53.

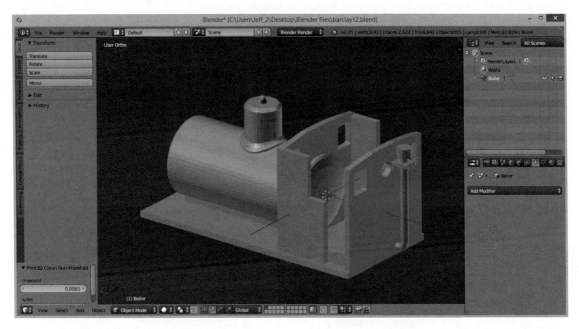

Figure 5-53 The main components assembled

Having reached this point, we had a go at printing the locomotive in 4mm scale. The result, as can be seen in figure 5-54, was pretty disappointing. Printing the cab sides, front and rear in situ was particularly unsuccessful – the successive layers were not precisely aligned and this gave rise to the fairly messy edges to these components. A great deal of tidying up with a file would be required to get the model anywhere near acceptable quality.

A far better plan would have been to print the parts as shown in Figure 5-52, i.e. as separate entities, rather than trying to print them joined together as in Figure 5-53. However, at around this time the project for which a fireless locomotive might have been appropriate was shelved, so the loco was abandoned!

Figure 5-54 The fireless loco printed

Printing a 'C14'

We have shown how to create some of the more complex parts of a locomotive and how we can sketch out the main parts of a body shell in 3D CAD. If we had the perfect 3D printer we need only waft our CAD model at it and the job would be done but, as Figure 5-54 demonstrates, we don't, and neither will you. Instead, we will create a model in separate sections that can then be assembled with superglue.

For this, we will take a look at an LSWR 'C14' loco model created in *DesignSpark Mechanical*. It's not the most accurate of models, but then it is intended to show building techniques rather than the ultimate in finescale modelling. Figure 5-55 shows our 'C14' CAD model in all its glory. Some might think it looks a bit like the old Triang 'Polly'!

There aren't many details in the model – no pipework, handrails, boiler bands, etc. This is deliberate as this model has been designed to be printed at 4mm/1ft scale, and these smaller items will be added using conventional modelling techniques. The underframe and wheels are simple outline placeholders to allow us to judge the proportions and placement of other parts. Where parts such as the tanks, cabsides and toolboxes are mirrored from one side to the other, we have only modelled one.

The key thing is that in order to get a good printed result there is no way we can print the whole thing in one go. As we saw in the previous example, we have to consider carefully the alignment of parts when we print to avoid printing aberrations such as graining and in order to get the required strength.

Although we need to break up the model to print it, having the whole thing together has several benefits. First it's a lot simpler to draw the whole model as one item and compare it to our drawings, etc. In addition it allows us to see how all the pieces fit together. In the case of this little loco it also allowed us to hollow out parts of the model easily to accommodate a motor. Breaking the model up into components can be easily done using the Boolean operators to cut one part from another and to combine bits together.

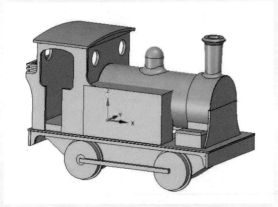

Figure 5-55 The complete 'C14'

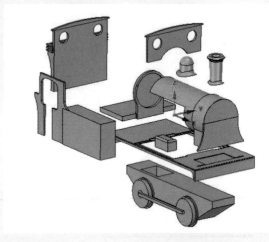

Figure 5-56 The exploded CAD model

Figure 5-56 shows an exploded view of the model showing the components we will print. Disregarding the dummy underframe and wheels, there are nine separate entities to print. Each is saved as a separate stl file, which can then be brought back into our chosen slicing program, *slic3r*, and aligned appropriately. Figure 5-57 shows the parts arranged in *slic3r*, and Figure 5-58 shows the same parts on the printer build bed (note the failure to print part of the boiler!). In these views it can be seen that we have oriented the larger flat areas – the cab side together with the tank sides and the footplate – so that the most visible areas are face down to the build table, which gives us the best chance of a smooth finish.

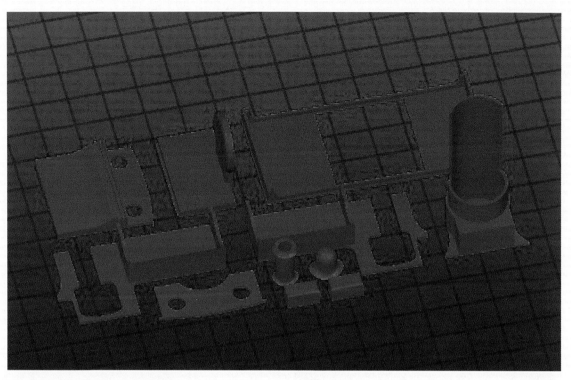

Figure 5-57 The 'C14' parts in *Slic3r*

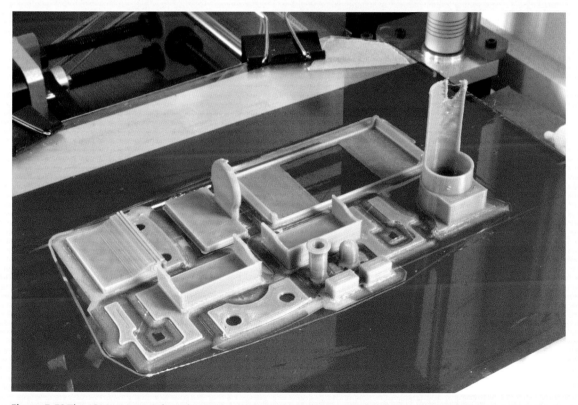

Figure 5-58 The 'C14' parts on the printer

The boiler presents a particular challenge as it has been hollowed out. If it were solid we could simply print it with one end on the build table, but as it is hollow we will need a lot of support structures if we print it in this way. An earlier attempt at doing so failed miserably, not because it didn't print cleanly but because it was well nigh impossible to remove all the support material without damaging the part. A dual extruder printer and water-soluble support material would work well for this. Figure 5-59 is the boiler printed with the support material.

Figure 5-59 The boiler buried in support material

To get round this problem the boiler was split into two parts: the majority of the barrel and the smokebox, which was printed in the same orientation as before, and the backhead joined with the cab floor. This allowed the parts to be printed with no support material at all, as seen in Figure 5-60.

Figure 5-60 The boiler split in two

Another part that was troublesome to print successfully was the curved cab roof. If we had printed it in its natural orientation we would have had the curved roof surface uppermost, which would have resulted in a markedly ridged surface that would need considerable work with files and filler. In addition we would need to have a fair amount of support material. The best solution we could come up with was to print the roof with the front edge downwards. Printing thin objects vertically is often not the most reliable method, so this is a real compromise. To help with stability the underside of the centre section of the roof was thickened so that only a small amount of support

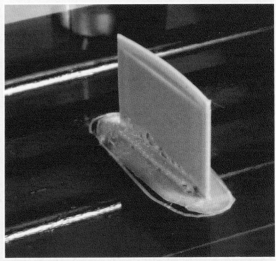

Figure 5-61 The printed loco cab roof

material was required along the edge in contact with the print bed. Figure 5-61 shows the result. It would probably have been a better plan to use a simple rectangle of plastic card!

By splitting the loco into these components and orienting them carefully, we are able to print a set of parts that can be assembled into a reasonable model without the need for too much surface preparation. We still needed to use fine files and emery paper to improve some of the surfaces, but nothing drastic was required.

Having had reasonable success with building the loco body, we went on to see if we could build a basic chassis for the loco. The approach taken was to build a solid chassis block with openings for the axle bearings, motor and gearbox. To facilitate assembly and the inevitable need to strip down the model at some point, the chassis block was split in two with a keeper plate that kept the motor and axles aligned.

Figure 5-62 shows the components in the CAD program. The upper orange part is the keeper plate, which locks the axles and motor in place. The driven axle has brass bearings as part of the gearbox, while the unpowered axle is carried in a brass tube that bears on the chamfered block on the rear of the keeper plate. This provides a three-point suspension system that allows the wheels of the unpowered axle to rise and fall around 0.5mm as a form of crude compensation. These components were printed at a 100-micron resolution upside down, with the upper faces on the build plate. Figure 5-63 shows the components on the printer.

Figure 5-62 Chassis components in the CAD program

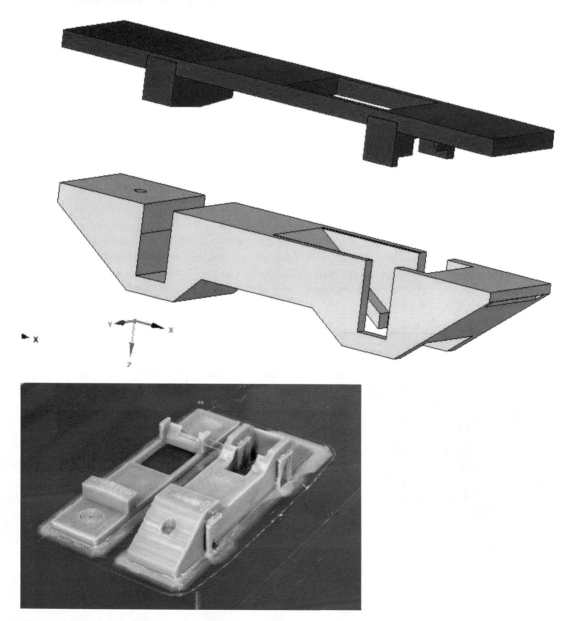

Figure 5-63 The printed chassis components

As can be seen, the chassis block parts have been printed with a hole running vertically at the unpowered end. This is to accommodate a bolt to secure the chassis parts to the body, and a nut has been melted into the cab floor to keep it captive. Figure 5-64 shows the cleaned and prepared chassis parts together with the hardware for the running gear.

Figure 5-64 The chassis parts ready for assembly

With the body and chassis parts assembled, the basis for the 'C14' loco model is shown in figure 5-65, warts and all. Extra parts such as cylinders, coupling rods and valve gear still need to be built and much of this will have to be created using old-fashioned modelling skills. Some of the joints need attention with some filler and a file.

Building this loco was not a 5-minute exercise and many of the parts had to be redrawn and/or reprinted several times in order to find the best way of tackling the problems. Don't expect to get it all perfect at the first attempt. As they say, it's not the parts you use for the model that take the time, it's the ones you throw away! See figure 5-66

Figure 5-65 The partially complete locomotive

Figure 5-66 Plastic mayhem!

Although printing loco parts in this scale with a low-end printer is getting near the limits of the technology, it is possible to get some reasonable results. Figure 5-67 shows the loco body shell after a spray coat of primer and after some filling and filing. A rudimentary shallow-cone smokebox door has been printed and fitted, together with some printed water tank fillers. The handrails, safety valves, whistle, lamp irons. etc, have been fabricated using wire and tube. After some paint, glazing and transfers we end up with a pretty much complete loco body as shown in Figure 5-68.

Figure 5-67 The loco ready for painting

Figure 5-68 The completed loco bodywork

6

3D printing technologies

In this chapter we will review some of the technologies available to translate our 3D design into a physical model. Until recently the very idea of a 3D printer, a machine that could construct physical objects from nothing more than a sequence of computer instructions and raw materials, was, to most people, something straight out of science fiction. In fact, 3D printing has been around since the 1980s, though until very recently the machinery required has been large and hugely expensive, putting it out of the reach of all but a few large corporations.

In 2005 the *RepRap* project was started at Bath University with the somewhat grand, and to some unbelievable, aim of building a machine that could replicate itself. The name of the project is an acronym for 'Replicating Rapid Prototyper'. Version 1.0 of the machine, which was named 'Darwin', is illustrated in Figure 6.1.

It is not possible yet to replicate a complete machine, but the plastic bits of a RepRap machine can be built using a RepRap machine! This proved a very useful feature when, as happened to one of

the authors, he managed to break one of the parts of the printer kit while assembling it! The *RepRap* project and other commercial projects have dramatically brought down the price of 3D printing technology to the point where it is now accessible to ordinary people, not just large corporations.

The world of 3D printing is one of rapid progress, so any book on the subject is almost certain to be out of date by the time the ink dries. So here we are going to cover the principles behind the technologies and introduce some of the options for modellers hoping to use them for creating stuff at home. The techniques used in the preparation of 3D CAD models are applicable whatever physical printing device and process is used. Hopefully we will be relevant for some time to come!

Currently there are three main groups of technologies used for 3D printing. Let's start at the bottom end of the market and look at the sort of printers that railway modellers are most likely to be able to afford and use, at least initially.

Fused Filament Fabrication (FFF)

This is also known as Fused Deposition Modelling (FDM), but since that name has been trademarked by a commercial company, FFF is the preferred generic term. These are two rather grand names for the simplest of the 3D printer technologies, and the one used in the *RepRap* project. Basically the idea is to extrude some form of plastic, commonly PLA (PolyLactic Acid) or ABS (Acrylonitrile Butadiene Styrene), at a highish temperature, around 200°C, to form very thin filaments. These filaments are laid out next to each other and, as the plastic is molten, they fuse together to form layers. Multiple layers are laid on top of each other, being fused together to form a 3D object. Typically each layer of plastic is around 0.2mm or less thick, so there are a lot of layers in the average model. Figure 6-2 shows the general idea.

The printer takes as input a 'slice' file or set of instructions that tells it how to lay down each layer of plastic, giving specific instructions as to how to move the extruder head in the x and y directions and how much plastic to extrude. Between each layer the extruder head is moved up, or the build table is moved down, by small amount. The input file is generated by a piece of software that takes as input the 3D CAD file, usually as an stl file, and knowledge of the target 3D printer. As with many things in the 3D printing world, there are a number

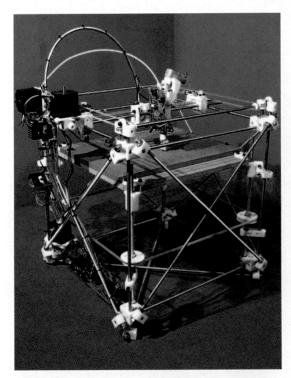

ABOVE *Figure 6-1* 'Darwin', the first RepRap printer.
From Wikimedia Commons under a GNU Free Documentation Licence confirmed by Professor Adrian Bowyer, founder of the RepRap project

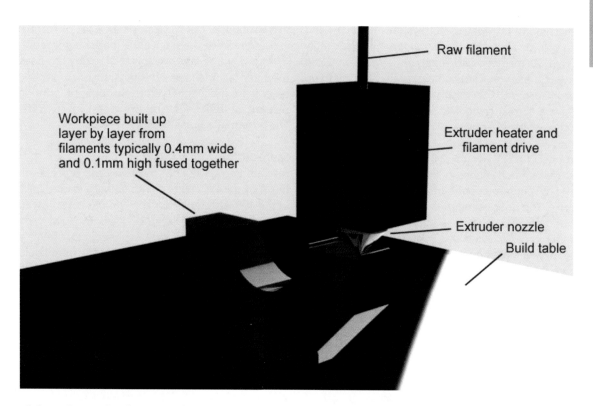

Raw filament

Workpiece built up
layer by layer from
filaments typically 0.4mm wide
and 0.1mm high fused together

Extruder heater and
filament drive

Extruder nozzle

Build table

of free pieces of software such as *slic3r* and *cura* that do this job without too much hassle. *Slic3r* was reviewed in Chapter 2

In Figure 6-3 we see a typical *RepRap* FFF printer set up and ready to go. This is a design known as a Prusa i3 after its creator, Josef Prusa, and it is the third iteration (i3) of the design. Being a RepRap design, all the yellow plastic parts were of course printed on a 3D printer. The solitary white piece on the left shows where the author had to print a replacement for one that got broken during assembly! This particular printer was purchased as a kit of parts from a single supplier and took around 8 hours to assemble and get working. It does rather have the look of an enthusiast's toy rather than a ready-to-go product, but don't be fooled, it can do clever stuff.

You can clearly see a spool of white PLA plastic filament, the raw material from which things are built, running down to the extruder assembly. The object being built is printed onto the glass plate at the bottom of the machine. This plate is able to move backwards and forwards and provides movement in the y axis. The extruder assembly itself is able to move left and right on the polished steel rods from which it is suspended, providing movement in the x axis. The whole of the extruder assembly and the x axis movement mechanism can be moved up and down providing movement in the z axis.

The printer has a small LCD display panel and a couple of control buttons mounted at the top of the

ABOVE *Figure 6-2* Fused Filament Fabrication.

BELOW *Figure 6-3* The Prusa i3 RepRap printer.

machine to provide access to various functions and to provide status feedback. Hidden in the assembly is an SD memory card reader into which you can insert a memory card containing the slice files you wish to print. This means that you don't need to have a computer hooked up to the printer all the time, which is just as well, because large complex models can take several hours to print! You can connect to a PC using a USB cable and print directly, or make modifications, or install software updates.

The biggest benefit of this technology is the price. The printers themselves can be had for a few hundred pounds and raw materials are widely and fairly cheaply available. Printers can be bought ready assembled from a number of companies, you can assemble one yourself from a kit, or you can buy all the bits separately and really drive down the price. There is also a huge community of enthusiasts who share their knowledge and designs, together with a range of suppliers of bits and pieces to allow you to repair and/or upgrade your printer.

The downsides are the limitations in the layer resolution that can be achieved and the length of time the printers take to do the job. For models in small scales the time factor is less of an issue, but potentially rough surfaces can be a problem; we'll discuss what you can do to limit this later on. Another issue is that of supporting structures. The technology relies on one filament sticking to its neighbour; however, if your model requires something akin to a bridge between two pillars, the first filament between the two has nothing to stick to and will sag. Programs like *slic3r* can put in

extra supports, but this can mean a lot of manual work to remove them once the model is printed.

As a point of interest, this technology has been used for all manner of things such as printing objects in chocolate (yum!) through to printing sections of buildings (full-size ones) in concrete. The potential is huge, literally.

Stereolithography (SLA)

Next up in the range of machines and processes in terms of price is where things actually started back in the 1980s, stereolithography. In this case, instead of extruding plastic layer by layer to build up a shape, ultraviolet light is used to fuse a photopolymer, a material that changes from liquid to solid when exposed to particular frequencies of light. Again the technique of slicing the 3D CAD model up into layers is used, but this time each layer is solidified by exposing it to UV light from a laser or projector, thus removing the need for physical movement in the x and y axes. Often the liquid photopolymer resin is exposed through the bottom of an optically clear vat and the model lifted layer by layer out of the vat. Other variations have the top layer of the photopolymer exposed and the model dropping down after each layer. Once completed the model is often given a final cleaning, then hardened under UV light – see Figure 6-4.

The main advantage of this process is an increase in resolution, i.e. a reduction in the thickness of each layer and thus the ability to print much finer detail but with increased build speed. The fact that

BELOW *Figure 6-4* Stereolithography.

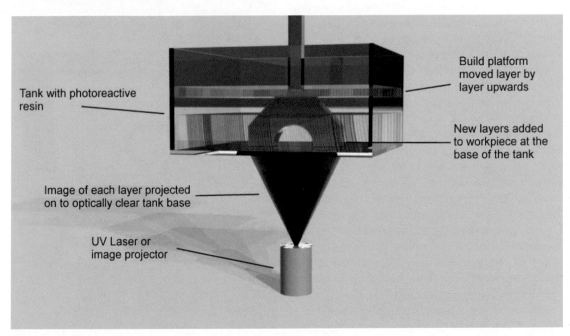

Tank with photoreactive resin

Build platform moved layer by layer upwards

New layers added to workpiece at the base of the tank

Image of each layer projected on to optically clear tank base

UV Laser or image projector

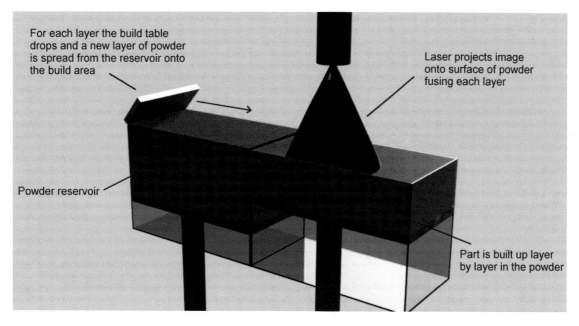

For each layer the build table drops and a new layer of powder is spread from the reservoir onto the build area

Laser projects image onto surface of powder fusing each layer

Powder reservoir

Part is built up layer by layer in the powder

ABOVE *Figure 6-5* Selective Laser Sintering.

the material is instantly solidified by the laser beam means that, unlike FFF, this process does not require supporting structures. The downsides are that the printer itself tends to be much more expensive and the photopolymer is also expensive and can be messy to clear up. It also requires careful handling and storage. But if you can find the cash the results can be very impressive.

Recently a number of Chinese companies have entered the market and have dramatically reduced the price of machines using stereolithography. There are also a number of companies around the world working on new designs with the aim of making this technology much cheaper and more accessible. At the time of writing there are printers of this type that can be had for less than a thousand pounds.

Selective laser sintering (SLS)

This is a process whereby the surface of a vat of granular material, which is mechanically levelled and smoothed, is scanned by one or more lasers causing the surface of the material to melt and bond to material underneath it. Layers are built up by progressively lowering the object being built into the vat of material, smoothing over a fresh layer of unprocessed material and again firing the laser at it. Powdered plastics can be used and also some metals. Alternatively metallic material may be sintered using an electrical arc rather than a laser. Figure 6-5 illustrates the process.

There are also machines that use combinations of the techniques described here, such as depositing layers of photopolymer resin, much like the FFF plastic extrusion, but curing with ultraviolet light during and/or after completion.

This sort of machinery is large and hugely expensive, costing thousands of pounds. This means it is unlikely that any modeller is going to invest in one, but there are a number of companies that will provide you with access to this sort of technology as a service. Several such are listed in Appendix 1.

Practical 3D printing

In this chapter we will review the success (or otherwise!) the authors have had in printing the various designs described in Chapters 3, 4 and 5. Hopefully, this will enable us to give some useful advice to other modellers and to warn of potential pitfalls.

A Chamber of Horrors

Early in our 3D venture, we had a very useful visit with our friend Iain Henderson, who has been 3D printing for longer than most. Iain kindly showed us his extensive collection of early failures from which we learned a lot. The following are some of the highlights!

Figure 7-1 illustrates the importance of a securely mounted print head. When Iain's printer (a Makerbot Replicator 2) was first delivered, its print head, which should have been secured by two screws, turned out to be fitted with only one! The result was that successive layers were not accurately aligned, so did not stick together properly. Fitting the second screw solved this problem.

In Figure 7-2, the effect of differential cooling can be seen – one corner of the building has lifted from the print bed. This is not uncommon when printing with PLA on an unheated bed, and longer prints are more prone to this effect. The effect can

be alleviated, to some extent at least, by using a 'raft' with pads at each corner of the model to hold it down while it cools, as shown in Figure 7-3.

In Figure 7-4 the effect of too high a temperature on the extruder nozzle can be seen. When the extruded material is too hot, threads of it can be dragged along with the nozzle when the latter is moving to its next print position. Notice the threads on the end wall, and the 'bobbles' on the roof.

In Figure 7-5 we see the building as it should be, with support material cleared away. This is an N-gauge (2mm/1ft) model of a pair of semi-detached houses.

In Figure 7-6, another N-gauge building has suffered from lack of supporting structures. Because the FFF process relies on the molten filament fusing with its neighbour before it solidifies, the process works best when the filaments are vertically above one another, and gravity can assist the process of fusing. When the filaments are side by side, there is only fleeting contact, and gravity will generally overcome whatever small amount of fusing takes place. At intermediate angles, the effect is graduated. In general, you can print sloping surfaces up to an angle of 45° to the vertical or thereabouts;

BELOW *Figure 7-1* The result of a loose print head.

any angle greater than that will require a supporting structure. In Figure 7-6 the roof has been printed at 60° to the vertical with the result that successive filaments have failed to fuse.

Finally, we have in Figure 7-7 a truly spectacular failure. This is what can happen when the first layer doesn't stick to the print bed! This could be due to the wrong bed height, wrong extrusion temperature or maybe a dirty bed surface.

TOP *Figure 7-2* Corner lifting due to differential cooling.

ABOVE *Figure 7-3* Raft and corner pads.

Chastened by these salutary lessons, we will now see how successful our attempts to print the designs described in earlier chapters were.

Cable ducting

In Chapter 3, we constructed a very simple model consisting of a sprue containing eight cable duct sections with eight lids. Figure 7-8 shows our CAD model loaded into *netfabb Basic*. One issue is that the CAD file describes the model in real-world dimensions, i.e. more than 6,000mm long! Given that our printer only has a build platform approximately 200mm by 200mm, and that the ducting was to go on a model railway, we felt that we ought to do something about the size. Luckily, netfabb has a scaling option, accessed by clicking the icon that looks like a sphere with vertical and horizontal arrows, about two-thirds of the way across the toolbar. This will scale the part in all axes to a particular size or to a percentage of the original size. We used the percentage option and made it for 4mm/1ft; the percentage was 1.315, which equals approximately ¹⁄₇₆th.

As we are resizing the model we need to check that it still sits at the origin of the z axis. Fortunately this is really easy to do with netfabb as one of the options on the Move dialog, accessed by clicking the icon of a sphere with a horizontal arrow

TOP *Figure 7-4* Too high a temperature, causing threads and 'bobbles'.

ABOVE CENTRE *Figure 7-5* What it should look like!

ABOVE *Figure 7-6* Insufficient support for a sloping roof.

RIGHT *Figure 7-7* The first layer didn't stick!

BELOW *Figure 7-8* The cable ducts in *netfabb Basic*.

BOTTOM *Figure 7-9* The cable ducts ready for slicing in *slic3r*.

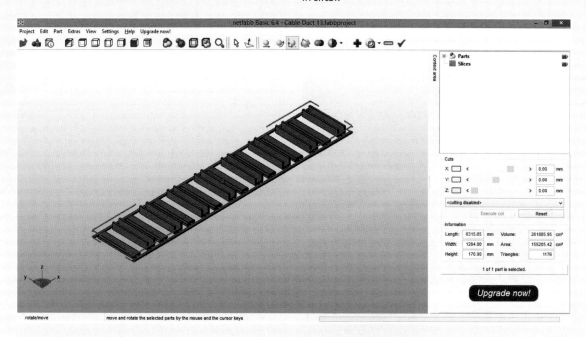

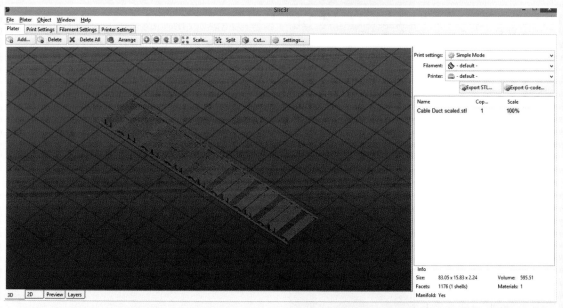

underneath, is 'Move to origin'. Having checked it and scaled it, we can save the new 4mm version to a separate stl file ready to slice for printing by clicking **Part > Export > As stl**.

To slice the model and save it as a set of instructions for the printer, we will use yet another piece of free software, *slic3r*. In *slic3r* we can define the details of the printer we wish to use, the plastic filament type and a huge number of other options to get the right result. We'll skip over most of this at this point, but there will be more later. Figure 7-9 shows our 4mm model loaded up into *slic3r*.

To the left of the *slic3r* screen we see the model positioned on a representation of the printer workspace. You can see there are buttons for adding in further parts to be printed and options to further scale, rotate, etc. There are also tabs to get access to the array of settings for printing the model, the filament type and the printer itself. The thing we really want at this stage is the big button on the right marked 'Export G-code', which generates the file of instructions for our printer. Having generated the instructions, the file is transferred to a memory card, which is then

LEFT *Figure 7-10* The cable duct sprue on the printer.

BELOW *Figure 7-11* The cable ducts after some basic cleaning-up.

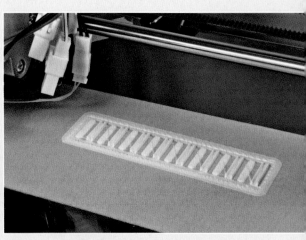

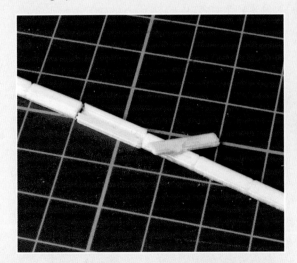

ABOVE CENTRE *Figure 7-12* The cable ducts installed on the layout.

ABOVE *Figure 7-13* The cable ducts in close-up.

inserted into the printer and we are good to go! Figure 7-10 shows what we get after a few minutes of whirring and beeping from our *RepRap* printer.

You can see that there are extra bits of plastic surrounding the model. This is known as the 'brim', and was defined in the print settings in *slic3r*. Using this brim around the model helps prevent it from warping while it is being printed. It is very thin, so fairly easy to remove. There will be more about brims and other things later.

The eagle-eyed will also spot that the author hasn't quite got the printer settings right and there are a few printing aberrations with this model! We will discuss these and how to avoid them later. Once the parts have had the brim removed and a bit of basic cleaning up has been done we are left with a basic set of components ready for use on the layout. The squares on the cutting mat in Figure 7-11 are 1 centimetre across.

After giving the plastic parts a splash of greyish acrylic paint, they can be assembled into something on the layout. On the author's layout 'Cramdin Yard', a few of these ducts have been added to represent a section of cable duct being installed. Figure 7-12 gives an overall view, while 7-13 provides a close-up with off-the-shelf figures added to set the scene.

Drawing and scaling

When drawing your object in your favoured 3D CAD program, what scale should you use? In the example of the cable duct above, the CAD model was built based upon the manufacturer's specification and drawings for the prototype. In this case it is really convenient to draw the model using the dimensions of the full-size object then scale it down to our chosen modelling size when we come to print it. That way we don't have to do any mental arithmetic or mess about with a calculator as we create each part. This reduces the potential for error and also ensures that we have the proportions of the object spot-on.

So why wouldn't I do that all the time? First of all, the CAD program may not support the real-world units we want to use. Surprisingly, *Blender*, at the time of writing, only supports arbitrary units, which can be anything you want them to be. *SketchUp* always converts everything internally into imperial (feet and inches). In the former case this isn't a big deal as we can simply say that each Blender unit is a millimetre or inch, whichever is more convenient, then we can scale things later to get the right size based on a known dimension and using a manual calculation. In the case of *SketchUp*, if we choose to use metric units, errors can creep in as the program converts everything and we don't get to see what it has done.

Another problem can be more of an issue and is due to the limits of the printing technology we are using. Consider the CAD model in Figure 7-14. This is a section of Southern Railway trestle platform that was produced in concrete at the Exmouth Junction works. The rear upright has holes for the rear guard fence wires, the largest of which is 1⅛ inches in diameter (the rest are even smaller), which equates to 28.6mm. If we scale this for 4mm/1ft the dimension is ¹⁄₇₆th of this, i.e. 0.38mm. If we print this on a 3D printer with a 0.4mm extruder nozzle how big will the resultant hole be? Basically it won't be a hole!

In addition, with the platform model we can see that the surface of the platform is made up of concrete slabs. These are 2½ inches thick, so when we scale for 4mm/1ft it will be only 0.84mm – pretty

BELOW *Figure 7-14* A section of SR trestle platform.

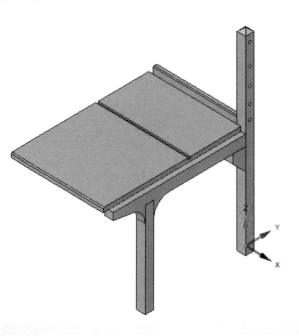

thin to be printed, especially if we want it to have a reasonably smooth surface. There is little chance that the printer will manage to render the rebate between the slabs or indeed create a usable part unless we can get down to 100-micron layers or less.

So what do we do to avoid this and get a result with the technology we have at our disposal? First of all, we can be a bit sensible about what we are doing. Most of us will probably only print objects to one particular scale, so we could just simply avoid adding details that quite clearly will not be printable after scaling down, in this case the holes for the fence wires in the upright. Also in this example, why wouldn't we simply create the concrete slabs of the platform in *Plasticard*? This isn't a matter of admitting defeat but being realistic and using the technology where we will get the most benefit.

Another option is to draw the model at the size that the final item will be printed. If we do this, and we have in the back of our mind the minimum dimensions that our printer can render, we will have to do a bit of adjustment with dimensions, but we can be fairly sure that the final model will print. If we are using a CAD program that doesn't allow us to accurately express real-world dimensions, this can be a bit tricky. However, it is not an insuperable problem as long as we know what scaling factor we are using to get the units from *Blender* (or whatever program) to our final size.

With some objects we can simply 'wing it'. We can draw the object to the prototype dimensions, then scale it down and print it. This is what we did with the cable duct and it printed OK, even if the final model might be a bit fragile. Often, though not always, the absence of the unprintable details will not be noticeable in the final model except under a microscope due to the small size. This is not a general solution but sometimes it's worth knocking out a test print and assessing it before spending ages fixing problems that may not exist.

Figure 7-15 shows four prints of the same 3D model, in this case one downloaded from *Thingiverse*, a website that has thousands of models for download. The figure on the extreme left is printed at half original size, the next one at around 7mm/1ft, then 4mm/1ft and, on the far right, 2mm/1ft. These are not printed at a particularly fine quality and the model has simply been scaled down in netfabb to the desired size, assuming that the figure is about 5ft 9in tall, before being sliced. You can see that the level of detail holds up fairly well until you get to the 2mm/1ft version, where the poor chap has lost his arms! To print this small the model would need some tweaking, or we would need to use a much finer print technology.

Orientation and printing limitations

While 3D printing is a powerful tool, we have to accept that it is not a magic bullet and there are limitations. There are a lot of things we need to worry about to get good results. An important one is the orientation of your model when you print it.

As we have outlined in the description of the various 3D printing technologies, all the current techniques build up the model in layers that are in some way fused together. Depending on the technology you are using, the layers may be anything from a few microns to 200 microns thick. Thicker layers, certainly 50 microns upwards, are clearly visible, as can be seen in the largest model in Figure 7-15. Painting and finishing can obscure the layers to some extent, but the orientation of your model can cause this effect to be exaggerated and give you poor results. Careful orientation of your model at the printing stage can radically improve your results.

Consider Figure 7-16. Here we show two versions of our sleeper stack from Chapter 3, which has a layer of sleepers arranged in a shallow slope to act as a sort of roof to the stack. The example to the rear and right of the picture has been printed in the obvious orientation with the foot of the stack flat on the print bed. With the model in this orientation the uppermost sleepers will be at an angle to the print bed, and in order to create the slope the top surface will be deposited across multiple layers. The effect is that the sleepers look more like a tiled roof! This was not what we were looking for, and we will have to file/sand the model substantially to reduce the effect to an acceptable level.

The example in front of it was printed in an orientation that meant the top surface of the sloping sleepers was parallel to the printer bed. The orientation was set in *slic3r* so that appropriate supporting material could be generated. If we had printed the complete stack in this orientation the results would probably have been good enough with little effect on the rest of the model, but in fact the 'roof' of the stack was printed separately and the rest of the stack printed in the conventional orientation. This gave us a good rendition of the sloping sleepers while eliminating the use of lots of support material and problems with its subsequent removal from the main stack.

This highlights another aspect we should consider. If you look around the internet you will find lots of intriguing models created on 3D printers that are printed in one piece and clearly impossible to assemble in a normal way. While this is a clever aspect of the technology, we should not consider that printing the whole of a model in one piece is the aim of the game, or indeed desirable. Taking this route limits us and almost always means that we have to accept poor quality in some aspect of our model. We are railway modellers, so we can glue a few bits of plastic together – after all, many of us were brought up on plastic kits! Splitting the model into assemblies can allow us to get good quality out of low-cost printers.

In fact, we can produce quite complex structures using a low-end FFF printer if we put a bit of thought into how the model is split up and how each part is oriented on the printer. Consider Figure 7-17, which shows a couple of roof trusses that have been produced for a 4mm/1ft model. The prototype truss is built from 'T'-section steel for almost all parts. If you think about this there is no practical way to print this model on a cheap printer without using huge amounts of support

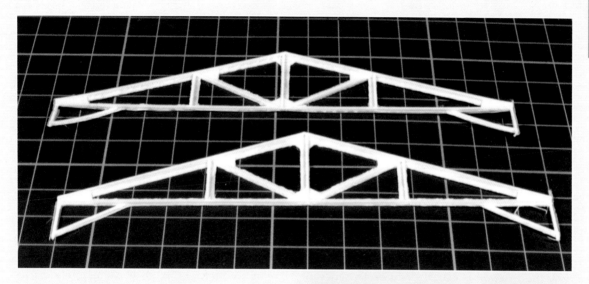

ABOVE *Figure 7-17* Roof truss components.

RIGHT *Figure 7-18* The assembled 4mm roof truss using mirror-image parts.

material, as whichever way you orient the model on the print bed there will be large parts of it running parallel to the print bed but above it.

The solution is simple: draw the CAD model as a series of 'L' sections rather than 'T' sections. Print this, then a mirror image of it with the long sections flat against the print bed. Stick the two together and you have your 'T' section. Figure 7-17 shows the two parts and 7-18 shows the two glued together with cyanoacrylate (superglue). As the final building model requires upwards of a dozen of these roof trusses, using the 3D printer saves a huge amount of time.

As well as avoiding nasty layer lines, you need to consider the structural strength of the parts of your model. The interface between the layers of the model is potentially a weak point. If your model has a wall thickness of a few millimetres then the orientation, in strength terms, probably doesn't matter. If, however, parts of your model are thin, you need to think about whether they will be strong enough when printed. The actual limit to the thickness will depend on the technology and print material you are using. If the details of your model are too thin, you may find that parts will snap along the layer lines!

Figure 7-19 shows a model where the weakness in the layer interface has caused a major problem. The model is a section of 7mm wagon underframe that has been printed complete with 'W' irons, axleboxes, springs and solebar details. The model has been printed with the top of the underframe flat on the printer bed, so the layers run along the length of the model. The 'W' irons and spring, even

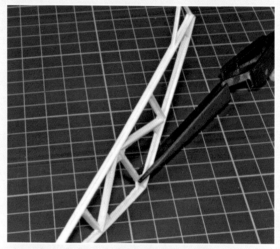

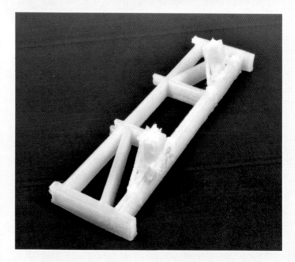

ABOVE *Figure 7-19* Lack of strength between layers.

in a 7mm model, are fairly thin at the point that they meet the solebar and in this case the model was not even strong enough to allow the support material to be removed.

Also bear in mind another potential issue associated with the orientation of the model. You have carefully drawn your model in your favourite CAD program so it is exactly correct in terms of dimensions, but when it comes to printing it you may find that a millimetre in the x axis is not the same as a millimetre in the y or z axes. They should be the same, but there are a number of factors that may introduce errors.

One place where errors can be introduced is in the slicing process. The resolution of the printer in all three axes has to be dealt with by the software. The resolutions are rarely the same, as some may be determined by an optical process, while others are physical, controlled by toothed belts or screw threads. Also, the slicing software must deal with how the material is extruded, cured or sintered. There's plenty of room for error.

The different mechanisms for movement in the x, y and z axes within the printer may also introduce errors. The z axis may be controlled by a screw thread or lead screw that can provide accurate movement down to the tens of microns we need for the layer thickness. However, movement in the x and y axes is more likely to be controlled by a toothed belt mechanism or something similar, which provides much quicker movement but with less precision. Even a system with the x and y axes controlled through a laser or projector may have a degree of error at the outer edges of the build area. Add to this errors introduced by the rate of curing of the resin or variations in material extrusion, and it seems surprising that we can print anything!

The bottom line of all this is that we need to think about many things when orienting the model for printing, and we may have to make some adjustments to the CAD model or split it into components to actually get a satisfactory print.

FFF techniques and issues

At the cheap end of the 3D printer range are the Fused Filament Fabrication (FFF) machines, which use some form of heated extruder to lay down layers of molten plastic filaments. As this is probably where anyone looking to have their own printer is likely to start, we'll provide some specific guidance in the use of these machines.

These low-end machines typically have a vertical (z axis) resolution of 100 microns (0.1mm) or more, although some can get down below this. In addition they tend to use an extruder nozzle diameter of around 0.4mm. These two dimensions determine the smallest size of detail that the printer can create and the thinnest wall that can be printed.

Even though these cheaper printers may not be able to create objects with super-fine detail and perfectly smooth surfaces, this does not mean that they can't be very useful to railway modellers. Hopefully some of our examples show this.

One of the things that frustrates many new users to FFF printing is that whatever problems you first encounter the answer from those in the know is 'level the build plate'. Everybody who buys a new printer will have followed the instructions in setting it up and will have been through the process of levelling the build plate, so getting this answer from an 'expert' when your first prints fail is not what you want. Unfortunately this fairly simple process is absolutely crucial.

FFF printers work by laying down layer after layer of molten plastic, so it is absolutely crucial that the first layer sticks to the build plate. If it doesn't, at best the print will warp and get out of shape, and in the worst case you will end up with a whole bunch of filament all over the place and very likely wrapped all round the printer machinery (recall Figure 7-7).

Levelling the bed

So what exactly does levelling the build plate mean? Forget spirit levels and getting things perfectly horizontal – strictly it's not levelling at all! What you are actually doing is ensuring that when the extruder is at its lowest point, i.e. when it is closest to the build plate, it is exactly the same distance above the plate at all points across the plate, and crucially the gap is less than the thickness of the layer we plan to extrude. The gap needs to be about 50-100 microns.

Each printer will probably have its own levelling process but, unless the printer has a self-levelling bed, you will need some sort of feeler gauge for measuring the gap between the extruder and the bed. Many recommend using a sheet of ordinary printer/copier paper for this, but if you are an oldie who used to do their own car servicing you may have some metal feeler gauges. Make sure that wherever the extruder is positioned in relation to the build table the paper/feeler gauge is a squeaky fit between them – not so tight that the extruder is lifted up by inserting the paper, but not a loose fit either.

Figure 7-20 shows a failed print where parts of the model have warped away from the build plate, and other bits have come unstuck completely and wrapped around the extruder! In this case the build plate is not far out of adjustment, as much of the model was printing reasonably well, but the gap is not consistent across the whole of the plate.

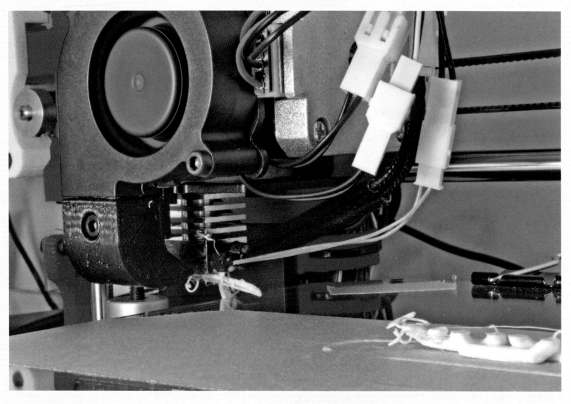

ABOVE *Figure 7-20* The result of a build plate not levelled correctly.

While levelling the bed is crucial, unfortunately there are one or two other things to think about to ensure that the first layer is laid down perfectly.

Making it stick

Your printer will probably have a build platform made of aluminium or some form of glass, and it may or may not be heated. A heated bed gives you more flexibility in what types of material you can print with; also, if it's at the right temperature, it helps to get the first layer to stick securely. An unheated table doesn't mean you can't get good results, but it limits you to using material such as PLA.

The machine's build table will (hopefully) have a nice smooth surface on which to lay the first layer of the print, but this is almost certainly not enough. Many people swear by a light dusting of the cheapest 'firm hold' hairspray on the build table to ensure that the first layer sticks. The author's experience is that this does indeed work sometimes, and with some models, particularly if you have a heated build plate. It's not the solution for every model and not the authors' first choice, though it does make the workshop smell nice!

Another popular alternative is to cover the build plate with a single layer of Kapton tape; this is lightweight insulating tape that has a smooth surface and is tolerant of high temperatures. Kapton tape is becoming more widely available in the UK and is available in a range of widths, but it's not the cheapest option.

If you are really working to a budget you can use plain old masking tape, which again is available in various widths. You don't need to cover the whole of the build table with tape if you are only printing a small object in the centre of it. The downside to masking tape is that it usually has a slightly textured surface, so if the first layer of the object you are printing is going to be visible and needs to be really smooth, you should use Kapton tape or print directly onto the build table surface.

Figure 7-21 shows the difference between the surface finish produced when using both cheap masking tape and Kapton tape. The nearer part has a much smoother finished surface, but is still not perfect, although a coat of spray paint may be enough to even out any minor flaws. The part printed on masking tape will require more surface finishing.

The authors have used ordinary masking tape for most of our prints with great success and, as it's cheap, it's not a disaster if you have to rip it off to release the print from the printer. Importantly, if you are using some form of tape make sure you level the build table with the tape in place, not before, otherwise the gap between the table and the extruder will be too small – an obvious point but easily overlooked.

ABOVE *Figure 7-21* A smoother surface is created by using Kapton tape (foreground).

BELOW *Figure 7-22* Using masking tape on the print bed.

Figure 7-22 shows the printer after completing a print when masking tape has only been laid on the centre of the bed with some small bits in the corners. The levelling process for the printer involves adjusting with the extruder in each corner and the centre, hence the extra bits of tape in the corners.

Whatever tape you use or don't use, it is worth making sure that the surface you are going to print on is clean and grease-free. Just before you start your print give it a quick wipe over with Ispopropyl Alcohol (IPA), also sometimes referred to as Isopropanol, or something similar. It takes seconds, yet can make a huge difference.

If you are using tape on the print bed it is worth investing in one of the many household cleaning products for removing sticky label deposits, etc, often called sticky stuff remover. When you need to replace the tape on your printer it will make getting the build plate clean much, much easier.

Extruding the right amount

The low-price end of the 3D printer market is still largely the domain of the hobbyist experimenting with the technology and you will find that much of the hardware and software has seemingly innumerable options for adjusting things. Unfortunately there is no magic 'push to set-up' button. Some of the options you may have to worry about are those dealing with the rate at which the plastic filament is extruded, and these are often defined in the slicing program.

First, you need to ensure that the diameter of the filament you are using is correctly set. The most common filament sizes are 3mm and 1.75mm diameter and, although the various suppliers will

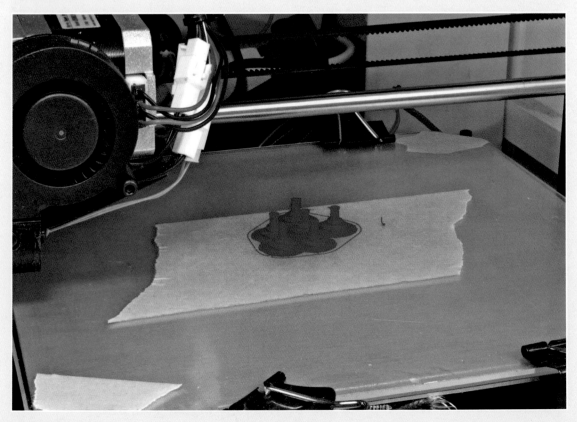

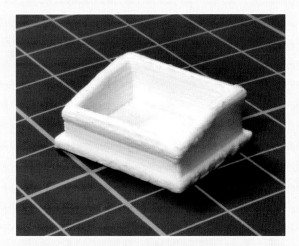

advertise their filaments with a specific size, you need to check it. Don't just measure the diameter in one place – take a number of measurements. The odd 0.1mm variation may not seem much, but it can make a big difference to the quality of your prints.

If you are using *slic3r* you will find the filament size defined on the **Filament Settings** tab. Also on this tab is an 'Extrusion Multiplier' setting. This allows you to increase or decrease the rate at which plastic is extruded. Unfortunately you will have to figure out any changes to this by trial and error. Leave it at the default 1.0 setting when you try out a new spool of filament and make adjustments if the initial prints are not up to scratch. Too little plastic extruded will give you overly defined layers or layers that don't stay stuck together (delamination). Too much plastic extruded will give you a rough or bumpy surface, as in Figure 7-23.

In addition, the **Filament Settings** tab lets you adjust the extruder and, if you have one, the heated bed temperature. You can specify different temperatures for the initial layer, the one that needs to stick firmly to the build table, and subsequent layers. You will probably use a slightly higher temperature for the initial layer. With PLA you should be looking at an extruder temperature of between 180 and 220°C. Start off with 200 and adjust up or down based on your prints. If you have a heated build plate, 70 degrees is a good number. If you are using ABS, you will need an extruder temperature around 230° and a heated build plate at around 110°.

If the extruder temperature is too low, your prints may have a rough surface, the layers may not stick together well, and the final print may turn out to be brittle. If the temperature is too high you may find excess plastic weeping from the extruder when the head moves from one point to another on the print, which can also leave 'hairs', as seen in Figure 7-24.

Brims, skirts and rafts

Sometimes just having the printer set up correctly is not enough. We are working at the cheaper end of the market so we sometimes have to give the printer a bit of a helping hand. Slicing programs such as *slic3r* have a number of options that help getting that first layer firmly stuck to the build table, so it is worth looking at them here.

A 'skirt' comprises one or two lines of extruded filament drawn around the outside of the print but not touching it. It is usually drawn 2 or 3 millimetres away from the model and one or two layers deep. The skirt is useful as it primes the extruder and gets the filament flowing before printing any important bits, and by observing the printing of the skirt you can quickly see whether the bed is levelled adequately. If the skirt doesn't stick, there is little chance that the rest of the model will print successfully. We therefore recommend using a skirt for all your prints. Figure 7-25 shows a skirt around a print of the LNER ballast bin.

A 'brim' is another very useful feature. This is an outline 2 or 3 millimetres wide, usually one layer thick, attached to the model and effectively increasing its footprint. Figure 7-26 shows a print with a brim. This helps greatly with getting the first layer to stick firmly to the build table and keeping it stuck down to avoid warping as subsequent layers are added. As the brim is only one layer thick it is easily trimmed off when the completed print is cleaned up. We recommend using a brim for all your prints, as it can make a dramatic difference. Figure 7-27 shows two prints where one shows distinct warping and the other almost none – the only difference is that one was printed with a brim.

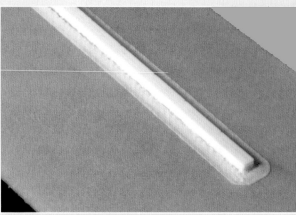

ABOVE LEFT *Figure 7-25* Use of a skirt.

ABOVE RIGHT *Figure 7-26* Use of a brim.

RIGHT *Figure 7-27* The effect of using a brim.

A 'raft' is a number of extra layers laid down underneath the first layer of the model, and is used when you are having real problems getting a print to stick to the bed, usually because your model has a very small footprint or is inherently unstable. The slicing software generates the raft automatically and uses a filament thickness and fill pattern that makes the raft easy to snap away, with care, from the finished print. Objects like standing figures can benefit from the use of a raft, but it's not something you need all the time. Figure 7-15 shows a raft below the feet of the printed figures.

Support material

Ideally we would like to print every model or component as a single entity without anything added, but in the real world there are many occasions where this is simply not possible. As we have already said, we can often get better-quality prints through careful orientation and/or subdividing the model into components, but at times this still isn't enough, and we need to print using supporting structures.

In situations where we have overhanging structures as part of our model, such as the overhanging eaves of a building, the printer will struggle or completely fail to print successfully – it simply cannot print elements that are held up by fresh air. This is a more frequent problem with low-end FFF printers, whereas some of the more sophisticated technologies have built-in support mechanisms as part of the printing process.

As the modeller you have options as to how to create adequate support structures for your models. Some slicing programs such as *slic3r* can automatically create various patterns of support structure, which more often than not do an adequate job. Picking the right patterns is, however, something of a black art. Other mesh repair and manipulation programs also have various tools for creating supports, requiring varying levels of user input. The structures that these programs generate are designed to be easily broken away from the model.

If all else fails you can create supports manually using your CAD tools, and sometimes this is the only way to get good results.

Commonly, the support structures are printed using the same material as the model, though if you are fortunate enough to have a printer with multiple extruders you can use different materials. There are various support materials available, including some that are water-soluble. These are ideal where you need to remove supports from delicate models or those in hollowed areas that are difficult to access.

Figure 7-28 shows a model of a house in *DesignSpark Mechanical*, which has a number of overhanging structures such as the eaves and several window and door frames. Figure 7-29 shows the same model in *slic3r*, with automatically generated supports shown in green.

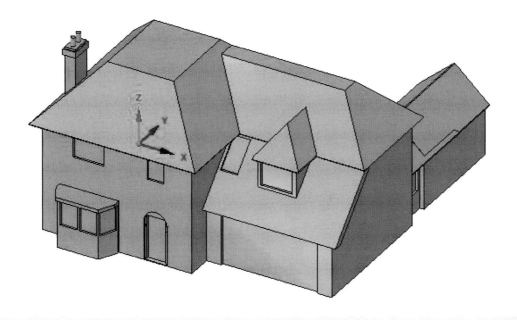

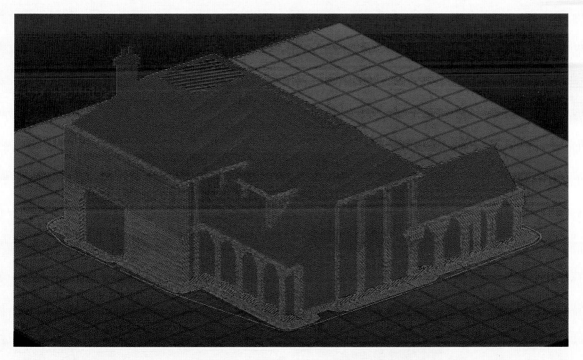

Keep on pushing!

The reader may by now have gained the impression that 3D printing, on a cheap printer at least, is a nightmare of one problem after another. Not so! With a little patience and practice, you can overcome most of the problems. Over time you will be able to design your models within the limitations of your chosen technology so that your prints work first time. Hopefully this chapter has given you a few tips that will shorten the learning curve.

TOP *Figure 7-28* A CAD model of a house.

ABOVE *Figure 7-29* The same house previewed in *slic3r* with supports.

Laser cutting

In this chapter we will investigate laser cutting and etching/engraving. A laser beam – a powerful, coherent and very narrow beam of light – is used to provide extremely accurate and narrow cuts in a variety of materials. The light beam delivers energy to a very small spot, which burns, melts or vaporises the material being cut.

The machines available range from tiny examples that can barely scorch cardboard through to industrial machines capable of cutting through substantial thicknesses of steel. The sort of machines we are looking at typically have a CO_2 (carbon dioxide) laser tube of 40 watts or more and are capable of cutting paper, card, fabrics and acrylics, and MDF or plywood up to a thickness of a few millimetres. Figure 8-1 shows a typical layout of the key components of a laser cutting machine.

The cutter head, which focuses the laser beam onto the surface of the workpiece, is moved in the x axis (left and right) and y axis (forwards and backwards) using stepper motors controlled by a microprocessor. It can usually also be moved through a small range in the z axis to allow for differing thicknesses of material, but this is only done during setting up rather than during cutting.

The laser beam itself is generated by a laser tube, often mounted at the rear of the machine, and the beam is directed to the cutting head by bouncing it off mirrors. This allows the large laser tube, usually equipped with water cooling, to remain stationary.

If a laser beam is capable of cutting through materials, it certainly won't do humans any good

so, with anything other than a very low-power machine, all of this will be carefully encased and have cut-outs to turn off the laser if any doors or covers are opened. A CO_2 laser produces light in the infrared part of the spectrum, so is invisible to the naked eye.

The machine may also have air jets on the cutting head to blow away dust and debris from the work surface, and some form of extractor fan to remove smoke and dust. Most machines connect to a PC via a USB cable to allow downloading of cutting instructions, and they can often store multiple files in an internal memory card.

Figure 8-2 shows the laser cutter owned by our friend Roger Stonham. This has a 40-watt CO_2 laser and a cutting area of 500mm by 300mm. Notice that there is a fire extinguisher to hand! You should never leave a laser cutter unattended while cutting – lots of energy is being directed to burn material, and it should be treated with great respect. Figure 8-3 shows the cutting space of the machine. The material to be cut is positioned on the knife-edge bars, which can be moved up and down to allow for different material thicknesses. The cutter head is at the rear left corner. Figure 8-4 shows the laser tube at the rear of the machine; the plastic tubing is for water-cooling.

Figure 8-5 is the view through the machine's left-hand side access panel, showing the cutter head carriage. The square block to the left is the

Figure 8-1 Schematic of a laser cutter.

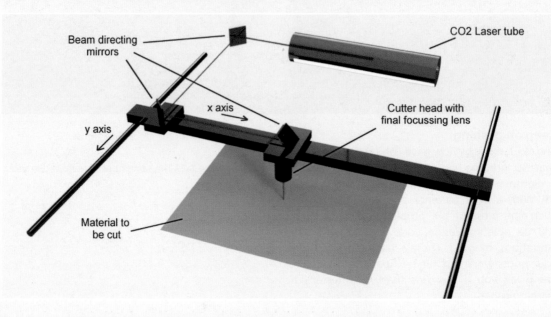

ABOVE *Figure 8-4* The laser tube.

CENTRE RIGHT *Figure 8-5* The xy carriage.

BELOW RIGHT *Figure 8-6* The cutter head.

stepper motor that controls movement along the x axis, and on the right is the mirror reflecting the laser beam in the x direction towards the cutter head. The brass knurled screws allow fine adjustment of the mirror position.

Figure 8-6 shows the cutter head from the front, and the mirror that turns the beam through 90 degrees down onto the workpiece can clearly be seen. The plastic tube towards the front is an air feed to clean away dust and debris from the cutting process.

There are three basic modes of operation. First, the machine can perform vector cutting, i.e. cutting along lines. The width of the cut is known as the 'kerf' of the laser and can be from around 0.1 to 0.5mm. This narrow cut means that we can create very fine detail.

Second, by reducing the power of the laser we can engrave or etch into the surface of the material (vector engraving) rather than cutting through it.

Finally the machine can raster engrave by filling in outlined areas. Rather than drawing continuous lines the machine pulses the laser, working backwards and forwards across the workpiece. This is typically how things such as text are formed.

Let us now look at three examples demonstrating each of these techniques.

Laser-cut gable ends

For our first attempt at laser cutting, we will cut a pair of ornamental barge boards for the gable ends of a station building. First we need to create a two-dimensional CAD drawing in the dxf file format, and to do this we will use the DraftSight program reviewed in Chapter 2.

The barge boards are to fit an existing model, and the measurements required are as follows: the total span of the roof (including overhang) is 160mm, and the total rise is 68mm. A quick look at a table of tangents (or a calculator) reveals that the roof angle is therefore 40.36°.

We start by drawing a line from the origin to a point x=80 (half the span) and y=68 (the rise). This will get us a line of the correct length as in Figure 8-7. However, it will be easier to do the next part of the drawing with the barge board horizontal, so select the line with the left mouse button and click **Modify > Rotate**. Click the origin as the centre of rotation, and pull the line down so that it is horizontal. You can make sure it is absolutely horizontal by clicking the Properties icon with the line selected and setting the y coordinate of the line's end to 0 (Figure 8-8).

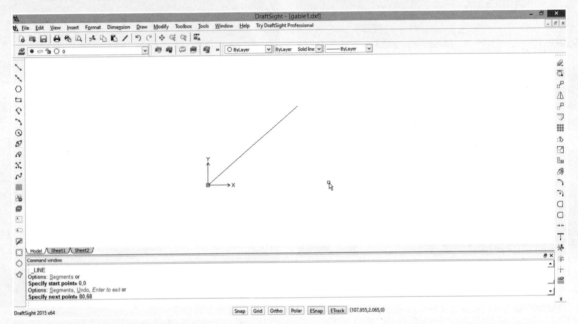

Figure 8-7 The roof line

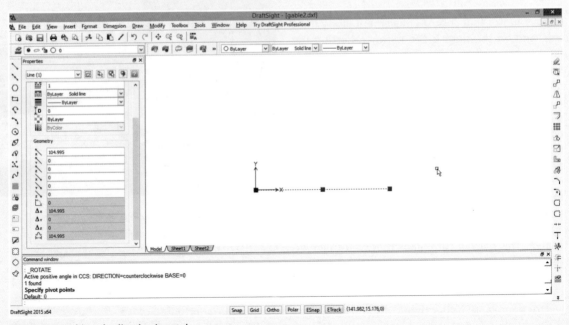

Figure 8-8 Making the line horizontal

Next, we draw a line to represent the top of the barge board, 10mm above the first line. Rather than use the mouse, it is easier to type in the coordinates of this line directly. Noting that our original line runs from (0,0) to (104.995,0), we type 0,10 and 104.995,10 in the command window as the start and end points of our new line (figure 8-9).

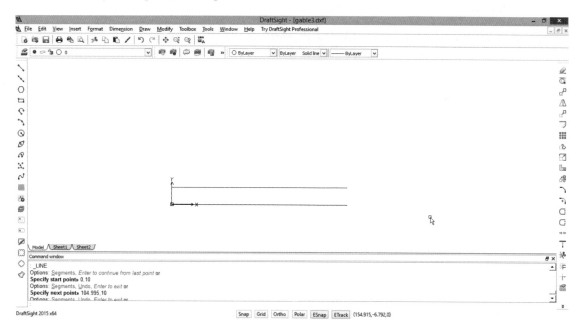

Figure 8-9 Typing the line coordinates

The next part of construction will be easier to follow if we move away from the origin, so click **Edit > Select All** and drag both lines away. Draw two lines to represent the ends of the barge boards (figure 8-10).

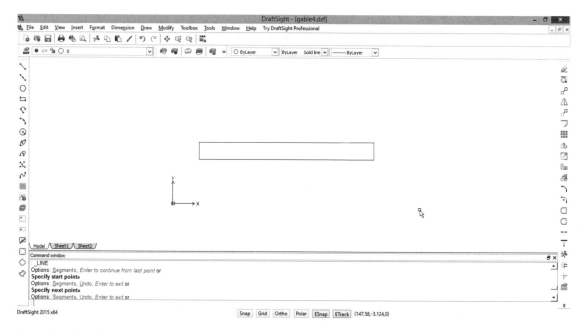

Figure 8-10 Complete the outline

Next, we want to round off what will be the bottom corner of the barge board. **Click View > Zoom > Window** and zoom in on the left-hand end of the board. Click **Modify > Fillet**, type R in the command window, press **Enter**, and change the fillet radius from the default value (10) to 5 and press **Enter** again. Then click the left and bottom sides of the barge board to indicate where we want the fillet to be (figure 8-11).

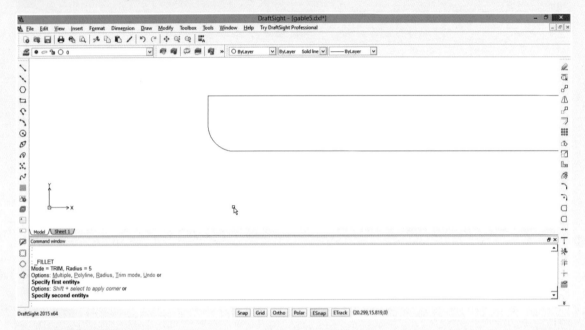

Figure 8-11 Fillet the end

We will now make the first of the decorative cut-outs. Draw a horizontal line near the left-hand end of the board, then a vertical line of about half the length rising from the centre of the horizontal line. Use the **Shift** key to keep these lines horizontal and vertical. Using the line ends, draw an arc using the **3-point Arc** tool (figure 8-12).

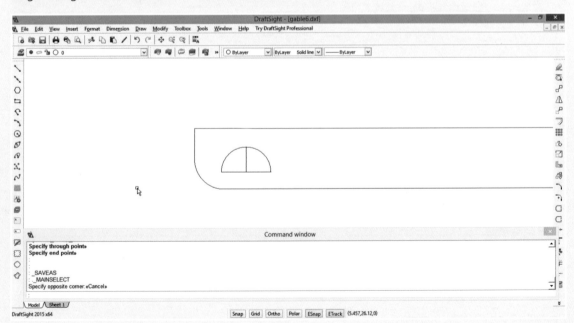

Figure 8-12 Starting the cut-out

We want to make a fillet between the ends of this arc and the horizontal line, so click **Modify > Fillet**, then type R into the command line, press **Enter**, set a new fillet radius of 1, and again press **Enter**. Click the horizontal line and the arc at the right-hand side of the cut-out. Repeat for the left-hand side. Delete the vertical line, which has now served its purpose (Figure 8-13). We need to repeat the cut-out right along the board, so click and drag the mouse to select the cut-out, then click **Modify > Pattern** (Figure 8-14). Set vertical copies to 1, horizontal copies to 10, vertical spacing to 0 and horizontal spacing to 10 (you may have to adjust some of these numbers depending on the exact size of the cut-out you've made). Press **OK** and there are your remaining cut-outs (Figure 8-15 overleaf).

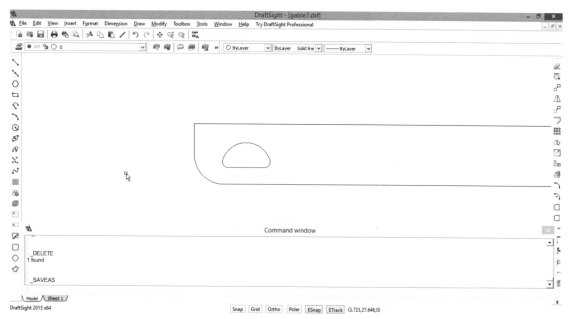

Figure 8-13 Completing the cut-out

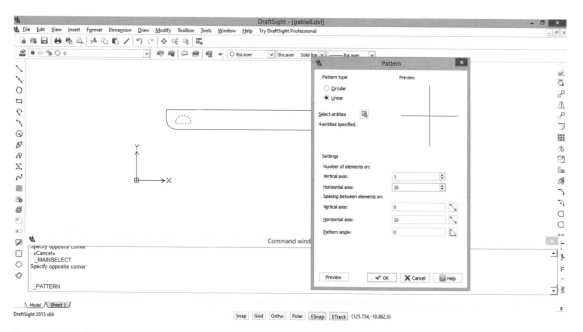

Figure 8-14 Making a pattern

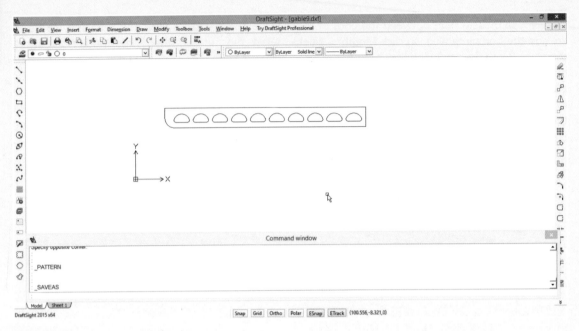

Figure 8-15 The cut-outs copied

We now need to rotate the barge board through 40.36°. Click **Edit > Select All**, then **Modify > Rotate**. Select the top left corner as the pivot point and, as we know that the roof angle required is 40.36°, type this value into the command window (figure 8-16).

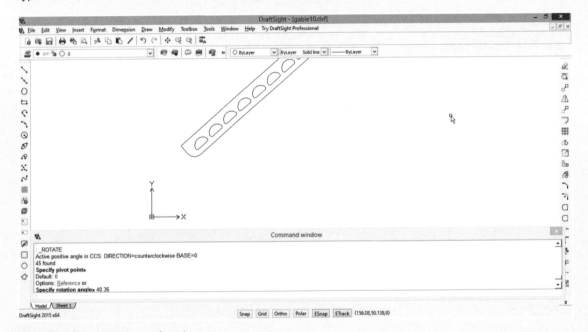

Figure 8-16 Rotate to the roof angle

Next, we want to get rid of some surplus bits at the top of the barge board. Draw a vertical line from the top of the board downwards (use the Shift key). Click **Modify > Trim**. Select the vertical line you've just drawn as the cutting edge, then just press Enter when prompted in the command window, for a second line. Click on the bits of arc and line that we wish to remove (figure 8.17), then delete the vertical line, the stray fillet and the line that used to be the end of the barge board.

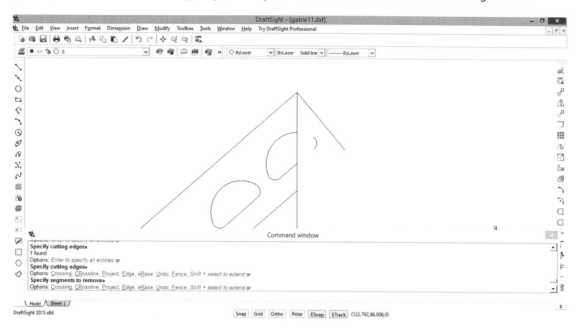

Figure 8-17 Trimming the surplus lines and arcs

We will now use the Mirror modifier to make the opposite barge board. Click **Edit > Select All**, then **Modify > Mirror**. Select the upper and lower end-points of the barge board edges as the ends of your mirror line and, when asked whether you want to delete the source, type N in the command window and press **Enter**. The result should be as figure 8-18.

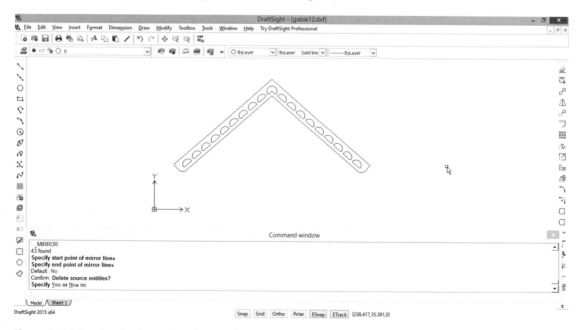

Figure 8-18 Mirroring the barge board

There remains just one minor job, then our barge board is complete. As it stands, if we tried to cut out Figure 8-18 we might end up with a sloppy piece of work. This is because we have a continuous line around the barge boards, and once this is fully cut the barge boards could move around while the cut-outs are being cut. Therefore we make a few small gaps in the cutting line to hold the barge boards in place. To do this, draw two horizontal lines close together right across the gable end as in figure 8-19.

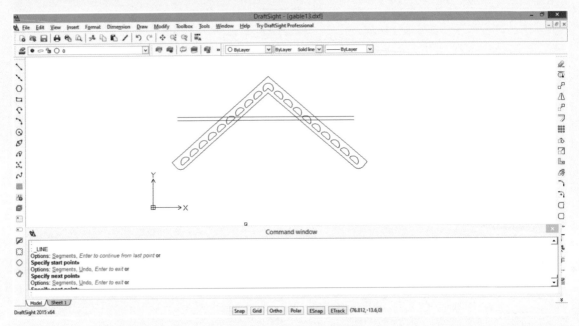

Figure 8-19 Making gaps in the continuous line around the barge boards

Next, click **Modify > Trim**, select both of these lines to be cutting edges, then press **Enter**. Zoom in if necessary, and by clicking on the barge board edges between these two lines, make four little gaps. These will be sufficient to hold the barge boards in place while the ornaments are being cut out. This done, delete the horizontal lines and our item is completed (figure 8-20).

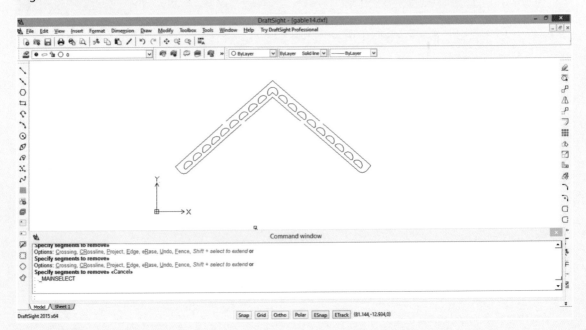

Figure 8-20 The finished drawing

Make as many copies of the item as you need using the **Pattern modifier** as described earlier. It is also a good idea to have a line of an exact length, say 100mm, which can be easily measured to ensure that cutting is to exactly the right scale. Figure 8-21 shows the gable ends cut out, and Figure 8-22 shows them *in situ* on the station building.

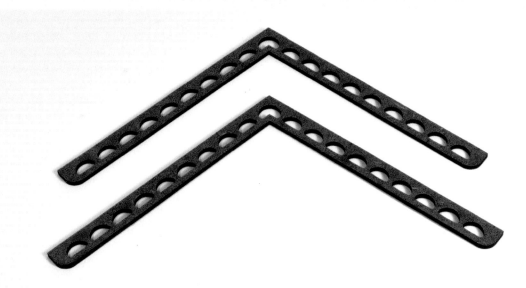

Figure 8-21 The gable ends completed

Figure 8-22 The gable ends in situ

Brickwork

Brickwork presents a challenge to the railway modeller, and most use plastic card embossed with a brick pattern. Problems start to arise when we come to corners; it is difficult to align the bricks accurately and to join up the edges of the card perfectly (see Figure 8-22 for an imperfect corner!). However, a laser cutter can produce excellent brickwork. The laser is first set to a low power to draw the mortar courses on the surface of the wall (vector engraving), then to full power to cut it out. For this example, we shall make the brick base for a small Saxby & Farmer signal box, which would typically house the locking equipment. Above the brick base the lever frame would typically be housed in a wooden superstructure.

First, some technicalities: brickwork is composed of bricks, beds and perpends. The 'bed' is the horizontal layer of mortar upon which the bricks are laid, while the 'perpend' is the vertical mortar join between the bricks. A typical brick size during steam railway days, when many of our stations were built, was 8½ inches by 4 inches by 2½ inches deep.

Allowing half an inch for mortar between the bricks, this gives us repeating intervals of 9, 4½ and 3 inches in each of the three dimensions. The reader will no doubt spot the symmetry between these numbers, which facilitates nice neat corners, as in Figure 8-23.

The pattern of brickwork shown in Figure 8-23 is known as 'stretcher bond'. A brick laid so that its long narrow side is exposed is known as a 'stretcher', while a brick laid at right angles to this is known as a 'header'. All of the bricks in Figure 8-23, except those at the end of alternate rows, are stretchers. Where a wall is one brick-width thick, this is the only way it can be laid. However, when a wall is thicker than this, other possibilities arise. For example, in Figure 8-24 we see the corner of a wall laid in 'Flemish bond'. This has alternate headers and stretchers along each row, and makes for a more decorative effect than stretcher bond, as well as being a lot stronger. Notice that to maintain symmetry, a 'queen closer' is employed immediately after a header at the start of a row. This is a brick divided in two along its width, marked by an asterisk in the first drawing in Figure 8-24. The third layer of bricks is the same as the first, and so on.

Another common bond is 'English bond', illustrated in Figure 8-25. Unlike Flemish bond, in which stretchers and headers alternate along each row, English bond has alternating rows of all headers then all stretchers. Again, a 'queen closer' (*) is employed after the first header on the all-header rows. There are numerous other bonds, so if you are reproducing the brickwork of a particular prototype it is worth trying to get it right. Wikipedia has a helpful article on 'Brickwork', which describes most of the bonds you are likely to find on the railway.

We will build our signal box base in Flemish bond at a scale of 7mm to 1 foot using 2mm MDF, which is inexpensive and cuts well. This time we will use LibreCAD to make our CAD drawing, and Figure 8-26 gives a rough outline of what we will build. The

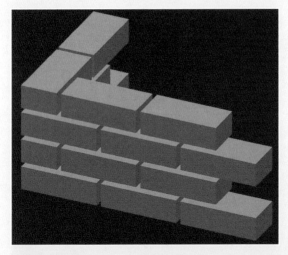

ABOVE *Figure 8-23* Corner brickwork.

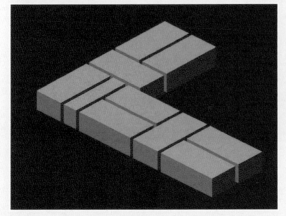

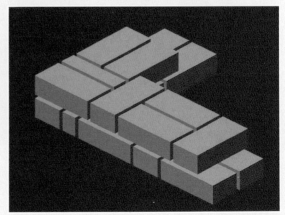

ABOVE, LEFT AND RIGHT *Figure 8-24* Flemish bond – first and second layers.

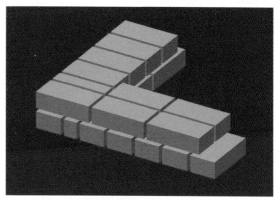

ABOVE, LEFT AND RIGHT *Figure 8-25* English bond – first and second layers.

RIGHT *Figure 8-26* General outline.

window may appear to be very low down, but this is a platform-mounted signal box, so the floor of the locking room will be well below platform level.

We will start off with a plain wall and, as we have done with many of our previous examples, we will build half of the wall then make a mirror image of it. It will make things simple if we start our half-wall at the origin, and (for reasons that will become clear later) it will be advantageous if the origin is in fact the centre-point of the bottom of the wall. We will also (again for reasons that will be made clear) work in units of millimetres at scale size, i.e. 7mm to the foot. In these units, a stretcher plus its share of the half-inch mortar gaps either side is 5.25mm. A header plus its mortar is half of this, i.e. 2.625mm. Perpends will be 1.75mm tall. We start up *LibreCAD* (figure 8-27) and click '+' on the layer list to create a

new layer in addition to the default Layer 0. Call this Layer 1 and set its pen colour to red so as to distinguish lines drawn on this layer from those drawn on Layer 0. We will use Layer 1 for the low-power 'mortar' courses and Layer 0 for the right-through cuts.

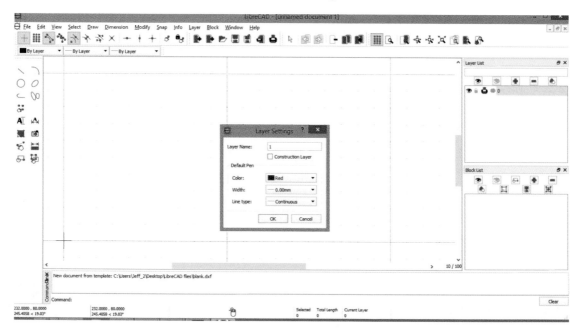

Figure 8-27 Creating a new layer

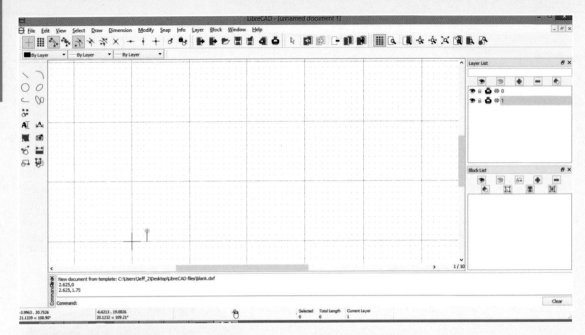

Figure 8-28 The first perpend

Incidentally, take care when you are switching between layers not to click the little icon to the left of the layer number. You have turned the layer into a construction layer, and it has the rather scary effect of extending all your straight lines to infinity! It's purpose is to help line things up with other things on distant parts of the drawing, but the sudden extension of all your lines to infinity can be disconcerting. Click the icon again to turn off the effect.

In the centre of the base of our wall we will have a stretcher, so we draw the perpend representing its right-hand end as a line from (2.625,0) to (2.625,1.75). On the menu bar at the top click **Draw > Line > 2 points**. Then click in the 'command' window at the bottom and type in the coordinates of the first and second points (figure 8-28).

We now have to press **Esc** to start a second line, because if we don't *LibreCAD* will assume that our next set of coordinates are a third point of the same polyline. So press **Esc**, click again in the 'command' window and type in the coordinates of the start and end of our second line, which are 5.25,0 and 5.25,1.75. This gives us our first header brick. The right-hand end of our first full stretcher will be from (10.5,0) to (10.5,1.75), so repeat the procedure with these coordinates. You should now have something like figure 8-29.

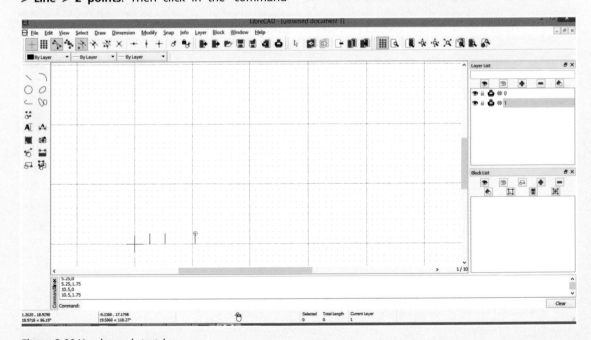

Figure 8-29 Header and stretcher

154

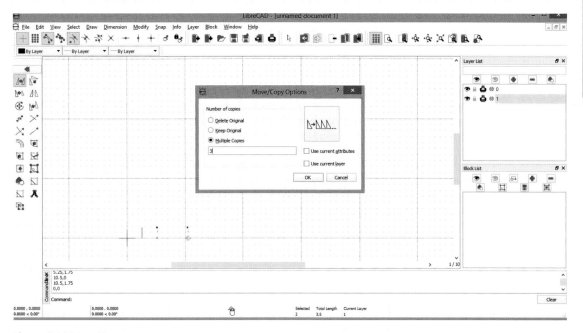

Figure 8-30 Move/Copy

Next, get out of Line-drawing mode by clicking **Edit > Selection pointer**, and select the second and third of our lines (but *not* the first) by dragging a selection rectangle over them. Then click **Modify > Move/copy** and select the base of our first line as the reference point and the base of our third line as the target point. Make sure that the Snap on end-points icon (just below the menu bar) is active to ensure that these points are exact. The Move/Copy options dialog will appear, so select Multiple copies and set the count to 3 (figure 8-30).

This will give us our first (half) course of bricks. Get into Line-drawing mode and draw a line from the origin to the bottom of our final perpend. To make sure we get the line exactly on the origin, click the 'Snap on grid' icon. We don't actually need this line here, since it will be cut through by a line on Layer 0, but we need it temporarily for copying purposes. This would be a good time to save our work, so save it as 'brickwork1.dxf' (figure 8-31).

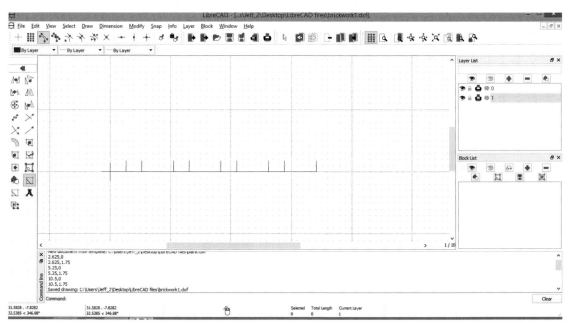

Figure 8-31 The first course

The next course will have a header at its centre, so now draw a line from (1.3125,1.75) to (,3.5) to represent the right-hand side of the central header. If you're wondering why 1.3125, it is half of 2.625mm. The other half of the central header will magically appear when we do our mirroring. Then draw further lines at x = 6.5625 and x = 9.1875 with the same y values (1.75 and 3.5). Again, copy the right-hand pair of lines using the base of the right-hand side of the central header as the reference point and the base of the line at x = 9.1875 as the target. Select **Multiple copie**s as before and make three copies (figure 8-32). Save as 'brickwork2.dxf'.

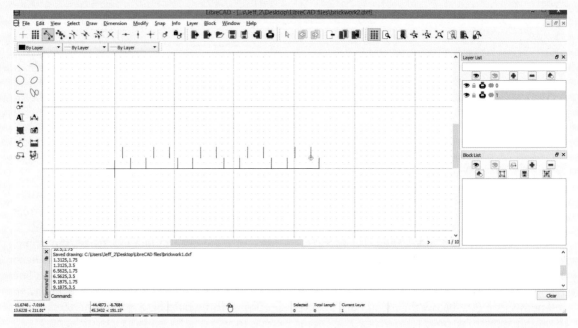

Figure 8-32 The second course

There is one obvious fault with the second course of bricks, as depicted in Figure 8-32. At the extreme right, we have a gap of half a header. This is because we haven't yet put a 'queen closer' in between the final stretcher and the final header. How we actually do this depends on what we are going to do about corners. There are two alternatives. Either we can cut our MDF so that alternate end bricks are missing and the corners fit together in what a carpenter would call a box joint (Figure 8-33a), or we could cut straight down the edge of the wall and file a chamfer on it to give us what a carpenter would call a mitre joint (Figure 8-33b).

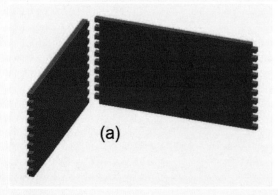
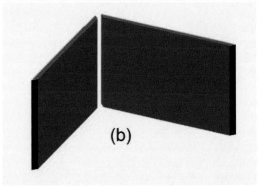

Figure 8-33 Box joint (a) and mitre joint (b)

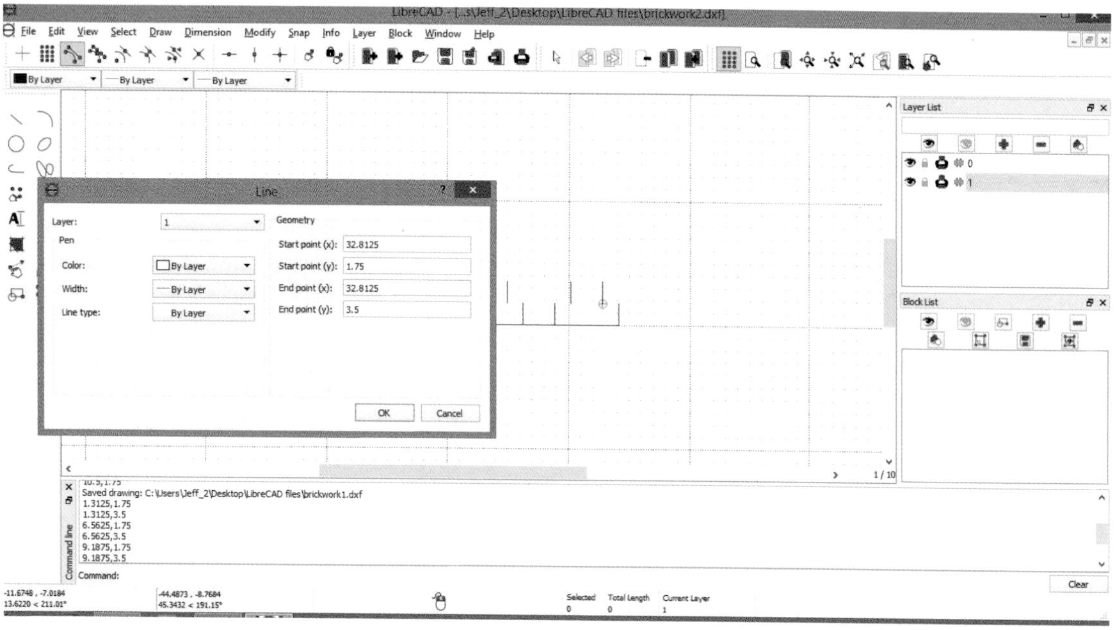

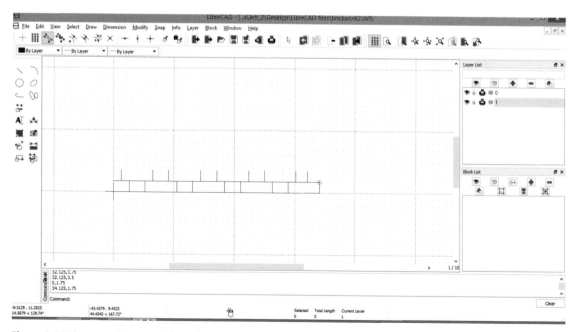

Figure 8-34 Line properties

The chamfer option (b) is certainly simpler from the CAD point of view. However, its success depends on the accuracy of your filing. If the resulting edges are not razor-sharp and at precisely 45°, the corner joint will be less than perfect. We shall therefore go for option (a) and have our bricks interlaced at the corners. However, there is one small problem with this option. Our MDF is 2mm thick, but if it was to accurately represent the headers it should be 2.625mm thick. We can allow for this by making a slightly non-scale queen closer. The last line on our second course is at x = 32.8125, as we can discover by clicking **Modify > Properties** then clicking on the line in question (figure 8-34).

In a similar way we discover that the last line on our first course is at x = 34.125, so the indent of the second course is 1.3125mm with respect to the first. Our MDF is 2mm thick, so this indentation needs to be larger, so delete the last line on our second course and draw another one from (32.125,1.75) to (32.125,3.5) in its place. This will be indented exactly 2mm as we require. If we were making a mitre joint corner, we could draw our new line at x = 31.5 and this would give us a more accurately-sized queen closer. Finally, draw a line from (0,1.75) to (34.125,1.75) to represent the bed of mortar between the courses (figure 8.35).

Figure 8-35 The second course adjusted

The reason for working in actual-size millimetres for the model is now clear. We know that our MDF is 2mm thick so this is the amount we would have to indent our final perpend on the second course. If we had managed to find some 2.5mm MDF we would indent by this amount instead, which would have given us a much more accurately scaled queen closer.

We now switch to Layer 0 and put in the lines for cutting through the MDF. Click Layer 0 in the layer list, set the Snap mode to Endpoints (not Grid) and draw over the right-hand edge that we wish to cut, as in Figure 8-36. The final point will have to be entered manually as 34.125,3.5 because we don't have an end point to snap to.

Now get rid of the lines we have just drawn on Layer 0 from Layer 1. Switch back to Layer 1 and click the little 'eye' icon against Layer 0 to hide the black lines. Click **Modify > Trim**, and as your limiting entity click the last 'perpend' line on the second

course. When asked for the entity to trim, select the horizontal line representing the mortar bed for the second course of bricks. Note that with *LibreCAD* we click on the part we want to retain, unlike *DraftSight*, where we clicked on the part we wanted to remove. Life's confusing, isn't it? Finally delete the two 'perpend' lines that we have gone over in black. Bring back the black lines by clicking the Layer 0 'eye'.

We now click **Select > Select all**, then **Modify > Move/Copy**. Set the reference point as (0,0) and the target point as (0,3.5), and set multiple copies to 9. A little tidying up is now required. Delete the short black line from the top right of the drawing and replace it with one on Layer 0 from (0.25,35) to (32.125,35). Then delete the red line along the bottom of the wall, and draw a black line at the bottom from (0.25,0) to (34.125,0). You should now have something like figure 8-37.

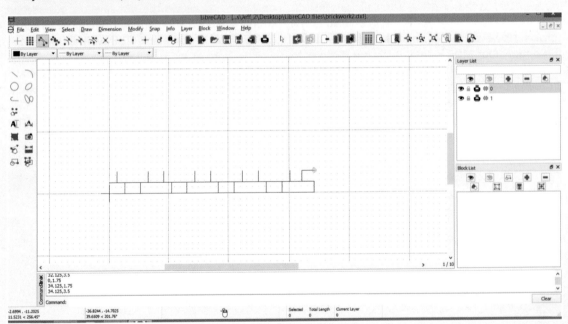

Figure 8-36 Layer 0 lines

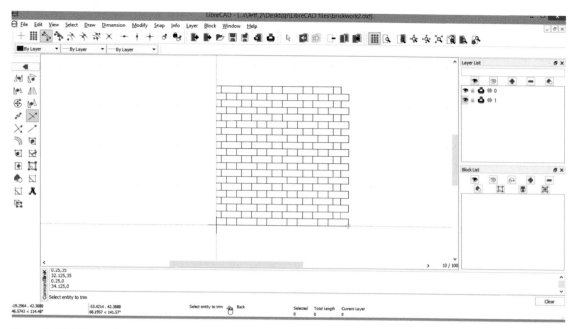

Figure 8-37 Half a wall

We now mirror the whole thing about the y axis. Click **Select > Select all**, then **Modify > Mirror**, and set the two mirror points to (0,0) and (0,35). In the **Mirroring Options** dialog, click **Keep original**, press **Enter** and you should have a complete wall as here. Save this as 'brickwork3.dxf' (figure 8-38).

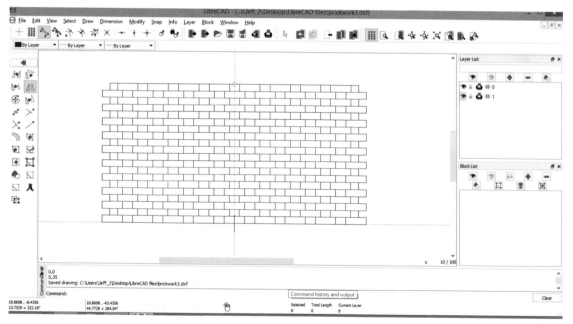

Figure 8-38 The complete wall

Now we make a second copy of the wall. Click **Select > Select All**, then **Modify > Move/Copy**. Set 0,0 as your reference point and 70,0 as your target point and you will end up with two walls as in Figure 8-39.

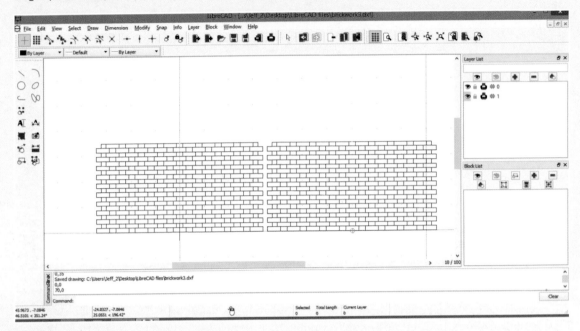

Figure 8-39 Two walls

As they stand, these walls are not much use as they obviously don't interlace. We need to turn the right-hand copy through 180°. Click **Edit > Selection pointer** and draw a selection rectangle around the right-hand wall. Click **Modify > Rotate**, set the rotation centre as (70,17.5) and the reference point as the same, and in the Rotation Options dialog box click Delete Original and set the rotation angle to 180°. You should end up with two walls that mesh nicely (figure 8-40).

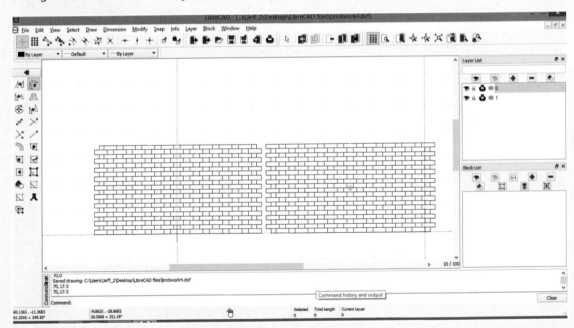

Figure 8-40 The second wall rotated through 180°

Now we could call these walls complete, but it will save laser cutting time if we put them together, making just one cut between them instead of the two shown. Hide Layer 1, then draw a selection rectangle round the black lines on the left of the second wall and delete them (figure 8-41).

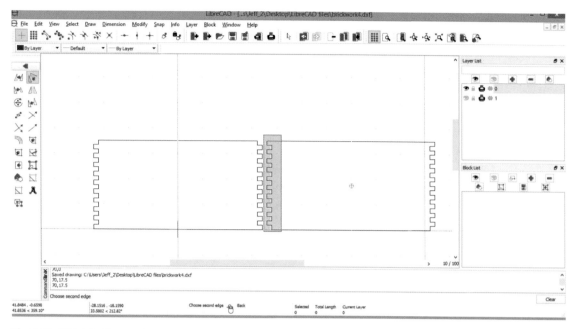

Figure 8-41 Delete these cuts

Click the Layer 1 'eye' so we can see the red lines again, then select the right-hand wall, click **Modify > Move/Copy,** and (making sure you are in Snap to Endpoint mode) click the left bottom point of the right-hand wall as your reference point and the right bottom point of the left-hand wall as your target. Opt to delete the original, and you should end up with figure 8-42. Don't forget to save your work regularly using a new number suffix.

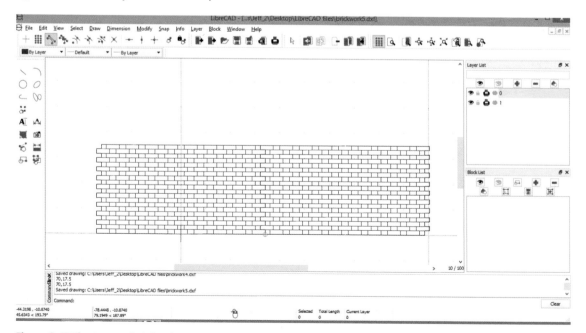

Figure 8-42 The two walls joined

We now make a copy of this pair of walls by clicking **Select > Select All**, then **Modify > Move/Copy** with reference point (0,0) and target point (0,50). The upper pair of walls are complete, but we still need to put a window in one of the lower walls and a door in the other.

Using the Snap to Endpoint option, draw two lines on Layer 0 as shown in Figure 8-43 to represent the sides of the window. Delete the verticals between them then, using these lines as the limiting entities, trim the horizontals on either side of them as shown in Figure 8-44. Click **Modify > Trim**, select the left-hand side of the window as your limiting entity, then each horizontal you need to trim, then press **Esc**, and repeat for the right-hand side. You should then delete the verticals behind the Layer 0 lines we've just drawn by hiding Layer 0, and deleting the offending red lines. Finally, again on Layer 0, draw a line to join the two sides at the bottom of the window.

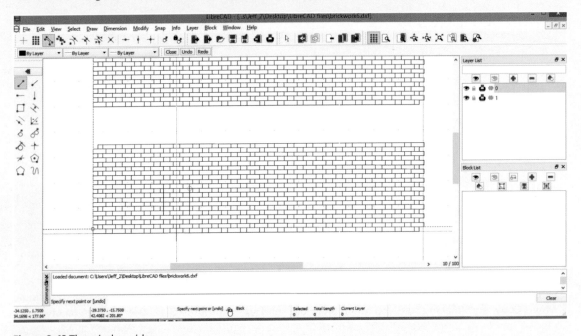

Figure 8-43 The window sides

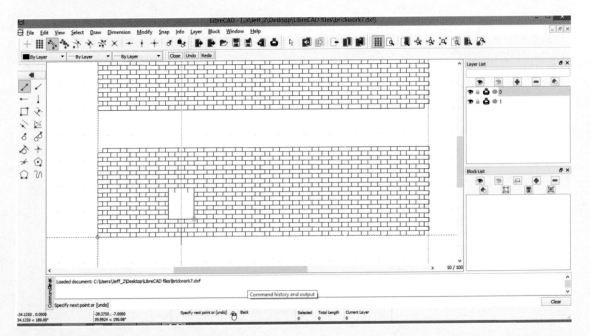

Figure 8-44 Deleting the 'window' bricks

We now draw an arch over the top of the window opening. To make an arch such as this, bricks would typically be laid vertically rather than horizontally (such a brick is called a 'soldier'). Arches would always have an odd number of bricks so that one brick was dead centre at the top of the arch – this was referred to as the 'key brick'. Click **Draw > Arc > Centre point, Angles**. When asked to specify the centre, click in the command window and type in 0,9.75. Where do we get 9.75 from? Well, the answer involves a bit of maths, which has been relegated to Appendix 5 so we don't get sidetracked here. Hit **Enter** and you will be asked for a radius. Click the top point of the right-hand 'window' line (make sure you're on Snap to Endpoint). *LibreCAD* will take the radius as the distance between the centre and this point. When asked for the start angle, click the same point again, then for the end angle click the top of the left-hand side of the window. You should now have something like figure 8-45.

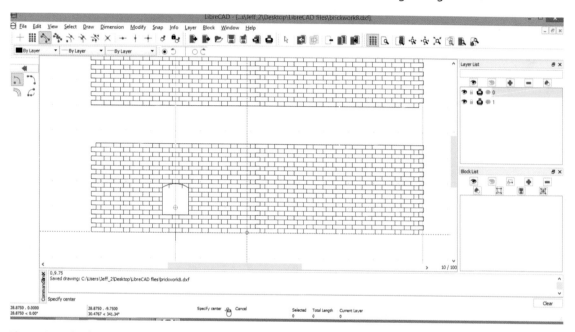

Figure 8-45 The first arc

Now, the radius of this arc is 9.36mm. We found this by clicking **Modify > Properties**, selecting the arc and reading off the radius. If we want our arc to be made of soldier bricks, we need another arc with a radius of 9.36 plus one stretcher, which is 9.36 + 5.25 = 14.61. This time we don't want to cut through the material, so switch to Layer 1. Again click **Draw > Arc > Centre point, Angles**. When asked to specify the centre, click on the **Snap to Centre** icon and use the same centre-point as the previous arc. When asked for the radius, click in the command window and type 14.61. Specify the start and end angles as before and you should have figure 8-46.

We can tidy this up a little by getting rid of some of the surplus perpend lines between the arcs. We now put in our 'soldier' bricks. We start with a line joining the two top dead centres of the arcs. An easy way to do this is to draw a random-length vertical line up the y axis, say from (0,0) to (0,35), then trim its two ends using the two arcs as limiting entities. Our central soldier needs to sit astride this line, so we **Move and Rotate** through an angle that will give us half-brick intervals. Again, we have relegated the maths to Appendix 5, but the angle we need is 4.875°. Click **Modify > Move and Rotate**, click on the arc centre as both reference point and target point, and specify 7 for the number of copies and 4.875° as the angle through which to rotate. You should end up with something like figure 8-47.

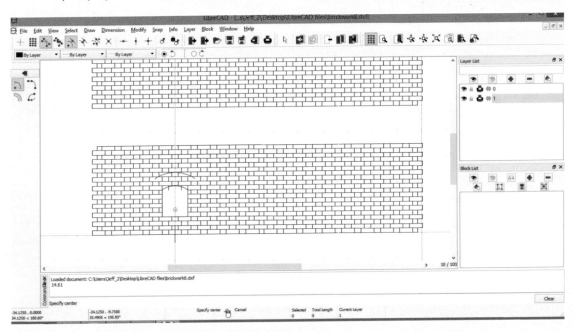

Figure 8-46 The second arc

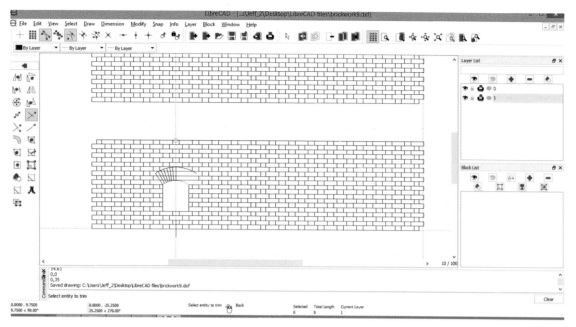

Figure 8-47 'Soldiers'

To make the right-hand side of the arch, repeat the procedure with a rotation angle of -4.875°. Finally, tidy up by deleting alternate radial lines and, using the upper arc and the side bricks of the arch as limiting entities, trim the horizontal lines on either side of the window (figure 8-48).

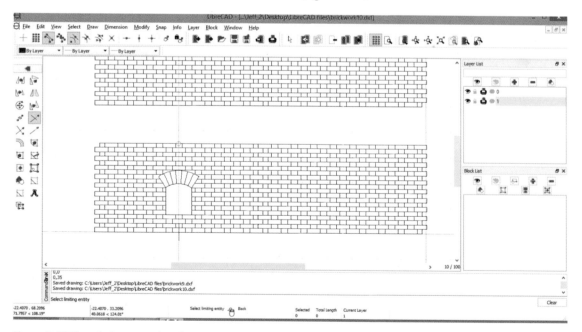

Figure 8-48 The window completed

We will now make the door in the wall to the right. This is a lot easier than the window, and employs the same techniques, so we will not describe it step by step. On Layer 0, draw the lines representing the door sides, delete all the 'perpend' lines within them, then use the door sides as limiting entities to trim the horizontal mortar lines on either side (tip: trim those to the right of the door first). See figure 8-49.

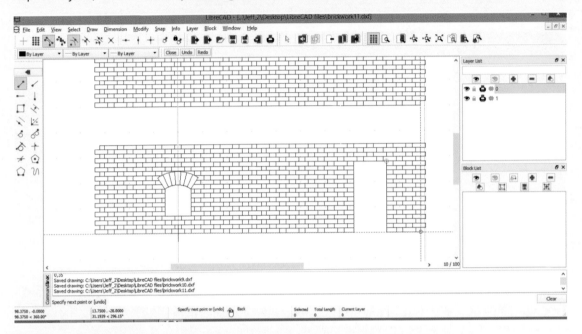

Figure 8-49 The door opening

Finally, make the lintel over the door by extending two perpends over two mortar beds, using these to trim the horizontals on either side, then delete the perpends within the lintel. A useful tip is illustrated in figure 8-50: if, instead of drawing a selection rectangle from top left to bottom right, we draw it from bottom right up to top left, we get a purple rather than a cream-coloured selection box, and this selects everything that lies wholly or partially within it.

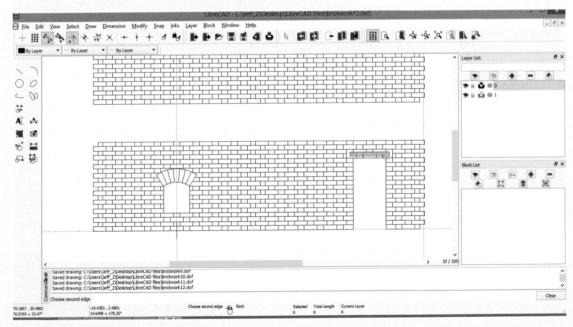

Figure 8-50 'Crossing' selection rectangle

Press delete to get rid of these lines and our drawing is done. It may be advisable to move everything into the positive quadrant, and it is useful to draw a rectangle of some exact dimension around everything. This will not be printed, but can be used to check that the scale of the drawing is correct on the laser machine and also to position it on the cutting bed. Figure 8-51 shows the finished drawing.

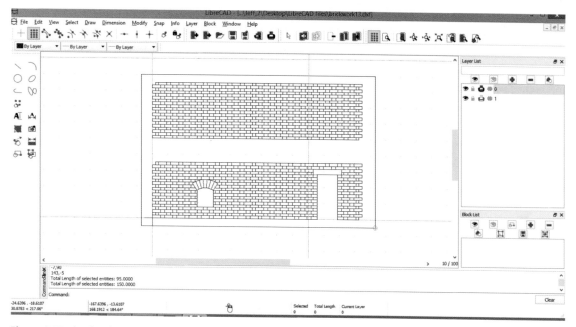

Figure 8-51 The finished drawing

In figure 8-52 we see the four walls assembled. Notice that where the laser has cut through the material, the edge is charred. This gives rise to the rather odd effect at the corners where the 'header' faces of the bricks on alternate rows are blackened. This effect will disappear on painting.

We hope the reader will agree that it would be extremely difficult to get this degree of accuracy using plastic card and a craft knife. Later in the chapter, we will see some even more impressive examples.

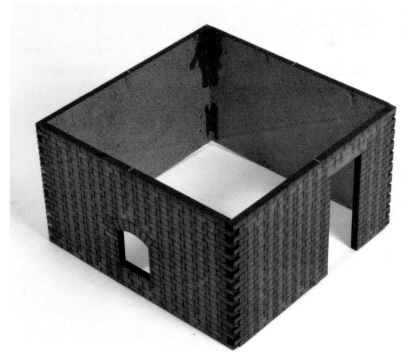

Figure 8-52 The walls assembled

Laser-etched and cut control panel

In this example we are going to use laser cutting and raster engraving
to build the graphics for a control panel. The final panel will be cut
into a two-layer acrylic material. The layers will be in contrasting
colours and we will etch through the top layer, exposing the lower
layer. This time we will use *Inkscape*.

Click **File > New**, then **File > Document Properties** (figure 8-53). Set
the page size to 500 x 300mm, and the default units to millimetres.
Strangely there is no 'Apply' or 'OK' button on this dialogue; changes
are adopted immediately. Simply close it when you are done.

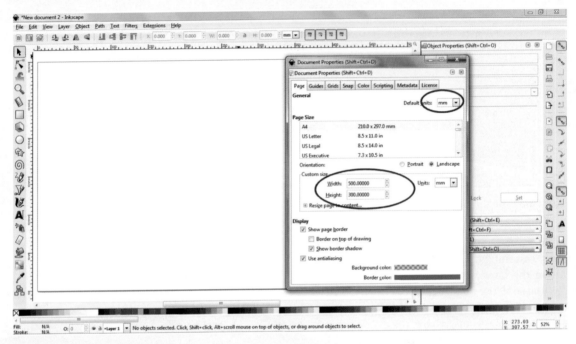

Figure 8-53 Setting the page size

Under the **Grids** tab in the **Document properties** dialogue, set up grids.
By default there is no grid: you use the 'New' button to set one up.
In figure 8-54 you can see we have created a grid with 5mm squares.

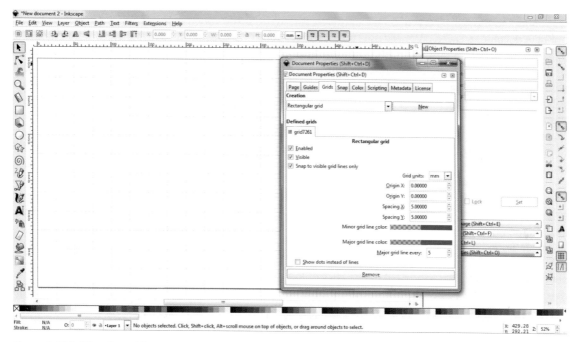

Figure 8-54 Setting the grid parameters

To allow us to set up the laser cutter it's very useful to have an object of a known size, so we will create a bounding box rectangle. To do this we use the rectangle drawing tool located on the left-hand vertical toolbar (figure 8-55). We can either drag to the required size (the size is shown in the bottom toolbar as you drag) or you can use the text entry boxes on the top toolbar to enter the exact values. We draw a box 400mm wide by 230mm tall.

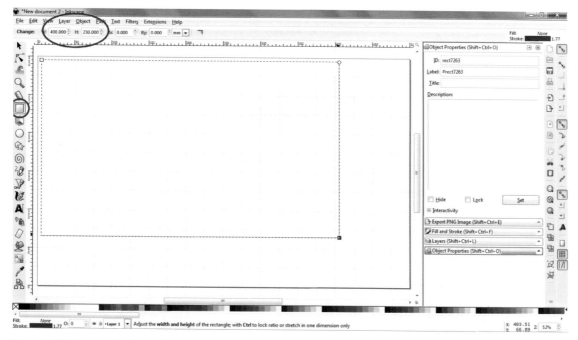

Figure 8-55 Drawing the bounding box

Our bounding box will be drawn on the only layer in our new document, Layer 1. We will use layers in our drawing to separate out different parts of the project, and we can give them names to make life easier. On the right-hand side of the Inkscape screen you may have noticed a panel that by default shows the properties of the currently selected drawing object. Below the properties panel are a set of buttons that reveal other panes. Click on the **Layers** button and a pane opens up showing the layers of the document. If you left click on a layer name it is selected as the layer to work on. If you right click on a layer name you are given more options that include the ability to rename it. We have renamed this layer 'Bounding box'.

We will not only use the bounding box to set up our cutter but also to cut the edge of the panel, so we need to set up a few parameters for the rectangle. Click on the **Selection** tool, the big arrowhead on the left-hand vertical toolbar, then click on one of the sides of our bounding box rectangle. The rectangle is then outlined with a dotted line and resizing handles at the corners. We can now go over to the right-hand pane and click on the **Fill** and **Stroke** button.

The **Fill** and **Stroke** pane comprises three tabs that set the way the shape is drawn. One pane defines the way the line around the outside of the object is drawn (Stroke style), one defines the colour of the outline (Stroke paint), and the final tab defines whether the shape has a fill colour (Fill). Figure 8-56 shows the three panes and the settings we are using for the bounding box.

It is generally recommended to use as thin a line as possible, so we use a blue outline 0.01mm wide. We have set a light grey fill colour so we can see the shape. We will use colours to determine whether a shape is cut or etched. For the bounding box we will be cutting, so we have selected blue to indicate this.

We are now ready to start drawing our track schematic, and to keep things orderly we will do this on a new layer. This is created by selecting **Layer > Add layer** from the top menu bar and name it 'Track'.

We are going to represent the track using lines 3mm wide, and we will be using the 'Draw bezier curves and straight lines' tool on the left vertical toolbar. Left click on the tool icon, then click and drag horizontally while holding down the **Ctrl** key and we get a straight line. When we have a line of the required length, double click the left mouse button. Figure 8-57 shows the line being drawn.

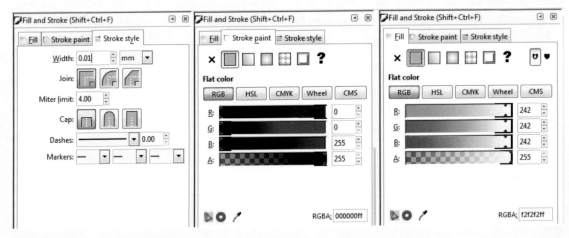

Figure 8-56 Bounding box properties

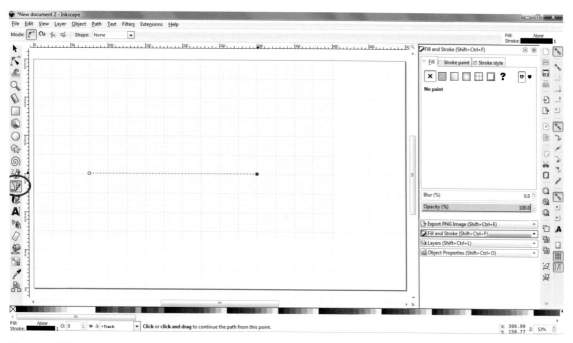

Figure 8-57 Drawing the first track line

This line will be etched rather than cut, so we need to set the colour to something different. As before we use the **Fill** and **Stroke** properties pane, but in this case we don't need any Fill parameters. Set the **Stroke** colour to black and the **Stroke** width to 3mm. If we need to adjust the length or angle of the line we use the 'Edit paths by nodes' tool button on the left-hand toolbar; it's the second icon down and looks like the selection arrow with a curve and three blue squares. If we click on the tool button, click on the new line, the 'nodes' that define the line appear as diamond shapes, and we can click and drag them (figure 8-58).

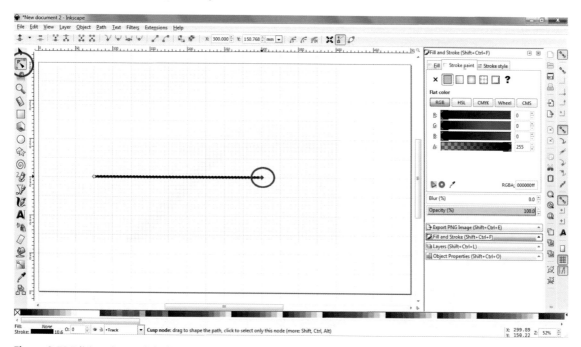

Figure 8-58 Editing the straight line

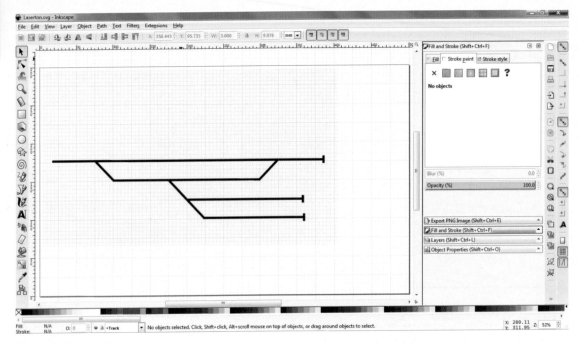

Figure 8-59 The track layout

Each line is an object in its own right and we can copy and paste it to create others. To copy and paste we use the **Select** tool (big arrow) to select the object, then right click to bring up a context menu that includes **Copy**. To paste, right click elsewhere on the page and select **Paste**. The object menu also allows us to rotate, flip and mirror objects. Figure 8-59 shows our basic track layout completed.

As it stands, our track plan won't successfully etch with most laser cutting software. What we need is an outline of the shape we want etched without any fill colour. Thankfully this is very easily accomplished with *Inkscape*. First, however, it is worth zooming in and inspecting the track layout to make sure all the lines meet up neatly. Figure 8-60 shows how, by zooming in, we can see where a couple of lines don't meet neatly, and figure 8-61 shows how by moving one of the lines this has been cleaned up.

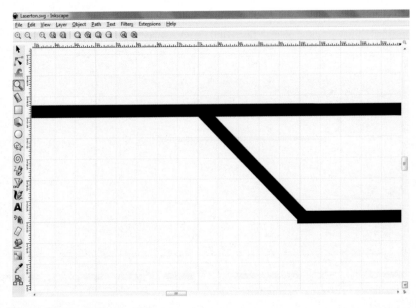

Figure 8-60 A scruffy corner!

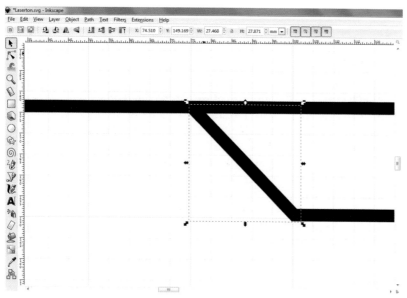

Figure 8-61 The corner tidied up

To turn our trackplan into an outline shape, select all the lines either by doing a click and drag selection or clicking **Edit > Select All**. A helpful hint here is to lock the bounding box layer before attempting to do a click and drag selection; do this by going to the layers panel and clicking on the padlock icon next to the layer name. If the layer is locked you can't select or move items in that layer by mistake.

With all our trackplan lines selected, use **Path > Combine** to turn all our track lines, which are currently defined as individual objects, into a single path object. Now we want to turn our 3mm-wide

lines into just the thinnest possible outlines with all the ends capped off. Assuming our trackplan object is still selected, switch to 'Edit paths by nodes' mode by either pressing **F2** or clicking on the tool icon, as we did when adjusting the lines.

With all the nodes visible, we can use the 'Convert selected object's strokes to paths' tool on the top toolbar. This is ringed in red in figure 8-62, and you will see that the nodes of the object have changed to define the outline of the trackplan rather than the starts and ends of the lines that were drawn. It still looks like a set of 3mm-wide lines, though!

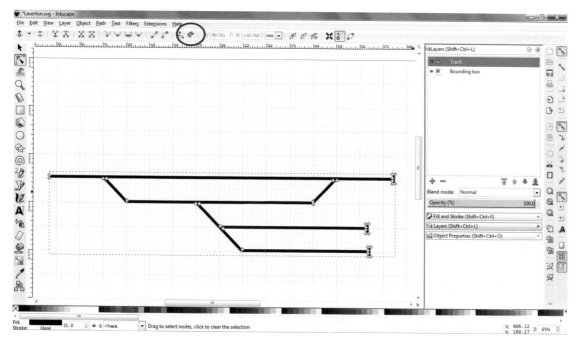

Figure 8-62 The trackplan with outline nodes

Finally, for these lines we change the stroke and fill parameters. Turn off **Fill**, turn on **Stroke** painting and define the stroke width as 0.01mm. Unfortunately the trackplan will now become practically invisible unless you zoom right in close! You might want to turn **Fill** back on to see the plan easily.

We now add some holes for switches to control our pointwork and for LEDs to show which routes are selected. To do this we add another layer (it might be worth locking the track layer at this point) using **Layer > Add**. In this case we are going to use miniature toggle switches to control our points, and these will need a 5mm-diameter mounting hole. We can draw 5mm circles by clicking on the 'Circles, ellipses and arcs' tool in the left-hand vertical toolbar. To draw a circle, hold down the

Ctrl key and left click and drag until you get the right size; if you do not hold down the **Ctrl** key you will get an ellipse. Set the **Stroke** colour of your new circle to blue with a stroke width of 0.01mm. As we did with the trackplan, select the hole object and use **Path > Object to Path**. If you don't do this you may find that your holes will not export properly later on.

You can position your switch hole wherever you need it, and copy and paste others. Similarly for LEDs you can create further holes, in our case of 3mm diameter. Figure 8-63 shows where we have got to. The LED holes have been filled with yellow so we can differentiate them from the switch holes, but their Stroke colour is blue, so they will be part of the cut operation.

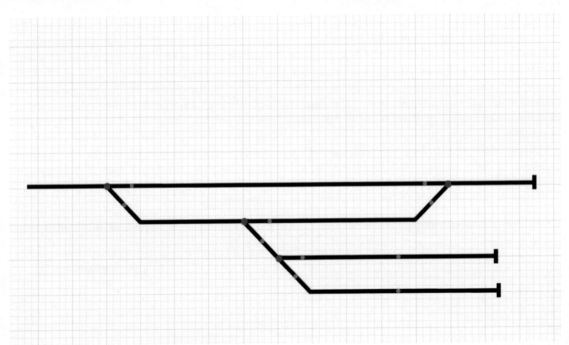

Figure 8-63 Track and switch layers complete

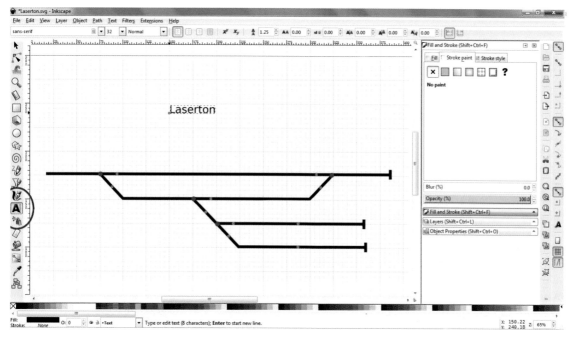

Figure 8-64 Adding text

You may well want to add text to etch into your panel, so we will add some to our example. In this case we will keep things simple and just add a station name. Again we create a new layer, then click on the **Text** tool on the left. We then click on the drawing and type the desired text (figure 8-64).

Our text is a bit small, so we need to access the 'Text and font' properties pane. For some obscure reason, even though we have a text object selected,

the required properties pane doesn't appear as an option on the right-hand panel as with other things, so we have to go to the **Text > Text and font** menu option. Lo and behold, the required pane appears on the right! Here we can change fonts and sizes and edit the text. Our text size increased and the Stroke and Fill colour changed to red (figure 8-65).

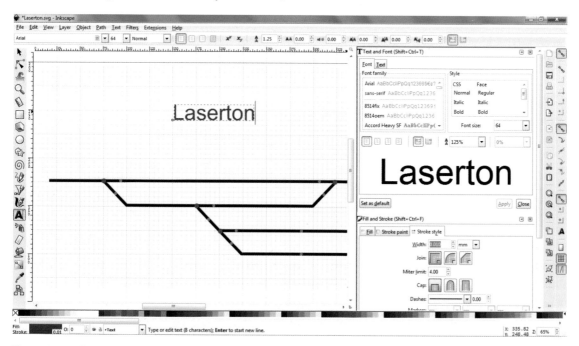

Figure 8-65 Adjusting text properties

We are going to etch our text, so there is an important step to perform, otherwise our text will not be exported properly or the laser cutter will do strange things to it. As we did with the trackplan, select the text object and use **Path > Object to Path**. Then convert from a set of nodes defining the lines forming the characters to a set of nodes defining the outline by once again switching to 'Edit paths by nodes' mode, then use the 'Convert selected object's strokes to paths' tool on the top toolbar. With text objects you will see no visual indication that anything has changed, but you may get problems exporting later if you don't do it.

Our drawing is pretty much done, so congratulate yourself and have a cup of tea, because the next bit can be tricky and somewhat frustrating! We need to export our drawing in a format that the software driving the laser cutter can understand. *Inkscape* can export in several formats, but there are a few 'gotchas'!

At the time of writing virtually all laser cutters, certainly the affordable ones, use proprietary software to drive them. There is no one-size-fits-all open-source driver. Unfortunately some of this driver software seems to be pretty flaky, with no regular updates, decent documentation or support. You will probably find that you have to spend a fair bit of time using trial and error to get your models cut as you would want them. Hopefully this situation will improve over time.

In our case the cutter is driven by *LaserCut 5.3* software, which is able to import drawings in dxf format. *Inkscape* can export in dxf format, but unfortunately there are several versions of this format, and the version *Inkscape* creates is later than the version *LaserCut* can read!

All is not lost, however, as there are several programs that can convert between different dxf formats, but it does mean we have to take an extra step. To create a dxf file in Inkscape we use the **File > Save As** menu option and select the 'Desktop cutting plotter (AutoCAD dxf R14)' file format. You are presented with a panel of options and figure 8-66 shows the options we used for the export.

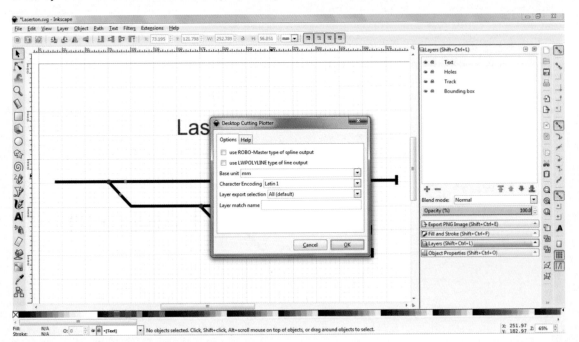

Figure 8-66 Exporting to dxf format

This creates a dxf R14 format file. To convert this to an earlier version, we used *LibreCAD*! Maybe we should have simply used *LibreCAD* for the whole job? We don't need to do anything in *LibreCAD* other than use the **File > Save As** menu option and select a file type of dxf 2000 as shown by Figure 8-67. This gives a dxf file that we can import into *LaserCut* as shown by Figure 8-68.

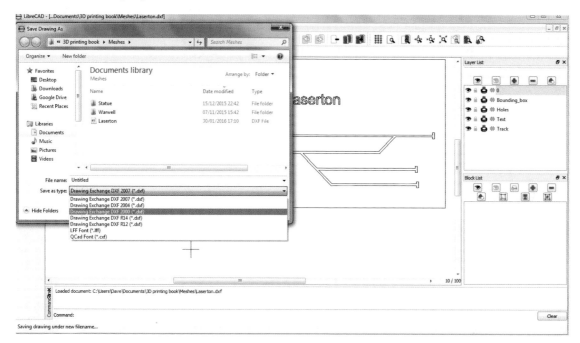

Figure 8-67 Converting the dxf format

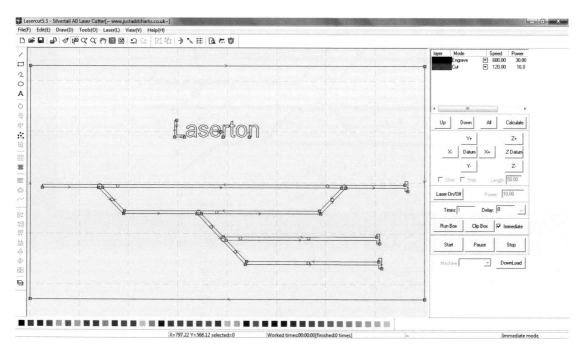

Figure 8-68 The drawing in *Lasercut*

In the top right corner you can see that we have assigned the operation to perform based on the colours of the lines. Black lines outline areas to be engraved/etched, while blues lines mark cuts. We order the operations such that the engraving is done before cutting to limit the likelihood of our workpiece moving before everything is done.

Unfortunately there is still a twist in this story. Although we now have the drawing successfully imported into the cutting software, you may well get some errors when you attempt to cut. *LaserCut* has a simulate mode that lets us try things out without firing up the cutter. If you get two objects that require to be engraved overlapping, the software will complain. In our case this happened when somehow we managed to get the outline colour of our switch holes set to black instead of blue, so *LaserCut* interpreted these as needing engraving. Whoops!

You may well get an error that isn't your fault. We frequently encountered the slightly cryptic message 'The polyline must be closed before it can be engraved'! Not sure why we got this, as looking at the dxf file all the shapes to be engraved seemed to have a continuous outline, but there is a fix. Select all the objects that are to be engraved, then use the **Tools > Unite lines** menu option. This will prompt you for a 'Unite tolerance' value. The default value of 1.0 seems to mess up some shapes, especially text, so we used 0.1, which seemed to work. Don't ask us why!

After all this you should find that your drawing will etch and cut correctly, and you can get a feel for what will happen by using the **Laser > Simulate** menu option before finally firing up your laser cutter.

Figure 8-69 shows a slightly more complex control panel laser-etched and cut.

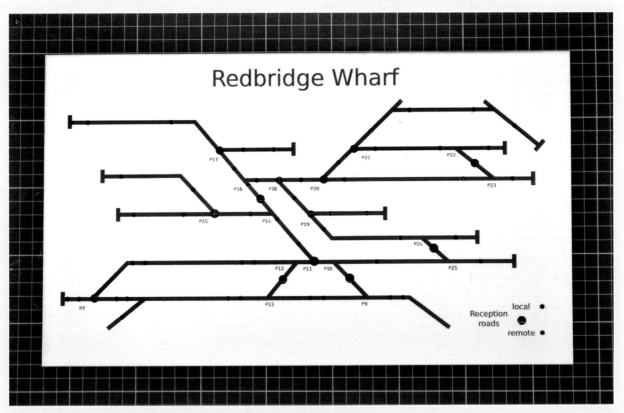

Figure 8-69 Redbridge Wharf control panel, laser etched and cut

Conclusions

Hopefully our examples, though simple due to space constraints, have shown how to prepare cutting files for the majority of situations. We have been fortunate in having access to a fairly sophisticated laser cutter to prepare our examples, but the cost of such a machine is still probably outside the budget of most individuals and even clubs. Rather as with 3D printers, the prices of smaller laser cutting machines are reducing significantly, so it may well be that they will soon become affordable to more modellers.

At the lower-price end of the market, many of the machines may take significantly more time and effort to set up and keep in adjustment than the more expensive ones. They are likely to lack features such as air jets to keep the cutting area clean, and other less important but handy bits. Having said that, a search of the web will reveal that resourceful folks have documented how these cheaper machines can be used and upgraded to provide good results.

If you don't have a friend with a laser cutter and don't fancy spending serious money, there are a number of companies that will take your CAD files and do the cutting for you. It may also be worth looking for local hackerspace or makerspace groups or technical colleges that may allow you access to laser cutting technology.

BELOW *Figure 8-70* The brickwork on the cutter.

Our first example of the ornate barge boards was a simple cutting operation. To perform the cut all that needed to be done was to convert the dxf file to a series of cutting instructions for the laser cutter, set an appropriate power level, position some 1.5mm plywood, and press the go button. The cutter then just performed a series of vector cuts.

For the brickwork example we added some vector engraving to the mix. In this case we identified the colour of the lines to be engraved, the mortar courses, and set a low laser power level so that we had just a scoring of the surface. The kerf of the laser provided enough width of scoring to be convincing. The cuts around the edges of the walls and the window and door were drawn in a different colour, so we were able to tell the cutter to use a higher output for these to cut cleanly through the material. In this case we used 2mm MDF, and Figure 8-70 shows the cut parts still on the machine.

For the control panel example we had no vector engraving, but used raster engraving together with cuts for the holes and around the edge of the panel. In this case, instead of just reducing the laser power level to engrave, we had to tell the machine that we wished to use an engraving operation, and which colour in the drawing represented these areas. To perform the engrave operation the software scans the drawing in a series of lines from left to right, turning the laser on when it encounters

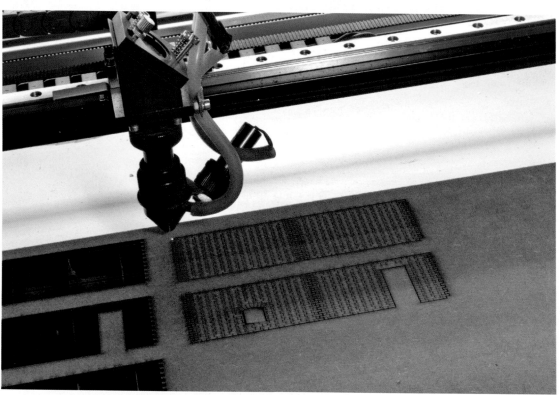

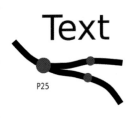

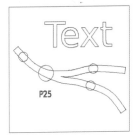

a line and off when it encounters the next line. If our shapes weren't closed we would have an odd number of lines and the ons and offs wouldn't match, leaving us with a mess!

Figure 8-71 shows a simple file with wide lines and text to be raster engraved. The drawing on the left is a screen capture from Inkscape, and that on the right the dxf version. In converting to dxf format we have lost the fill information and are left with just the outlines that we need. The circles are cut lines that, being in a different colour, are

ABOVE *Figure 8-71* Raster engraving outlines.

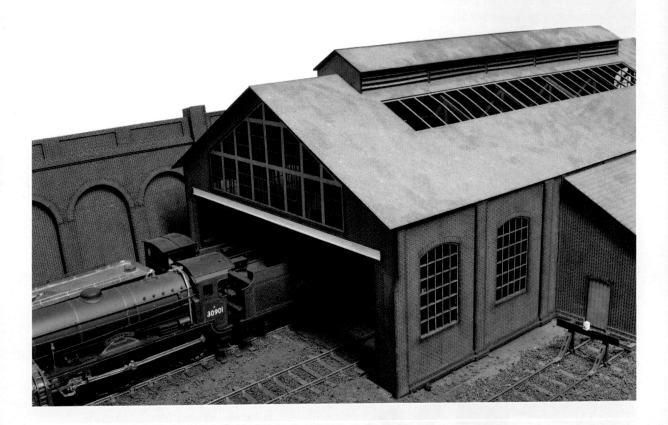

ABOVE *Figure 8-74* A coaling stage.

CENTRE LEFT *Figure 8-72* The front of the engine shed.

BELOW LEFT *Figure 8-73* A side view of the engine shed.

ignored. In this example we have done as we did in our control panel project and converted the lines and characters into paths, then outlines, before exporting to dxf. If we hadn't done so they would have been lost in the export operation.

Now we have used all the capabilities of the cutter, but haven't really explored just what can be achieved by combining several cut parts. Our brickwork example is very simple and the walls are basically flat with just the mortar courses providing relief. More often than not, especially with larger brick structures, there is far more to it than that. Many buildings have buttresses, cornices and all manner of ornamentation added into the brickwork. The Victorians, who built much of our railway infrastructure, loved a bit of ornamentation.

If we used thicker materials we could probably etch/engrave away large areas to get perhaps two layers of brickwork relief, but that would take an age to cut and be madly wasteful of material and laser tube life. A much more sensible approach is to laminate layers of laser-cut material together to obtain the relief. Figures 8-72 and 8-73 show two views of Roger's O-gauge engine shed. This is a work in progress but is still a mightily impressive structure, not just because of its sheer size (it's a metre long) but also for the range of ways in which

material that has been laser cut and engraved has been brought together.

Almost all of this building is constructed from laser-cut pieces, each having been designed to interlock with its neighbour. The windows are an impressive example of the fine detail that can be cut. The size of the structure means that large flat areas such as the roof panels had to be cut in pieces even on a fairly large machine with a 500mm cutting area. Panels interlock with dovetails and the narrow kerf of the laser means that they are a good fit without having to make allowances in the drawings. The retaining wall section behind the shed is yet more laminated laser-cut sections.

Figure 8-74 shows another of Roger's buildings, a timber coaling stage, finished and painted. The planks for the sides were individually cut, which of course could be done easily enough, if somewhat tediously, with a craft knife and ruler. Look, though, at the internal framing visible through the wagon access doorway to the left. All those diagonals and cross braces would be a fair technical challenge by hand, but are cut clean as a whistle by the laser!

Hopefully this chapter has at least given the reader a hint of the possibilities afforded by laser cutting and also afforded some basic CAD skills. Unfortunately, one of the railway modeller's favourite building materials, plastic card, does not cut well with a laser as it melts too easily, but the CAD techniques we have described also create cutting files for craft cutters that use a physical blade. Go forth and use your new skills!

Appendix 1
Web resources

One of the problems with including a list such as this is that things change. On the web they change frequently, and websites can appear and disappear without trace, software versions can become out of date or incompatible with current operating systems, and so on. Nevertheless, at the time of writing the following are useful websites to find software to download, designs, advice, tutorials, etc.

www.blender.org
This is the official website of the Blender Foundation, where you can download *Blender* and find *Blender* documentation, tutorials, etc

www.Sketchup.com
The *Sketchup* website, from which you can download *Sketchup Make*, or arrange a free trial of *Sketchup Pro*.

www.rs-online.com
The RS website, from which you can download *DesignSpark Mechanical*.

www.autodesk.co.uk
The *Autodesk* website, from which you can download *Fusion 360*.

www.openscad.org
The *OpenSCAD* official website, from which you can download the software, look at user forums, etc.

www.tinkercad.com
Tinkercad offers a web-based 3D design and modelling tool that you launch in your browser – no need even to download any software!

www.meshlab.sourceforge.net
This is the site from which to download *Meshlab*.

www.youtube.com/user/ MrPMeshLabTutorials
An entertaining series of tutorials on using *Meshlab*.

www.slic3r.org
The website from which you can download the *slic3r* application.

www.netfabb.com
The *netfabb* website from which you can download *netfabb Basic*.

www.librecad.org
The official website of the *LibreCAD* community, where you can download *LibreCAD* 2D software, access the manuals and other resources.

www.inkscape.org
The website for the *Inkscape* 2D CAD software.

www.3ds.com/products-services/draftsight-cad-software
This is where to find the *DraftSight* 2D software.

www.rmweb.co.uk
A vast source of modelling help. In particular look at the 3D Printing, Laser Cutting, CAD & CNC forum.

www.railalbum.co.uk
Greg Martin's Rail Album website holds a great many useful photographs and drawings, including that used to make the Warwell wagon in Chapter 4.

www.44090digitalmodels.co.uk
Paul Hobbs has written some fine tutorials on building 3D locomotives in *Blender*. Although these are designed to go into the *Trainz* simulator, rather than for 3D printing, his tutorials contain a wealth of useful information.

www.thingiverse.com
The *Makerbot Thingiverse* website contains thousands of 3D designs you can download for free.

www.shapeways.com
Shapeways offers a 3D printing service to modellers who don't want the expense of buying their own 3D printer. In addition, you can put your design in the *Shapeways* shop and sell online to other modellers.

www.i.materialize.com
Like *Shapeways*, this is a comprehensive 3D printing service offering a variety of technologies to the modeller.

www.sculpteo.com
Another 3D printing service, which, like *Shapeways* and *i.materialize*, lets you upload your 3D CAD file, then ships you the printed result in a few days.

www.cwrailways.com
Chris and Christine Ward offer a specialist 3D printing service to railway modellers and a range of kits and components in various scales.

www.modelshop.co.uk
Look for Modelshop's bespoke services, under which you will find their very reasonably priced laser cutting and engraving service.

www.graingeandhodder.co.uk
Grainge and Hodder supply laser cutting services to the model trade, but are also happy to help with 'one-off' modeller's projects.

www.greenwoodmodelrailwayproducts.co.uk
Bespoke and product line laser-cut models, storage boxes and baseboard items.

www.yorkmodelmaking.co.uk
York Modelmaking supplies a range of laser-cut kits, but also offers a bespoke cutting service to railway modellers.

Appendix 2
Separation of celestial bodies

This is an example of serendipity. It turns out that our steam exhaust pipe bending problem in Chapter 5 is neatly solved by a formula designed to measure apparent distances between stars!

In Chapter 5 we encountered a requirement to determine the angle through which a steam exhaust pipe must be bent in order that, when rotated so that one section pointed upwards at 37° in the yz plane and the other downwards at 6° in the xz plane, the projection onto the xy plane is exactly a right angle. This kept one of the authors scratching his head for some time until he suddenly realised that the problem was exactly the same as one in astronomy, namely the angular separation of celestial bodies. Referring to Figure A.1, at (a) we see an observer at the centre of the celestial sphere. In order to describe the precise location of a star in the sky, we conventionally use two angles. The first, angle 'a', is the azimuth angle measured from due north. The second, 'd', is the altitude measured from the horizon. Now consider diagram (b). Given two stars at locations a_1,d_1 and a_2,d_2 what is the angular separation between them, i.e. the angle 's' in the diagram? Luckily, your author happens to be a keen amateur astronomer as well as a railway modeller and had to hand his copy of *Astronomical Algorithms* by Jean Meeus, from which the fearsome looking formula shown in the figure was obtained!

At (c) we have placed point B at the centre of the diagram – this corresponds to point B in Figure 5-16, where we need to make our bend. Points A and C take the place of the two stars. If we take the 'North' direction as meaning straight towards the cab from point B, then we can say that point A is in direction $a_1 = 0°$, $d_1 = -6°$. Point C is in direction $a_2 = 90°$, $d_2 = 37°$. Substituting the various sines and cosines of these angles into Meeus's formula, we find that the angle 's' is 93.6°, therefore we would require to bend a straight pipe through 86.4° to achieve this.

There may be other applications for this useful formula, for example in the exposed pipework of the BR Standard classes, which is why we have included it here.

BELOW *Figure A-1* Angular separation.

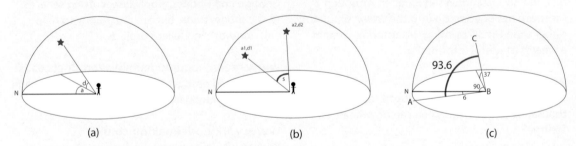

(a)　　　　　　　　(b)　　　　　　　　(c)

$$\cos s = \sin d1 \sin d2 + \cos d1 \cos d2 \cos (a1 - a2)$$

Appendix 3
Rotation around axes

A frequent operation in 3D CAD is to rotate an object around the x, y and/or z axis. We saw this in Chapter 5 in building our steam exhaust pipe. The question sometimes arises 'How do the co-ordinates x, y and z of a specific location on a body change when that body is rotated round the x, y or z axis through a specific angle?' The answer is given by the following standard equations, where Θ denotes the angle through which the body is rotated. Note that Θ is measured anti-clockwise when viewed from the origin looking along the axis of rotation in the positive direction, x, y and z are the coordinates *before* the rotation, and x', y' and z' denote the coordinates *after* the rotation.

Rotation around the x axis:

$$x' = x$$
$$y' = y \cos \Theta - z \sin \Theta$$
$$z' = y \sin \Theta + z \cos \Theta$$

Rotation around the y axis:

$$x' = z \sin \Theta + x \cos \Theta$$
$$y' = y$$
$$z' = z \cos \Theta - x \sin \Theta$$

Rotation around the z axis:

$$x' = x \cos \Theta - y \sin U$$
$$y' = x \sin U + y \cos U$$
$$z' = z$$

We mentioned in Chapter 5 that the initial rotation of the steam exhaust pipe around the x axis should be 36.85° rather than 37°. Only after a second rotation of 6° around y would the upwards angle be exactly 37°. We can see why this is by using the above equations and doing the rotations in reverse. To keep the arithmetic uncluttered, we will assume that the pipes are each one unit of length rather than the 22 inches plus the 'bend' at the end. Lengths are irrelevant to the issue – only angles matter.

Our 'final' desired position is with points A, B, C at these locations:

A is at (-cos 6, 0, -sin 6)
B is at (0, 0, 0)
C is at (0, cos 37, sin 37)

To see where the points A, B and C were before the final turn of 6° around the y axis, we apply this rotation in reverse to xA, yA, zA, etc, and find that they must have been as follows:

A was at (-1, 0, 0)
B was at (0, 0, 0)
C was at (sin 37 sin 6, cos 37, sin 37 cos 6)

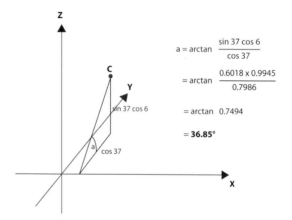

ABOVE *Figure A-2* Determining angle a.

Referring to Figure A-2, the point C is shown in its position immediately before the final 6° turn. To get to this position, the initial turn must have been through angle a, since initially C lay on the xy plane. The tangent of this angle is the z coordinate of C divided by its y coordinate, so we see from the figure that the angle is 36.85°.

Of course, this is so close to 37° that it would make little difference in this case. However, this is only because 6° is a very small angle and its cosine (0.9945) is very close to 1. If the angle were larger, this might make a significant difference.

Appendix 4
Background images

For the benefit of readers who wish to try the examples in Chapters 4 and 5, we reproduce here, with the kind permission of the publishers, the diagrams to be used as background images for the Stanier chimney, the 50-ton bogie well wagon and the fireless locomotive. To use these images, scan them and save in jpeg format, then follow the instructions given in the appropriate chapters.

RIGHT *Figure A-3* The Stanier chimney. From *Historic Locomotive Drawings in 4mm Scale* by F. J. Roche (Ian Allan, 1976), reproduced with permission

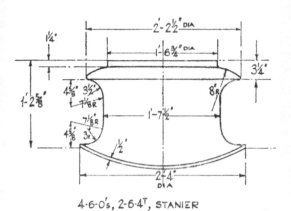

BELOW *Figure A-4* The Andrew Barclay 0-4-0 fireless locomotive. From *Fireless Locomotives* by Allen Civil and Allan Baker (Oakwood Press, 1976), reproduced with permission

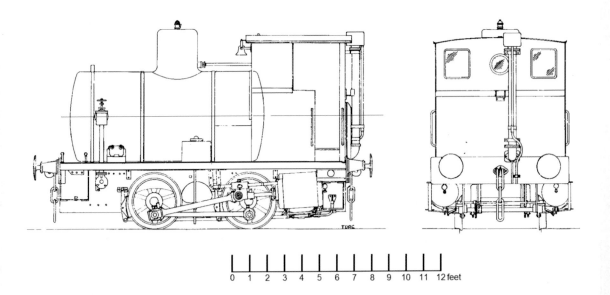

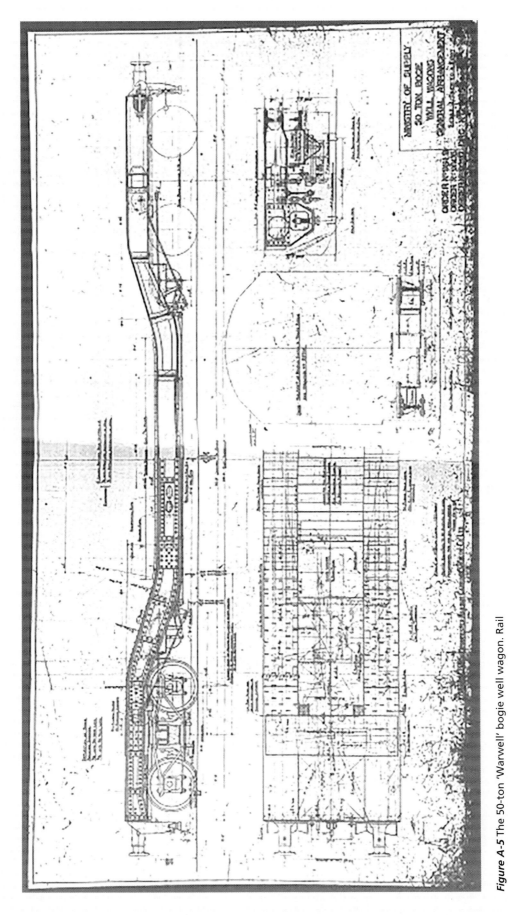

Figure A-5 The 50-ton 'Warwell' bogie well wagon. Rail Album website (http://www.railalbum.co.uk) by kind permission of Greg Martin

Appendix 5
Brick arches

The brick arch is a very common feature on railways – above windows and doors, on bridges and tunnel entrances, and so forth. It is worth getting these right, so we present here some of the basics. First, some nomenclature. Referring to Figure A-6, the centre of the curvature of the arch, shown as a green dot, is called the 'striking point'. The distance from this point to the arch is its radius. The width of the opening over which the arch sits is called the 'span'. The points at which the arch begins are called the 'springing points', and the line between them is the 'springing line', shown dotted. The vertical distance between the topmost point of the arch and this line is called the 'rise'.

We wish to find the relationship between the span, the rise and the radius of the arch, and to ensure that the arch can be built of a whole number of bricks. This number should always be odd, to ensure that our arch will have a central key brick. Although at first glance the formulas in Figure A-7 look a bit scary, they are in fact no more than a simple application of Pythagoras's theorem.

In Figure A-7, S is the span, h the rise and R the radius. We will assume that S has been determined by the required width of our window, door, tunnel or whatever. We decide on a figure for the rise, h. These two will determine the value of R. Note in the figure the triangle (shown in green) formed between the striking point, the (left-hand) springing

point and the centre of the springing line. Formula (a) in Figure A-7 is the theorem of Pythagoras applied to this triangle, namely that the hypotenuse (R) squared is the sum of (½S) squared plus (R – h) squared. A little simple algebra turns this into a formula for R, as in equation (b). We now can discover the angle Θ, since its cosine will be (R – h)/R as in equation (c). Finally, the length of arc a is given by equation (d) in terms of R and Θ.

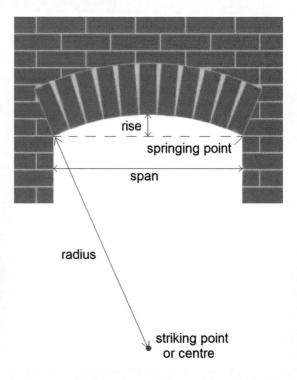

RIGHT *Figure A-6* Arch terminology.

BELOW *Figure A-7* Arch geometry.

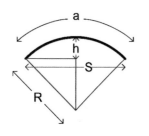

(a) $R^2 = (½S)^2 + (R - h)^2$

(b) $R = \dfrac{S^2 + 4h^2}{8h}$

(c) $\theta = \cos^{-1}\left(\dfrac{R - h}{R}\right)$

(d) $a = \dfrac{4\pi R\theta}{360}$

We want the arc length a to be an odd multiple of the width of a brick, to ensure that there is one brick dead centre as our key brick. If the arc length a turns out to be a little longer than we would like, we can lower the rise (use a smaller number for h). Or, if it is a little shorter, we can raise h and do the sums again. We continue this iterative process until a is exactly an odd multiple of a brick width.

You can cheat, however, by using 'bricks' of a different width. If you are going to do this, simply determine Θ by using the equations above, then pick an odd integer by which to divide it, in order to get the angle between successive mortar lines in the arch. Provided your choice is reasonable, the results should be perfectly adequate for all but a perfectionist!

Index